TOKYO

A CULTURAL GUIDE

to Japan's Capital City

TOKYO

A CULTURAL GUIDE

to Japan's Capital City

John H. and Phyllis G. Martin

CHARLES E. TUTTLE COMPANY

Rutland, Vermont & Tokyo, Japan

All photographs were taken by the authors except the cover photograph and the photographs facing pages 128 and 129, which were taken by Narumi Yasuda.

Published by the Charles E. Tuttle Company, Inc.
of Rutland, Vermont & Tokyo, Japan
with editorial offices at
2-6 Suido 1-chome, Bunkyo-ku, Tokyo 112

LCC Card No. 96-60059
ISBN 0-8048-2057-0

First edition, 1996

Printed in Japan

Contents

TOUR 2: Otemachi, Imperial Palace East Garden, and Yasukuni Shrine

TOUR 3: Kasumigaseki and Akasaka

TOUR 4: Tsukiji and Hama Detached Palace Garden

TOUR 5: Yurakucho, Ginza, and Nihombashi (1)

TOUR 6: Nihombashi (2), Fukagawa, and Ningyocho

TOUR 7: Yanagibashi, Asakusabashi, Kuramae, and Ryogoku

TOUR 8: **Asakusa, Senso-ji, Kappabashi, Yoshiwara, and Tsubouchi Theater Museum**

TOUR 9: **Shitamachi, Ueno Park, and Nezu Shrine**

TOUR 10: **Yushima, Kanda, Akihabara, Jimbocho, Korakuen, and Tokyo University**

TOUR 11: **Atago Shrine, Zojo-ji, Tokyo Tower, Shiba Detached Palace Garden, and Sengaku-ji**

TOUR 12: **Roppongi, Meguro, and Shinagawa**

TOUR 13: **Meiji Shrine, Harajuku, Omote Sando, and Aoyama**

TOUR 14: **Shibuya, Shinjuku, Ikebukuro, and
Rikugien**

ILLUSTRATIONS

Preface

TOKYO has been a major city for centuries, surpassing in size the great capitals of Europe since the seventeenth century. It is a city which, prior to 1868, had seen the pageant of the shogunate as the daimyo, the great lords of Japan, progressed in state behind their retainers along the Tokaido Road to their sumptuous mansions in the shadow of the shogun's castle. In more modern times, the city has seen the manipulations of the military in their attempt to make Japan a world power by employing the same, and sometimes more brutal, imperialistic means as used by the nations of the West. It has faced as well devastation by earthquakes and by the "Flowers of Edo," those all-consuming fires which have periodically swept over Edo, old Tokyo, and left it but ashes and a memory.

The *Edokko,* the sons of Edo (and they were mostly sons since men until recent times have always outnumbered women by two to one) have always risen to the challenges which have rained upon the city either by the forces of nature or by the actions and laws of those who ruled over them. Despite the destruction in the twentieth century which has leveled much of Tokyo, first in the Great Kanto Earthquake of 1923 and then in the fire-bombing raids of the spring of 1945 (which in each case left more than

13

100,000 dead and saw a city of wood disappear in flames), there is a history and a continuity of tradition which has not died. Tokyo since the 1950s has been a rising phoenix. It is a city which offers to visitors one of the most modern façades and boasts towering skyscrapers which, it is claimed, can withstand future earthquakes. Yet past traditions are retained despite all the modernism of the second half of the twentieth century.

It is the intention of this volume to explore present-day Tokyo through a series of "tours" that have a view on the past, whose memory still lingers in the urban life of this ever-changing city. This guide is designed to explore the various intriguing areas of Tokyo on foot, describing the buildings and the history behind them. It does not offer a compendium of restaurants (which can be found at every hand) or shops, with their infinite variety of fine or inexpensive wares. On a few occasions particular department stores or specialty shops will be mentioned, for these cannot be ignored in areas such as Ginza, Shibuya, or Shinjuku, but the listing is not meant to be comprehensive. Museums are noted in the course of a tour, but many of these require a separate visit in order to enjoy their extensive holdings. Each tour is so organized that one may leave it at a specific subway station and then return at another time if a tour is longer than desired.

Part of the pleasure of walking in Tokyo comes from viewing the architectural variety expressed in many of the unusual structures within the city. In the last quarter of the twentieth century, Japanese architects (and some foreign architects with Tokyo commissions) became more imaginative and daring in their architectural designs. Experimentation, innovation, creativity, and sometimes even extravagant conceptions have appeared on the face of the city. Witness the façade on one building on Meiji-dori near Togo Shrine which has a jagged crack built into its construction, as though it had been damaged by an earthquake. Or view the building near Ebisu Station whose lower façade is seemingly missing, again as though a cataclysmic stroke had exposed a portion of the inner building.

The purpose of *Tokyo: A Cultural Guide* is to bring to life the continuing pageant of historic Edo which lives on in today's Tokyo and which can always surprise and delight those who are willing to explore it on foot and by subway. In some cases a tour can be covered in more than one visit. On the other hand, more than one of these tours can be combined, depending on the time one spends along the way. Before striking out into "unknown territory," one can always purchase sandwiches from the many convenience stores in order to have a picnic lunch en route at a park or shrine. These stores can also provide food for breakfast or dinners should one find restaurant or hotel dining too expensive.

No book on Tokyo, nor any individual who is interested in the capital of Japan as a living city with its roots in the past, can afford to ignore the scholarly yet popular volume by Paul Waley in his *Tokyo Now and Then* or Edward Seidenstecker's *Low City, High City* and *Tokyo Rising*, or Sumiko Enbutsu's *Old Tokyo*. These volumes are essential reading for anyone wishing further information on a most fascinating city. Additional reading materials are listed in the Bibliography at the end of this volume.

Introduction
Tokyo and Its Heritage

IN 1590, Tokugawa Ieyasu, the powerful warlord of eastern Japan, was beholden to Toyotomi Hideyoshi, the military ruler over all the nation. Hideyoshi, anxious to remove Ieyasu from Kyoto and the center of political power, offered to exchange certain of Ieyasu's territorial holdings near Kyoto for a grant of extensive lands in the underpopulated area in eastern Japan. Ieyasu's followers were aghast at their leader's acceptance of the isolated land at Edo Bay in exchange for his more valuable lands near the imperial capital. Ieyasu, however, had a vision he had not as yet shared with them. Here at the tiny village of Edo (Mouth of the River or Estuary), where the Sumida and other rivers poured into an almost completely encircled bay at the edge of the great Kanto Plain, he would create a mighty civil capital, and from here he and his heirs would rule all of Japan.

With the passage of time, with patience, with guile—and with force—Ieyasu would bring this vision to reality. By 1598 Hideyoshi was dead, and, in the ensuing struggle among the contesting daimyo, the feudal lords who coveted power, Ieyasu had by 1603 conquered all who stood in his way and now ruled as shogun over all Japan. As victor, Ieyasu moved the seat of civil and military power from an effete aristocratic court in Kyoto to the land at the head of the large and sheltered bay where he would build his capital. Thus Edo, the future Tokyo, began its modern existence. Here as shogun he ruled over Japan in the name of the powerless emperor and over the 176 Inside Lords (Fudai Daimyo) who had sided with him before his decisive and victorious battle at Sekigahara in 1603. He also ruled over the 86 Outside Lords (Tozama Daimyo) who had not been farsighted enough to be his allies.

Ieyasu forced both the inside and the outside daimyo to supply labor, materials, and funds for the construction of an impregnable castle in Edo. The work of creating moats, canals, walls, and a fortified residence went on until 1640. From 1603, and for the next 265 years, Ieyasu's successors as shoguns were to rule the nation with unparalleled control from the Edo Castle.

Both to control and financially to weaken any possible contenders for power, Ieyasu enforced the rule of *sankin kotai* (alternate attendance) on his vassals. Alternate periods of two years had to be spent by the leaders of the great clans at their Edo residence. Thus the great daimyo made their compulsory biennial passage from their domains to Edo, a progression with all the panoply and display as required by the Tokugawa shoguns. It was an ostentatious progress which would keep them sufficiently impoverished. At the end of the period of attendance on the shogun, their return to their territorial homes took place with the same pomp. One half of the Outside Lords had to make their journey to Edo in March of each year while the other half returned to their homes that month. The Inside Lords made their biennial journey in alternate years in August.

In Edo, custom and honor forced these daimyo to live in splendid mansions befitting their rank. On their return to their domains they had to leave their women and children as hostage in their Edo palaces of Momoyama grandeur as warrant of their good behavior. The expense of maintaining their territorial seat of power and an elaborate establishment in Edo, with the incumbent costly procession between the two locations, financially precluded any attempts on their part to mount a threat by force against the Tokugawas.

As an additional precaution, the Tokugawa shoguns had barriers erected at points along the main highways into Edo, and here the rule of "no women out, no guns in" maintained the hostage system and kept the daimyo weaponless within the new civil capital.

For 265 years the Tokugawas ruled from their mighty Edo Castle, a fortress which only nature and time (but no military attack) would subdue. Its nemesis appeared in the form of earthquakes and fire, and these untoward events occurred on more than one occasion. When in time the rule of the Tokugawas came to an end (1868), Edo was renamed Tokyo (Eastern Capital). Then a sixteen-year-old emperor was moved from Kyoto to reign from the former castle grounds. Ostensibly power had returned from the shogun to the emperor, but time would disclose the powerless nature of imperial rule since the nation's new military leaders were the real power behind the throne and would both enhance and endanger the nation's place in the world. It is one of the ironies of history that in time a blue-eyed "shogun" in the guise of an American general would reign over Japan for a number of years before a new and more democratic form of governance would issue from the political and economic centers about Edo Castle, now become the Imperial Palace of Tokyo.

The walking tours which follow begin at that place from which many visitors arrive at Tokyo: Tokyo Central Station. The walks then spiral out from the palace to encompass the variety that the city has to offer. The subway or rail station from which each walk begins is indicated at the beginning of that walk. Thus with a map of Tokyo (which can be obtained from one's hotel or from the Japan National Tourist Office on Harumi-dori just down from the junction of the Palace and Hibiya Park) and a plan of the Tokyo subway lines, one can venture forth into a fascinating city.

TOUR 1

Marunouchi, Imperial Palace, and Hibiya Park

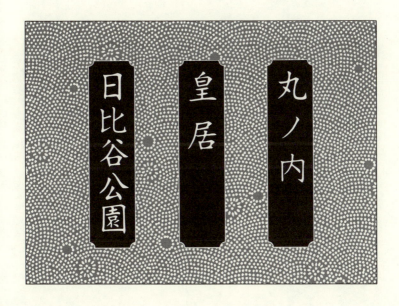

WHEN Tokugawa Ieyasu planned his castle in Edo in 1590, he chose to build it on the high ground above the Hibiya Inlet which spread inland from the great bay (Tokyo Bay) in front of his new capital. Under his direction, that inlet and various rivers in the vicinity of the castle were channeled so as to form canals and moats about the innermost portion of the city. Here, behind these watery barriers, the shogunal headquarters were to rise protected by fortified walls and water-filled moats.

The Hibiya Inlet in front of the eastern side of the castle was soon filled in, leaving an inner moat and, beyond the filled inlet, an outer moat. Earth for the project was taken from the higher terrain known as Yamanote (The High City) to the west and north. Upon the newly reclaimed land between the inner and outer moats, an area called Marunouchi (Within the Moats) housed the mansions of the daimyo most favored by the Tokugawa shoguns. Additional fill was used which formed the *shitamachi* (literally, the "low city") to the east in which lived the common workers who supplied the daimyo and their entourages with their daily needs.

Around the moated castle enclave, between the inner and outer moats, were placed the residences of Ieyasu's most trusted Inside Lords. Today, Uchibori-dori (Inner Moat Street) borders the Imperial Palace grounds on the palace's eastern side, and a portion of this moat is still in existence. Sotobori-dori (Outer Moat Street) has in the twentieth century become a ring road about the original central portion of Tokyo and the Imperial Palace grounds. It is only in the decades after the Second World War that the remaining portions of this latter moat were filled in, thus Sotobori-dori now varies between being a ground-level roadway and, in part, an elevated and then an underground roadway. In the northeast portion of the Marunouchi area, between today's Tokyo Central Station and the palace grounds, lay the mansions and dependencies of the Matsudaira lords. To the south, in front of today's Imperial Palace Plaza were the mansions of the Honda, the Sakai, and other favored daimyo.

For some 260 years, these lands housed the most powerful military leaders of Japan. By the 1860s, however, the political and military power of the last two shoguns gradually dissipated. The rule of *sankin kotai* (alternate attendance) which, after 1635, required both the Inside and Outside Lords to spend two years in Edo and two years in their own lands on an alternate basis, came to an end. Then in 1868, with the victory of the adherents of the Emperor Meiji over the Tokugawa shogunate, the mansions of all the daimyo were abandoned as the provincial lords returned to their home provinces. The deserted buildings were by 1871 either used for government offices when these offices were moved to Tokyo from Kyoto or were cleared for military drill grounds for a growing and ever more militaristic government.

By 1890, within twenty years of the imperial takeover of Edo (now Tokyo), the Meiji government and the military authorities required funds for the development of new establishments for their growing needs. Thus the land "within the moats" was put up for sale. The Imperial Household did not have the funds to purchase the land, and thus the Iwasaki family, a leading mercantile and growing industrial clan, were prevailed upon to purchase the vacant Marunouchi area in front of the palace grounds. Known derisively as the Mitsubishi Meadow or even the "Gambler's Meadow" by those who did not have the foresight to buy the land, the Marunouchi district was planned by the Iwasakis to become a Western-style complex of buildings for the industrial and commercial growth they foresaw for the nation. To this end they hired Josiah Conder, an English architect who came to live in Japan in 1877 and who worked not only as an architect but as an instructor at the College of Technology (later to become Tokyo University) to teach architecture. Here he trained the first generation of Japanese architects in the technicalities of Western architecture.

Conder's three-story buildings, which he designed for the Mitsubishi group, were red-brick structures with white stone quoins. Windows and doors were outlined in white stone. The new Western-style district he created was known as "London Town." Its streets were lined with trees and the newest of modern appurtenances, poles to support above-ground electric wires. London Town with its Queen Anne style architecture in Marunouchi, and the not-too-distant Ginza area with its newly paved streets and brick-built structures, were the pride of the Meiji era.

The sponsors of London Town hoped that it would quickly become the new commercial and financial center of Tokyo. The first building was completed in 1894, but unfortunately the Stock Exchange, the Bank of Japan, and other financial and commercial establishments remained in Nihombashi to the east. Success for London Town had to await the arrival of the railroad into central Tokyo.

The extension of the railroad from Shimbashi, south of the Ginza area, into Marunouchi finally became a reality in 1914. Dr. Tatsuno Kingo, a student of Josiah Conder, was named as the architect of the new Tokyo Central Station (where this walking tour begins), which opened in 1914. The 1,000-foot-long red-brick Renaissance-style station was modeled after the Amsterdam Zentraal station in the Netherlands. The new station faced toward the east, toward London Town and the Imperial Palace. The plan to have an entrance on the eastern side of the station was stymied for years since the Sotobori (Outer Moat) still ran parallel to the railroad right-of-way to the east, and the interests of the Nihombashi and Kyobashi officials could not be satisfied since each wanted a bridge over the moat to their district. The dispute was not resolved until 1929 when an eastern entrance to the station was created. This latter entrance was greatly enhanced in the 1960s when the high-speed Shinkansen Line with its "Bullet Trains" came into being, for then a whole new, modern terminal structure was built behind the existing station. Also the Daimaru Department Store was built, facing Yaesu Plaza, which covers a portion of the former Sotobori.

Tokyo Central Station, after its opening in 1914, was meant as a memorial for Japan's victory over Russia in the Russo-Japanese War of 1904–5, and its main entrance was reserved solely for royal use. The station remained central in name only, for it was the terminus for trains from the south while the station at Ueno (to the north) was the terminus for trains from the north and east. Not until after the Great Kanto Earthquake of 1923 could the two stations be linked, a possibility brought about by the earthquake's destruction of the buildings between the two terminals. With the completion of the elevated Yamanote Line in 1925, which circles a major portion of Tokyo, it was finally possible to link Ueno Station and Tokyo Central Station.

The early future of Marunouchi looked brighter when the Tokyo city and prefectural governments agreed to share a new building in the former daimyo quarter. A red-brick, Western-style structure was to arise in Marunouchi with the prefectural offices to the right while the city offices were to the left. Each had the image of its patron before its portion of the structure: Ota Dokan, the founder of the earlier Edo Castle in the mid-1400s, was placed before the city sector of the building. Tokugawa Ieyasu, the second founder of Edo in the 1590s, stood before the prefectural offices. (A new, modern city hall was erected on the site in 1957 under the direction of the noted Japanese architect Kenzo Tange. As with its predecessor, it was to be razed after 1991 as the city hall moved farther west to Shinjuku. The new city hall was also designed by Tange.)

The new station became the "front door" to the city, and gradually office buildings in Marunouchi, as London Town came to be known, filled the "Mitsubishi Meadows" between the railroad and the Palace over the next twenty-five years. The life of modern buildings is frequently all too short, and Conder's buildings gradually were replaced from 1930 on by newer and larger structures. The last remnant of London Town, Mitsubishi Building Number One, disappeared in 1967 in the post–Second World War construction boom. The limit of seven to eight floors (100 feet in height) for the buildings in Marunouchi, out of respect to the adjacent Imperial Palace, which it would not be proper to overshadow, was to go the way of many such traditions after the 1950s, and today the financial and commercial head-quarters of Japanese and international firms tower over the Imperial Palace grounds. Other traditions, such as the placing of an image of the Buddha under the roof of a building as protec-tion against lightning, are no longer recognized. According to Edward Seidensticker, one of these original Buddhas resides in the basement of the Marunouchi Building, hardly a protection against the deity of lightning.

This tour of Marunouchi and Yurakucho begins at the eastern side of **Tokyo Central Station,** a bustling center whose daily train traffic its original planners could not have envisioned. Twelve train platforms above and below ground receive three thousand train arrivals a day. A small park graces the area before the station with the Tokyo Central Post Office on the left and a bus terminal to the right. A broad street leads from the plaza in front of the station to Hibiya-dori and the park before the Imperial Palace that was created in 1926. The building on the left of the beginning of this boulevard was the **Marunouchi Building** (Maru Number One), completed just before the 1923 earthquake. It marked the beginning of a new era for Marunouchi, for this eight-story building was the largest one in Japan at the time, and it helped to attract financial and commercial firms to this area of geometrically planned streets. The district was fortunate in that it remained undamaged in the 1923 earthquake and from the major air raids of 1945, although it too is now gone.

A companion building on the right of the beginning of the boulevard is the New Marunouchi Building (Maru Number Two), which appears to be a twin to the original structure across the way. Its foundations were in place before the Second World War, but it remained a stagnant pool until 1951, when work finally commenced on its completion. The success of the one-time London Town is obvious from the number of high-rise buildings in the district. The 1958 Otemachi Building, which can hold forty-thousand employees, is a prime example of the change which has come over the "Mitsubishi Meadows."

Two streets along the boulevard bring one to **Hibiya-dori,** the **Babasaki-bori** (Moat in Front of the Horse Grounds), and the beginning of the Imperial Palace Outer Gardens. (The moat has this strange name since it derives from a 1635 display of horse-manship presented before the shogun by a delegation from the then dependent Kingdom of Korea.) When the capital was moved to Tokyo in 1868, three areas which were a portion of the castle grounds were gradually given to the public as parkland. These include the Imperial Palace Outer Garden along Hibiya-dori in front of the Palace, the Imperial Palace East Garden, which contains the remains of the former Tokugawa castle, and the Kita-no-Maru Park, which was once also a part of the castle grounds. The Outer Garden has seen momentous events since it was separated from the Imperial Palace grounds. Here refugees from the destruction of the 1923 earthquake gathered, and here in August of 1945 a number of Japan's officer corps committed *seppuku* (ritual suicide), their deaths supposedly atoning for Japan's loss in the Pacific War. In the 1950s and 1960s it became a place for public demonstrations against unpopular govern-ment decisions. Many of these gatherings were anti-American in nature.

Hibiya-dori extends along the Outer Gardens and the palace with a range of modern office buildings on its eastern side. Turning to the left from the boulevard leading from the Tokyo Station and heading south (to the left) on Hibiya-dori, the present buildings between the railway and the Outer Garden cover not only the site of the Matsudaira daimyo mansion and ancillary buildings but also the building in which the shogun's chief Confucian advisor, Hayashi Razan, once held sway.

Prior to the nineteenth century the shogunal fire department was located where the **Meiji Life Insurance Building** now stands across from the bridge over the Babasaki Moat. Edo never

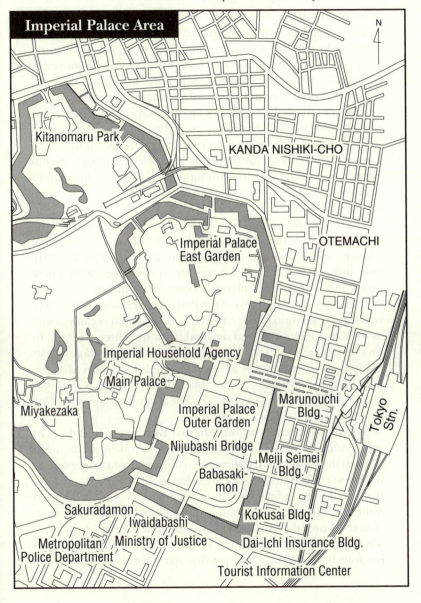

Imperial Palace Area

N

Kitanomaru Park

KANDA NISHIKI-CHO

OTEMACHI

Imperial Palace
East Garden

Imperial Household Agency

Main Palace

Miyakezaka

Marunouchi
Bldg.

Imperial Palace
Outer Garden

Nijubashi Bridge

Tokyo Stn.

Meiji Seimei
Bldg.

Babasaki-
mon

Sakuradamon

Iwaidabashi

Kokusai Bldg.

Metropolitan
Police Department

Ministry of Justice

Dai-Ichi Insurance Bldg.

Tourist Information Center

boasted an organization which could fight the "Flowers of Edo," outbreaks of fires which occurred all too frequently. Each daimyo and the shogun had men who could serve to protect their lord's property, but the common citizen was on his own in his warren of wooden houses in the *shitamachi* when fires broke out. Unfortunately, not even the firefighters of the daimyo were always successful, and in the Long Sleeves Fire of 1657 the shogun's castle was engulfed in flames and destroyed. The shogunal fire detachment can lay claim to fame even today on one score, however, for here at the location of the Meiji Life Insurance Building a son was born to one of the shogun's firefighters. He forsook his father's profession, and Ando Hiroshige chose to make his name through his woodblock prints instead.

One full street along Hibiya-dori beyond the bridge over the Babasaki Moat is the **Kokusai Building.** Within it is the Imperial Theater, which opened in 1911. It was the first major Western-style theater in Tokyo, and it was highly decorated with a generous use of marble. Splendid tapestries hung in it as well, reminiscent of the richness of the Paris Opera House. This 1,900-seat theater was initially intended for concerts and recitals as well as for Kabuki, but it proved unsuitable for this latter art form. In more recent years, after a 1966 renovation when the stage and its equipment were updated and a restrained decor pervaded the hall of the playhouse, it has been home to many popular contemporary American musicals. The theater occupies the first three floors of the Kokusai Building.

The main entrance to the Kokusai Building is found on its south side. Here are elevators which may be taken to the ninth floor to the **Idemitsu Art Museum,** a museum containing one of the finest collections of Asian art in Japan. (The museum is open from 10:00 A.M. to 5:00 P.M. No admission after 4:30. It is closed Mondays, but open on Monday if a national holiday and then closed the next day. Also closed over the New Year holidays. Entry fee.) Created by the president of the Idemitsu Oil Company, it has four large rooms which provide space for the display of the riches of the collection. The main room presents objects from the museum's fine collection of Chinese ceramics, which range from prehistoric times through to the eighteenth century. Japanese ceramics are also well represented with examples of Imari, Kutani, Seto, Nabeshima, and Kakiemon wares.

Another room shows selections from sixteenth and seventeenth century screens depicting episodes in *The Tale of Genji* as well as prints with scenes of Kyoto and Edo before 1868. The *ukiyo-e* woodblock prints in the collection illustrate an art form that was popular from the 1600s through the 1800s, and these prints are complemented by Zen paintings and fine examples of calligraphy. An additional room holds a varied and very large collection of ceramic shards representing a range of countries from Iran (Persia) to southeast and eastern Asia. Chinese and Japanese lacquerware of excellent quality are also on view. The labels in the exhibition cases are in English and Japanese. Since 1972 the museum has branched into another area of art with the acquisition of more than four hundred works by the French painter Georges Roualt.

Along with its artistic attractions, the location of the museum on the ninth floor of the Kokusai Building provides an excellent view of the Imperial Palace Outer Garden. In addition, a coffee shop offers a place to relax among the Asian works of art.

Continuing south on Hibiya-dori, across the street from the Kokusai Building is the **Dai-Ichi Insurance Building,** encompassing the full frontage of the street on which it sits facing the palace grounds. Built in 1938 to the design of Watanabe Matsumoto in what was a modern international style, particularly one favored by authoritarian governments of the day, ten huge columns of its façade supported two upper floors. One of the modern, fireproof buildings of pre–Second World War Tokyo, it managed to survive the bombings and firestorms of the war years. Today the façade of the building has been covered over with a bland end-of-the-twentieth-century facing while a new tower of twenty-one stories, designed by the American architect Kevin Roche, rises behind the original structure. Whatever character the front of the building once had has now been effaced.

Here in the original building, from September 15, 1945, until April 11, 1951, General Douglas MacArthur had his headquarters as the military and civilian representative of the victorious Allied forces at the end of the Second World War. His sixth-floor, walnut-paneled office was simply furnished with a conference table and a green leather armchair. The General's office virtually became a museum after his departure, and now it is used by the head of the Dai-Ichi Mutual Insurance Company. The room is preserved, and requests may be made to the Dai-Ichi Insurance public relations office to view the room.

Crossing the street to the **Imperial Outer Garden,** which lies in front of the walls of the palace, one can enjoy one of the few open spaces within this crowded city. This portion of Tokyo has seen many transformations in the 550 years since Ota Dokan in 1457 first built his fortified mansion and two other fortresses on the height above today's garden. At that time there was no garden, for the Hibiya Inlet, an extension of Tokyo Bay, once stretched this far inland, providing a natural moat before the fortified hill. The tiny town that Ota Dokan began below his hillside fortress received its name of Edo (Water Front or Mouth of the River) from its location. The town was to grow, but in the unpredictable politics of his day, Ota Dokan was assassinated at his lord's behest in 1486, and his fortified mansion and stronghold became derelict. One hundred years had to pass before a more massive castle would arise on the site and before Edo would begin to grow into a major city.

This present parkland was created when Tokugawa Ieyasu moved his headquarters from Shizuoka to the site of Ota Dokan's castle in the 1590s. Ieyasu had the Hibiya Inlet filled in with land from the hills of Kanda to the north, and the newly created land became the site of the mansions of the Inside Lords, who were his closest allies. After 1868, with the fall of the Tokugawa shogunate, the Meiji government established its government offices in the area in which the daimyo had lived. These offices were relocated from Kyoto into former daimyo buildings in Tokyo, a not very satisfactory arrangement. Relocation of the offices into more practical quarters was inevitable, and in the period after 1889 the Marunouchi area, as described above, was sold to the Iwasaki family in order to raise funds for the proper housing of govern-mental functions. In 1889 that portion of what is now the Outer Gardens had the government offices removed. Pine trees were planted there, and the land in front of the palace became a public park.

In 1897 a bronze equestrian statue of Kusunoki Masashige, given to the nation by the wealthy Sumitomo family of Osaka, was cast by Takamura Koun and placed within the Outer Garden. The creation of this statue by order of the Meiji government was part of its attempt to establish new heroes whose actions in the past showed devotion to the Imperial House and to the emperor. Such public images were meant to enhance the government's new creed of loyalty to the emperor and the need to be ready to sacrifice oneself for the emperor and nation. These two virtues were evident in Kusunoki's life and exemplified by the way he defended Emperor Go-Daigo and his imperial prerogatives in the 1300s and then committed *seppuku* when his defense of the emperor against Ashikaga Takauji's usurpation of power failed in 1336.

Reverence to the god-emperor reached such ideological heights in the late nineteenth and early twentieth century that at one time passengers in the trams that went by the palace were expected to rise from their seats and bow to the emperor within its walls. The fact that the Meiji defenders of Imperial rule were themselves governing in the name of a powerless emperor, whose image they were using, was completely overlooked. A much lighter element was added to the northeast portion of the Outer Gardens in the 1960s when a large fountain within a pool was created to celebrate the wedding of the then crown prince (Emperor Heisei).

At the far end of the Outer Garden from Hibiya-dori another moat separates the palace walls from the public park, these various moats encircling the 250 acres of the palace grounds. The Imperial Palace today is located in the Nishi-no-Maru (Western Fortified Area) in what was one portion of the shoguns' castle confines. The raised ground of the palace, beyond the Outer Garden and moats, is faced with walls of huge stones brought by boat in the early 1600s from the Izu Peninsula some sixty miles to the southwest of Tokyo. These massive stones were dragged by teams of laborers supplied by the daimyo, along paths covered with seaweed to ease the movement of the heavily loaded sledges, from the bay to the castle grounds. Such fortified walls, before the development of modern gunpowder and explosives, could only be breached by treachery from within, by natural forces such as earthquakes, or through a siege which might starve a defending force into surrendering. In the more than 260 years of the enforced Tokugawa peace that followed 1603, these walls were neither breached nor attacked.

Most of the shogunal buildings in the Tokugawa castle were destroyed by fire in the years before Emperor Meiji arrived in his new capital. His sojourn in the castle grounds was briefer than anticipated, since in 1873 the last of the Tokugawa buildings were destroyed by fire, and the emperor and empress were forced to move to the Akasaka Palace grounds, where they lived in a former mansion of a branch of the Tokugawa family until 1889 when a new palace was completed on the palace grounds. This 1889 palace was destroyed in the air raids of early 1945.

When facing the palace grounds from the Outer Garden, one sees on the right the Fujimi Yagura (Mount Fuji Viewing Tower), while to the left stands the Fushimi Yagura (Fushimi Tower), two of the three remaining fortified towers of the Tokugawa castle. Toward the south end of the Outer Garden (to the left), Nijubashi (Double Bridge) comes into view along with the Fushimi Tower, both of them rising out of the Imperial moat. In the militaristic era of the 1930s and 40s, the bridge, the Fushimi Tower, and the walls of the palace grounds became a symbol of mystical patriotism for the Japanese. So mystical or mythical became the palace site where the god-emperor resided that when Emperor Hirohito at the end of the Second World War announced the capitulation of Japan, the more fanatical of Imperial Army officers performed ceremonial suicide before the palace enclave as atonement for the loss of Japanese military honor.

The Imperial Palace grounds are not open to the public except on two occasions: on the emperor's birthday on December 23 (from 8:30 A.M. to 11:00 A.M.) and at the start of the New Year on January 2 (from 9:30 A.M. to 3:00 P.M.). On December 23 the emperor greets the public from the balcony of the Kyukaden (The Hall of State), while at the New Year holiday the imperial family receives the public from the same balcony. The "Hall of State" is a 1968 ferroconcrete, earthquake-resistant and fireproof structure which serves as a reception and banqueting hall for official imperial events. The Kyukaden consists of three buildings: the Seiden, in which is the Pine Tree Hall (Matsu-no-ma) where the imperial family receives greetings from the prime minister and his cabinet in the annual New Year reception; the Homeiden where formal dinners are held for foreign dignitaries; and the Chowaden, which has the imperial balcony for imperial public greetings. The imperial private residence is in the Fukiage Palace in the western portion of the grounds, a structure which was constructed (1991–93) to replace the unit built after the Second World War. (In Tokugawa times this twenty-eight-acre sector provided land for the mansions of the three main branches of the Tokugawa family.) The private residence area has a gateway to the city through the Hanzomon gate on the western side of the palace grounds.

On the two occasions when they may visit these private areas, the public may come into the palace grounds by means of the 1888 **Nijubashi** bridge. Although it is usually referred to as the Double Bridge, the name originally referred to the Double Layer Bridge, a wooden bridge and later a steel bridge with an upper and a lower level. A modern single-layer steel bridge replaced the double bridge in 1964. Today, two bridges, one behind the other, give the name "Double Bridge" a new meaning. In the foreground is a stone bridge of two arches, the Shakkyo-bashi, which is also called the Megane-bashi since its two arches when reflected in the water form a whole circle and resemble a pair of spectacles (*megane*). During the public visitation to the Palace, one moves through the massive gateway with its guard stations to the palace grounds, over the Nijubashi bridge, through the Seimon (Main Gate), into the Kyakuden East Garden in five minutes or so, and to the Hall of State from whose balcony the imperial greetings are given.

Two other gates at the north end of the Outer Garden lead into the palace grounds. The Sakashita-mon (Gate at the Bottom of the Slope) provides an entrance to the brick structure which constitutes the Imperial Household Agency offices, the very conservative bureaucracy which safeguards and controls the heritage and activities of the imperial family. The buildings of the Household Agency stand before Momijiyama, the hill named for its maple trees, an area which is more poetically known as the Hill of Autumn Leaves from the lovely color of the foliage of the trees at the end of the summer season. On this hill stood the Toshogu shrine to the spirit of Tokugawa Ieyasu, one of the many shrines raised to his spirit throughout Japan and which culminated in the highly ornate shrine in his honor at Nikko. The other gate, the Kikyo-mon (Bellflower gate), is the entry for visitors and officials to the palace and for the delivery of supplies by tradesmen. Its name is said to derive from the family crest of Ota Dokan, which contained a bellflower.

Leaving the Outer Garden grounds from the southwestern corner, one exits through the **Sakurada-mon** gate of the palace. It was one of the *masugata* gates that are described in the next tour, a tour which is concerned with the original castle and its present site. Here on March 24, 1860, occurred an event which was to weaken the Tokugawa shogunate and help to lead to its ultimate demise eight years later. At the Sakurada-mon (Gate of the Field of Cherry Trees) on a snowy morning, Ii Naosuke, Lord of Hikone, and his guards made their way to the castle grounds. Ii was one of the more important advisors to the shogun, and he had signed the unequal treaties with the West, treaties opposed by the emperor in Kyoto, his courtiers, and even some branches of the Tokugawa clan. Assassins from the Mito branch of the Tokugawa, opposed to the agreements with the "Western barbarians," fell upon Ii and his guards, leaving their bodies in the bloodied snow.

Ironically, walking through the Sakurada-mon gate and crossing the Gaisen-Hibiya moat today and then Harumi-dori, one is faced by the white-tiled exterior of the 1980 eighteen-story **Metropolitan Police Department** headquarters to the right and the 1895 **Ministry of Justice** building to the left. The present police headquarters stands on the site of a pre–Second World War jail, one in which the captured fliers of General Doolittle's raid on Tokyo were held in 1942 before being taken to Sugamo Prison to be executed. The Ministry of Justice building was designed by two architects from Germany. They wished to combine the best of traditional Japanese and Western architecture in this new structure, but in the press for modernization in the 1890s, government officials insisted on a more Western style to prevail. The original roof of the building was damaged in the 1945 air raids and was replaced with a flat roof which would have caused the architects even further unhappiness. It is one of the few Meiji era brick buildings still standing, and it and its grounds underwent extensive restoration in the 1990s.

Turning to the left along Harumi-dori, the northwest corner of **Hibiya Park** is at hand. Halfway down the street there is a path which leads through this forty-one-acre park which held daimyo residences before 1868. Whereas Shogun Ieyasu's most dependable allies had their mansions in front of the castle gate in the Marunouchi area, the Outside Lords who were not among Ieyasu's allies prior to 1603 were permitted to lease lands at a further remove from the castle main gate. Living in what is today's Hibiya Park area, they were close enough for the shogun's spies to keep an eye on them, but they were not so close to the shogun and his retinue that they could act upon any treacherous intentions. Here were the residences of the powerful Nabeshima clan of Saga on the island of Kyushu and that of the Mori clan of Choshu in western Japan, mansions located beyond the outer ramparts of the castle. Sixty percent of the land in Edo belonged to the daimyo and their followers, who represented less than half the population of Edo, while twenty percent was occupied by commoners, and another twenty percent was given over to temples and shrines.

The daimyo had to express their status by their show of splendor, and thus they built their residences in the extravagant, highly decorated Momoyama architectural style popular at the beginning of the 1600s. The original Momoyama mansions were destroyed in the Long Sleeves Fire of 1657, and the replacement structures were, of necessity, in a more simple style. New sumptuary laws and the alternate attendance requirement, with its costly journeys by full entourages and the expense of maintaining mansions in home provinces as well as Edo, were a crippling burden for the daimyo.

By 1871 the land once occupied by both the Inside and the Outside Lords had been confiscated by the new Meiji government, and the land was cleared, leaving but a vestige of the past in the northeast corner of Hibiya Park where a portion of the original wall of the Hibiya Gate of the former moat remains. What in 1903 was to become Hibiya Park was in the 1870s a dusty military parade ground, and here in 1872 Emperor Meiji reviewed his troops. With the military wishing to create a permanent Tokyo headquarters, their parade ground was moved to the edge of the city in the 1890s. Plans were drawn to build Western-style government offices on the former military parade grounds. The subsoil was found to be too soft to support modern brick and stone structures, however, and, given the engineering of the day and the fact that this had once been an arm of Tokyo Bay before it was filled in, construction of modern buildings was out of the question.

Plans were therefore made to establish a park on the site, and it was opened to the public in June 1903. It was one of the first Western-style parks in Japan. Through the years the park has accrued several amenities: the Hibiya Gallery on its Harumi-dori side, a Public Hall of 1929 with its art nouveau touches on its southern side for concerts, lectures, meetings and other cultural activities, a public library adjacent to the hall, a café, two restaurants, a lake, ponds, lawns, flower gardens, tennis courts, and a tiered outdoor area where today jazz, folk, and other popular music attracts young music lovers. In 1961 a large fountain was added to the park, and it is illuminated with seven colors at night. The park also is notorious for having become a trysting place for lovers, and thereby a resort for peeping toms. There is even a small museum devoted to the history of the park. The museum is open from 10:00 A.M. to 4:00 P.M. except on Mondays.

The park is noted for its cherry blossoms in April, for its wisteria and azalea blooms in May, and for its magnificent display of chrysanthemums in November, this latter a festive event which draws many visitors. The park also contains dogwood trees that were a gift from the United States in appreciation of the Japanese cherry trees which were given by Tokyo to Washington, D.C.

In the unhappy days of the 1930s and 1940s, the park became an artillery battery, the lawns were replaced by vegetable plots, and, after the first American air raid by General Doolittle in 1942, anti-aircraft guns were put into place.

The Imperial Palace Outer Gardens were not the only public spot used for dissent in the past. In 1905 some 30,000 protesters gathered at Hibiya Park to object to the terms of the peace treaty at the end of the Russo-Japanese War, and, as a result of the violence which ensued, the government declared martial law. Again in the 1950s and 1960s, protests against Japanese government relations with the United States were centered here. The **Hibiya Public Hall,** which has served as the site of political party meetings, has had its unhappy incidents as well, the most notable occurring in 1960 when Inejiro Asanuma, the chairman of the Japan Socialist Party, was killed at the podium by a sword-wielding student.

Across from the southern end of the park and the Public Hall and Library is **Hibiya City,** which is similar to New York City's Rockefeller Center in that it has a large, open skating rink, fountains, and statuary within the square of shops and corporate display centers.

If Hibiya Park represented an early Western-style influence, there was an even earlier attempt at "Westernization" across Hibiya-dori on lands once held by the Outside Lords of Satsuma. After the nation opened its doors to the world in the 1860s, Japan had been forced by the Western nations to grant certain extra-territorial rights to Western governments. These restrictions obviously rankled members of the Japanese government, and numerous attempts were made to remove these limitations on Japanese sovereignty so as to permit Japan in an international context to assume its status as an equal with the European nations and the United States.

One of the more futile of these attempts occurred in 1881 when Kaoru Inoue, then foreign minister of Japan, had the Rokumeikan hall erected to the south of where the Imperial Hotel now stands. This Western-style, two-story brick and stucco structure designed by Josiah Conder, the British architect whose influence was so strong in Meiji Japan, was a potpourri of Western architectural styles. As Paul Waley describes it, it had Mediterranean arcades on both floors, being of a Tuscan nature on the ground floor and of a vaguely Moorish nature on the second floor. Verandas ran the length of the building, and the mix of styles was then topped with a roof which had French overtones of the *belle époque* (a model of the Rokumeikan can be seen in the Edo-Tokyo Museum under one of the glassed floor panels).

The Rokumeikan was meant to be a social gathering place where foreigners and the cream of Japanese society (in Western attire) could meet, dance the popular Viennese waltzes, and enjoy one another's company. All the appurtenances of modern civilization were present: a ballroom, a reading room, a billiards lounge, and a music room. Other innovations of a Western nature occurred in these modern halls, such as invitations to gatherings that were addressed to both husbands and wives, garden parties, and evening receptions. There was even a charity bazaar in 1884 that ran for three days. Surely this must have indicated to the Europeans and Americans (whom some Japanese still referred to as "red-haired barbarians") that Japan was now an equal to the West and should be treated as an equal.

The building was also meant to serve as a state-owned guest house. The former guest house in the Hama Detached Palace in Shimbashi that had received American President Grant and his wife had now fallen into disrepair. The suites for distinguished guests in the Rokumeikan could even boast an alabaster bathtub six feet long by three feet wide. Unhappily, the significance of the name of the building was lost on the Westerners it was intended to impress. Rokumeikan means "House of the Cry of the Stag," a literary reference to a Chinese classic which, as any learned Japanese would have known, referred to "a place of convivial gatherings."

Alas, the Rokumeikan did not bring about the abolition of extra-territoriality. The building soon lost popularity among the Meiji era Japanese elite, and a clamor from political rightists called for its demise as "an affront to Japanese honor." Abandoned as a cultural center, it became the Peers' Club in 1889, a mere five years after it opened, and it eventually came into use as a bank and as an insurance office. In 1940 it was finally torn down. A remembrance of the Rokumeikan lingers in a most unusual location today. In a Buddhist prayer hall in Tomyo-ji temple at Hirai in Edogawa-ku, one of the Italian bronze chandeliers from the ballroom of the Rokumeikan, that nineteenth-century attempt at Western civilization, now adds the light of culture to the light of Buddhist faith.

The site of the Rokumeikan has with time been covered with more modern edifices. One of the more striking examples is the Dai-ichi Kangyo Bank Building across from the Hibiya Public Hall. This thirty-two-floor building was erected in 1981, and its eastern and western walls are covered with a gray granite while the front has a stepped, glass curtain wall. A sunken mall is entered from a plaza with a large clock, and the lobby holds the sculpture *Doppo la Danza* by Giacomo Manzo.

Despite the failure of the Rokumeikan to survive, a new Western-style hotel was being planned, and it came into being as the **Imperial Hotel** in 1890 adjacent to the Rokumeikan just to the north on Hibiya-dori. The new hotel soon became a center for both foreigners and Japanese. A three-story wooden structure with verandas and arches and a mansard roof, it resembled its ill-fated next-door neighbor. The hotel could only accommodate two to three hundred guests. Nevertheless, it became the center for the "smart set" of its day. Within a year of its opening it came into unexpected use when the nearby Diet chambers burned to the ground, and members of the Diet had to meet in the hotel until their new legislative meeting place was available.

The one hundred rooms of the Imperial Hotel proved to be inadequate as Tokyo moved into the twentieth century. In 1915 Frank Lloyd Wright was commissioned to create a new and more modern hotel on a portion of the site of the existing Imperial Hotel. "Westernization" reached new proportions in Wright's edifice since he reworked an earlier design in a somewhat Mayan style that he had made for a non-Japanese client in Mexico and which had been rejected as too unusual. The design provided a building which was Western and modern in ambience but pre-Western in its architectural design. The building was under construction for seven years, with the usual recriminations since it ran several times over budget as well as over its timetable for completion. Its opening occurred in 1922 just as the original

Imperial Hotel in front of it burned down and but one year before the Great Kanto Earthquake of 1923.

Wright boasted that his building had proved to be earthquake-proof during that 1923 disaster. He credited its underlying "dish" foundation construction, whereby the building could float on its underground basin which he had designed for keeping the building from collapsing. A similar design had been used elsewhere in Tokyo whereby a structure would "float" on piles sunk in the mud. A number of these other buildings successfully survived the earthquake, some without the unfortunate settling which affected parts of Wright's building.

The vicissitudes of use, of uneven corridors and floors, of other evidences of the 1923 damage, of wartime neglect in the 1940s, of its use by the U.S. military authorities after 1945, and of the rise in land prices brought this self-proclaimed monument to Wright's genius to an untimely end in 1967. Then it was razed for the new high-rise Imperial Hotel and its later tower addition, both in the international style of the late twentieth century. A "Society to Protect the Imperial Hotel" had been organized in 1967, but the Wright hotel closed its doors forever on November 15 of that year. A portion of the original Wright Building, including the forecourt, pond, and main lounge rooms, have been saved and scrupulously restored in Meiji-mura, the outdoor museum of Victorian architectural style in Japan near Gifu City. Again, here is one of those ironies of history since this post-Meiji era unit was built in the succeeding Taisho era and in a prehistoric Mayan architectural style, and is now saved among the Victorian architectural artifacts of Japan's early modern period which has been designated as the Meiji period (1868–1912).

The post-1968 Imperial Hotel provides the latest in luxury accommodations: it has a coffee shop and restaurants as well as an arcade of shops on the lower level. Among its unexpected amenities is a swimming pool on the nineteenth floor. It is a far cry from the original Imperial Hotel of a mere one hundred rooms. In 1983 an additional unit, the Imperial Tower, was added to the 1970s building, and its first four floors are given over to very expensive luxury shops. The later Imperial Hotel is overpowering in its attempt at grandeur and has the ambience of an international airport terminal striving for recognition.

Just to the north of the Imperial Hotel on Hibiya-dori is the 1963 **Nissei-Hibiya Building** which contains the 1,334-seat Nissei Theater. The theater offers ballet, opera in season, and concerts and movies at other times. It provides a rather showy theater interior with its ceiling flecked with mother-of-pearl, its walls of glass mosaics and lights flashing within the walls and ceiling. Its lobby boasts an art deco ceiling and a marble floor, making it as theatrical as some of the entertainment which appears in it.

Behind the Nissei-Hibiya Building is the **Takarazuka Theater** on the side street to the left of the Imperial Hotel. The street is now known as Theater Street, its sidewalks increased in width and its roadway narrowed in order to handle the festive crowds attending the theaters along its length. In the period of the United States military occupation of Japan after 1945, this theater served as the Ernie Pyle Theater for American troops, named for the famed World War II correspondent who was killed on Iwo Jima. The Ernie Pyle served as a movie-and-stage theater for almost a decade, its operation giving an exceedingly large Japanese staff employment which might not otherwise have been available to them in those post-war days. The theater was restored to civilian control as the Occupation ended.

The theater was eventually returned to Japanese control, and its spectacular music and dance extravaganzas in which all the parts, male and female, are taken by young women, were resumed after a wartime and post-war hiatus. Aside from the stage with its multiple possible uses, there is a *hanamichi* (flower path), as in Kabuki theaters, which joins the stage at the *ginbashi* (silver bridge). This brings the performers in closer contact with the audience. The Takarazuka revues are offered in the most lavish settings and ornate costumes, and these revues by this Osaka-based theatrical company have immense appeal for adolescent

Japanese girls and middle-aged matrons. The attraction of the theater can be attested to by an incident from the war years: when the theater was closed for wartime reasons on March 4, 1944, the crowd was so large and in danger of becoming unruly that the police unsheathed their swords to maintain order.

Continuing to the east on the street which runs alongside the Imperial Hotel, one arrives at the **International Arcade,** which extends under the overhead railroad right-of-way. The International Arcade extends for one street in either direction as an enclosed market with a variety of goods meant to appeal to tourists: from electronic gear to new and used kimonos to souvenir items of great diversity. The shops are open from 10:00 A.M. to 7:00 P.M. (until 6:00 P.M. on Sundays) and some offer tax-free shopping. To the north and still under the elevated structure are the *yakitori* stalls which are favored for snacks by both visitors and Tokyo residents.

At Harumi-dori to the north of the International Arcade and to the west of the overhead rail line is the **Tourist Information Center** on the south side of the street. Here maps, brochures, and general information for all of Japan may be obtained from English-speaking staff. The office is open weekdays from 9:00 A.M. to 5:00 P.M. and on Saturdays from 9:00 A.M. to noon. Across the street is the Hibiya Park Building, and in its northeast corner on the street parallel to Harumi-dori is the **American Pharmacy,** which offers American pharmaceutical supplies and can fill prescriptions. It is open from 9:00 A.M. to 7:00 P.M. Monday through Saturday and from 11:00 A.M. to 7:00 P.M. on Sundays.

At the intersection of Harumi and Hibiya-dori are stairs down to several subway lines: the Chiyoda Line, the Toei Mita Line, and the Hibiya Line, while a passageway connects to the Yurakucho Line. An underground passage runs a mile to the east under Harumi-dori from Hibiya Park, and it ends at the Shimbashi Embujo Theater and the Ginza Tokyu Hotel. There are numerous exits to the street along the way.

TOUR

2

Otemachi,
Imperial Palace East Garden,
and Yasukuni Shrine

THE Marunouchi financial district of Tokyo, which was explored in Tour 1, has been described as the onetime site of the mansions of the Inner Lords of the Tokugawa shoguns from 1603 to 1868. Just to the north of Marunouchi is the Otemachi district which also held the mansions of the Tokugawa's most trusted daimyo. This section is circumscribed by the main railway tracks on the east (to the north of Tokyo Central Station), by Uchibori-dori (Inner Moat Street) before the former castle walls on the west, by Eitai-dori on the south, and by the modern Shuto (Metropolitan) Expressway on the north. The mansions of the feudal daimyo have long since disappeared from Otemachi, and today Otemachi is the home of the "daimyo" of big business, for here may be found the offices of many banks, insurance agencies, and major commercial corporations.

The district is well served by subway and rail lines since Tokyo Central Station is just to the south of the district while the various Otemachi stations of the Toei Mita Line, the Hibiya Line, the Tozai Line, the Marunouchi Line, and the Hanzomon Line all exit into the area. The Marunouchi subway exit brings one to the first point of interest on this tour: the 1964 eight-story **Teishin Building,** which houses the **Communications Museum** on the first four floors of the building. Anyone interested in the various forms of modern communications will enjoy this museum, for the exhibits include matters pertaining to postal, telegraph, telephone, and other forms of telecommunication. Here one will find an extensive display of postage stamps (more than 200,000), thus it comes as no surprise to learn that there is a relationship with the Ministry of Posts and Telecommunications. The museum is open from 9:00 A.M. to 4:30 P.M. daily except Mondays. The exhibits are only labeled in Japanese, but an English language brochure is available upon request.

Across the street and further east toward the railway right-of-way is the **NTT Telecommunications Science Hall.** Here the wonders of the modern world of computers can be discovered through displays and the opportunity to use computers. This hall of science has an unusual host to welcome visitors: a mechanical robot.

An unusual location can be found in the midst of this modern area of Tokyo. On leaving the Communications Museum, the east-west street should be taken to the west toward the grounds of the Imperial Palace. Just before Uchibori-dori and the Otebori moat at the former castle grounds, surrounded by the Mitsui Bussan Building, the Long-Term Credit Bank of Japan, and the Sanwa Bank, is a small, open space upon which no modern financial organization has dared to build.

Here is the **Hill of Masakado's Head,** a shrine at what was once the top of the bay when the Marunouchi and adjoining areas were still under water. The object of veneration worshiped by the early fishermen of Edo at this shrine was Taira-no-Masakado, a headstrong warrior of the 900s. He not only took over eight counties in the Kanto (Tokyo) region, but he set himself up in his domains as the new emperor in defiance of Kyoto's traditional emperor, whose claim to the throne was said to be verified by the divine origin of one of his ancestors. As the old adage would have it, pride comes before a fall, and in 940 Masakado fell in battle. As was the custom of that and later times, the rebel's head was severed and sent to Kyoto as proof of the death of this usurper to royal power. True to his headstrong ways, it is said that Masakado's head flew back to Edo in one night to rejoin its body in its grave. The validity of the story was attested to at the time by the brilliant lightning and pealing thunder which accompanied the head on its flight. As was only proper under the circumstances, a shrine was raised to Masakado's spirit over the site of his grave in order to keep his spirit from raising new troubles.

Centuries later, Tokugawa Ieyasu was not one to take any chances. The location of so troublesome a spirit might even threaten his domains despite the passage of seven hundred years since Masakado was put in his place. No thought could be given to moving the body from its grave since this could rouse the vengeful spirit of this former warrior. Thus Ieyasu let the grave remain undisturbed—as have all the corporate chairmen of the present day. No structure has ever been raised over this very expensive piece of property. Ieyasu, however, took no chances: he had Masakado's shrine which honored his spirit removed to the Kanda Myojin Shrine not too far to the north where Masakado can still be honored today. There at Kanda Myojin, Masakado's spirit remains. However, the story does not end here, for the Meiji government also foresaw a threat from this wayward spirit, but that tale has to wait to be told until Tour 10.

The small area of the Hill of Masakado's Head is enclosed by traditional Japanese walls on three sides as well as by modern office buildings, but the slightly raised unit with memorial stones to the right at the rear of the plot is still a place of reverence. Offerings of flowers and the burning of incense still occur a millennium after this intrepid warrior's death. Greenery throughout the small plot makes the site a park. Ceramic frogs on either side of the memorial provide a lighter touch to this solemn spot.

While warriors of the distant past still need to be placated, noble statesmen are also not forgotten. In the year 769 Wake-no-Kiyomaro, a member of the Empress Shotoku's court, was sent on a mission. Her senior advisor (and lover), the Buddhist monk Dokyo, had designs on the throne, hoping to succeed his royal mistress as the next emperor. Shotoku sent Kiyomaro, a trusted member of the imperial court, to the Hachiman Shrine in Kyushu to see if the gods favored Dokyo's accession to the throne. Despite dire threats from the monk, Kiyomaro brought back the deity's pronouncement that only those descended from the imperial gods could sit on the throne. Kiyomaro suffered disfigurement at Dokyo's orders for bringing so untoward an answer from the gods. Sent into exile while the monk Dokyo lived, he was returned to imperial favor by the legitimate successor to the empress upon her death.

This diversion into ancient history is relevant, for the large bronze statue which stands in a small plot of greenery at the edge of the Otebori moat to the north celebrates this eighth-century defender of the Imperial House. In 1854 the Emperor Komei raised Kiyomaro quite posthumously to the first rank of the nobility and named him Go-o-myojin as a spirit to be honored. This was a powerless emperor's attempt at a slap at the Tokugawa shogun of his day, for it was his only way of showing his displeasure with those who ruled without consulting him. After Komei's death, his son became Emperor Meiji, who, on succeeding his father, saw his advisors and supporters bring to an end the two and one-half centuries of Tokugawa rule. The new emperor's advisors were not taking any chances as to a threat to the throne from either the living or the dead. Thus on March 18, 1898, the noble and divine status of Kiyomaro was once more confirmed by imperial edict.

Almost ninety years later, in 1940, this bronze image of Kiyomaro was raised at the edge of the Imperial Palace grounds by a later set of concerned advisors to Emperor Hirohito. In the 600s, this eighth-century scholar had saved the throne. In 1940 the militaristic government was taking no chances with any new threat to the throne. As a result, a **statue of Kiyomaro** was created, and it still stands guard over imperial affairs at the edge of the Otebori moat to the castle grounds.

In Japan, the placement of buildings should always honor the rules for auspicious location of structures lest they be built or oriented in a direction which is not favorable to their successful existence. In the case of Edo and the shogun's castle, this was a particular problem since the castle site did not have the proper geographical orientation, given the rules of Chinese geomancy which were observed in Japan. Shogun Ieyasu, if nothing else, was decisive in matters like this. He decreed that Mount Fuji, to the west of his intended castle, was truly to the north, and thus the castle site was properly oriented. Nonetheless, temples were built in Ueno to the true northeast (from which evil could flow, according to Chinese geomancy), as well as to the true southeast in the Shiba area, as additional protection for the castle.

Back along the Otebori moat to Eitai-dori, a bridge crosses the moat to the Ote-mon gateway and the shogunal castle grounds, the site where Tokyo had its beginnings. The story of Edo Castle begins with Ota Dokan (1432–86), who is credited with founding Edo. The top of the natural hill which overlooked the great bay of Edo and its inlets rose sixty-five feet above the water, providing a natural site for the largely earthen fortifications that Dokan created. Such fortifications had been erected some two centuries before Ota Dokan raised his stronghold here, but they had been of little consequence. Dokan's fortification did not have too long a life either, for his brutal murder in 1486, instigated by the feudal overlord of the Hojo clan of Odawara, led in time to the disintegration of his fort. By 1590 when Tokugawa Ieyasu chose the site for his headquarters, three small fishing villages and a few scattered farms at the foot of the future castle hill were all that composed the village of Edo. The naturally defensive nature of the hillside was obvious to Shogun Ieyasu when he entered Edo on August 1, 1590, and here he determined to build the strongest castle with the most intricate defensive system that Japan had ever seen.

The defensive stronghold that Shogun Ieyasu began in 1590 was not completed for another fifty years. By 1603 he had conquered all the contestants for civil power in Japan, and the work on the castle and its defenses could now be pursued with vigor since the daimyo who were subservient to him were forced to supply labor, materials, and funds to create the castle which would keep them in thralldom. The dimensions of the stronghold beggar description, for they encompassed a ten-mile circle which stretched from the Shimbashi area waterfront in the south to the hills of Kanda to the north. The outer protected area involved 110 entry gates, 30 bridges, an inner and an outer moat, and canals to serve as further barricades. The innermost moat was faced with stone walls sixteen-feet thick to protect the citadel where the shogun and his inner court resided. As has been the case in European cities, the nineteenth century in Tokyo was to see the dismantling of fortified walls as the city expanded and traffic increased. Thus the outer walls and gates of the palace began to be dismantled in 1873.

The castle grounds themselves were always a protected and private area to which the public had no entry. However, in 1968, to celebrate the construction of the new Imperial Palace which replaced the bombed imperial buildings, the inner grounds of the former castle complex were opened to the public as the East Imperial Garden (Kokyo Higashi Gyoen). (The inner walls of the complex divided the fortified hill into four areas called *maru*.) The East Imperial Garden includes the Hon-maru (the Central Keep), the Ni-no-maru (the Second Keep), and the San-no-maru (the Third Keep). The fourth fortified area consisted of the Nishi-no-maru (the West Keep) which today forms the Imperial Palace grounds and thus this sector is not open to the public.

The **Imperial Palace East Garden,** the former castle site, is primarily a garden complex today since the various buildings and fortifications of the shogunal castle have long since been destroyed by fires. The Long Sleeves Fire of 1657 was particularly disastrous for the castle, while the last major fire of 1872 wiped out the remaining Tokugawa structures. The East Imperial Garden can be entered through several gates (*mon*): Ote-mon, Hirakawa-mon, and Kita Hanebashi-mon, and these various gates can be reached from the Otemachi or Takebashi subways stations. This tour begins at the **Ote-mon** gate since it was the main entrance to the castle in its days of glory, and it provides an example of the type of defensive architecture which was employed in the 1600s. It is difficult today to envision the magnitude of the castle structures, for there were ninety-nine gates to the castle of which thirty-six were in the outer defensive wall which enclosed the 450-acre heart of the shogunate's power. There were within this complex twenty-one large watch towers (*yagura*), and twenty-eight munitions storehouses (*tamon*) aside from the residential buildings and ancillary structures.

To enter the castle grounds one crosses the moat before Ote-mon, one of three such waterways about the castle which varied in size but were generally 230 feet wide and between 4 to 10 feet deep. On entering the Ote-mon gate, the visitor is given a small token. Return it when leaving the compound by any of its gates. (There is no charge for visiting the castle grounds.) The grounds may be entered between 9:00 A.M. and 3:00 P.M. every day but Monday and Friday; the castle grounds are closed from December 25 through January 5. The grounds are closed at 4:00 P.M., at which time all visitors must leave.

The construction of the original Ote-mon gate was the responsibility of Date Masamune, the daimyo of Sendai, and it was in two parts: the first or smaller gate was known as Koraimon, the Korean Gate, while the larger of the two gates lay beyond a narrow courtyard. The inner Ote-mon gate was destroyed during the air raids of the spring of 1945, but it was rebuilt in 1967. Ote-mon was a *masugata* gateway. That is, the outer and inner gateways formed a "box." If an enemy was able to storm the outer Ote-mon, he then found himself in a walled, box-like courtyard with a second larger gatehouse before him. Here he was under attack from more than one side since slits in the gatehouse permitted the raining of arrows on the attackers. The chances of survival for attackers were slim. The roof tiles of these gates as well as other buildings often were topped with images of the mythical dolphin which would protect the structure against fire.

Beyond Ote-mon were four *maru*, keeps or fortresses. At the foot of the hill beyond Ote-mon was Ni-no-maru, the Second Fortress or Keep, while above it was Hon-maru, the Central Keep. San-no-maru, the Third Keep, and the Kita-no-maru, the North Keep, lay below Ni-no-maru. In Tokugawa days, Kanjosho, the main office of shogunal officers of administration and finance were on the right just beyond the gate, a tie with the past which the adjacent Otemachi and Marunouchi financial districts of modern Tokyo still maintain. Today the **San-no-maru Shozokan** (Museum of Imperial Collections) is on the right as one walks from the entry gateway. This modern, climate-controlled building of two large rooms is used as an exhibition hall for some of the

6,000 treasures of the Imperial Household which were donated in 1989 by the Emperor. Thus a portion of the private artistic holdings of the Imperial family, which are seldom otherwise available for public viewing, may be seen in this modern hall without charge. The National Police Agency's Martial Arts Hall is on the left while further along the Ote (Rest House) on the right has beverages, maps, and souvenirs on sale.

Hon-maru, the innermost sector of the castle, sat on the higher ground within the walls, and thus the progress within the castle grounds calls for an uphill stroll. Walking up the slope, one arrives at the site of Ote Gejo (Dismount Gate), at the point at which daimyo would dismount from their steeds or from their *kago,* those awkward "cages" in which a nobleman was carried on the shoulders of his retainers. Two walls remain, but the gate and the moat before it no longer exist. Here were two guardhouses to protect the inner castle beyond the Ote Gejo gate. To the right is the 1863 Doshin-bansho guardhouse while on the left is the **Hyakunin-bansho.** The latter is the "One-Hundred Man Guard-house," so named from the four platoons of one hundred men each who were drawn from the four major families or branches of the Tokugawa family to stand guard for the protection of the shogun.

To the left, a path leads to Hon-maru, while to the right the path leads to Ni-no-maru, which lies at the foot of Hon-maru. Ni-no-maru before 1868 was the residence of the retired shogun, and its gardens were originally planned in 1630 by Kobori Enshu, the famed landscape architect of the seventeenth century. Today's garden, of course, is a reconstruction, but it contains all those elements essential to a traditional Japanese garden: a pond, a waterfall, stone lanterns, and a bridge. At the far side of the garden is the early nineteenth century Suwa-no-chaya tea ceremony pavilion, a unit which once stood within the Fukiage Garden of the Imperial Palace.

Ni-no-maru stands beneath the wall that supports Hon-maru, a wall composed of the massive granite stones brought from the

Izu Peninsula, sixty miles away, in the early 1600s. At its base is Hakucho-bori, the Moat of Swans, twenty-four swans being a 1953 gift from Germany after the East Imperial Gardens were opened to the public. A path from the Ni-no-maru garden goes back to the Moat of Swans, and to the right of the moat is the Shiomizaka (Tide Viewing Slope), which leads up to Hon-maru. The Slope today offers no view of Tokyo Bay or its inlets (now filled in), for the rise of multistory buildings in the twentieth century have obscured any possible view of tidal waters. In the 1600s, however, the slope was true to its name.

At the top of the slope once stood Ote Naka, the Central Gate leading into Hon-maru together with its guardhouse (O-bansho). The 1657 fire and the later 1872 fire destroyed the grandeur which once topped this hill, and the foundations of the main donjon and the Mount Fuji Viewing Tower are all that remain today. A "Rest House" on the left of the path at the top of the slope site offers a contrast in photographs which are on display: one group shows the castle as it was in 1868; the other offers more recent photographs of the same sites.

Hon-maru contained the residence and other official buildings of the reigning shogun. At the southwest corner of Hon-maru is the previously mentioned **Fujimi Yagura,** one of three such towers which still exist out of the original twenty-one which surmounted the castle walls. It was seriously damaged in the 1657 Long Sleeves Fire, but it was reconstructed two years later. At that time the decision was made not to rebuild the rest of the fortifications of Hon-maru, Ni-no-maru, and San-no-maru. The nation was at peace, and such castles were neither needed nor supportable when faced with the destructive force of modern artillery. Further along the way is Fujimi Tamon (The Mount Fuji Viewing Armory), one of two remaining armories out of the twenty-eight which once existed. Behind this arsenal was a well to supply water to shogunate quarters. The well was almost one hundred feet deep.

There were three main groups of buildings in this innermost

complex. Closest to Fujimi Tower in an area now covered by a lawn was a group which contained the Halls for Affairs of State, the shogun's Audience Hall, and Ohiroma (Hall of One Thousand Tatami Mats). It was in this grand hall that on the first and fifteenth of each month the shogun received his feudal lords. It was here also that the Dutch from the trading station of Dejima in Nagasaki were required to make the journey every four years to do obeisance to the shogun, this being largely a political event that required them to bring gifts, and to demonstrate the foolish ways of the Southern Barbarians—the Europeans who were best kept at a distance.

A second group of buildings contained the shogun's private residence. A third group of structures consisted of the innermost quarters which were adjacent to the Central Keep itself. Here were the shogun's sequestered halls for the 500 to 1,000 women of his court, consisting of his wives, his concubines, the ladies-in-waiting, attendants, servants, and cooks.

The pride of the castle was its 5-story, 170-foot donjon that, given its location on the hill, soared 250 feet over Edo. It surveyed not only the bay but the five great highways which converged on Edo from throughout Japan. It had been erected under Tokugawa Hidetada, the second shogun, in 1607 and rebuilt in 1640. All the buildings of the castle were white, save the donjon which was a stark black. Its lead tiles were covered with gold leaf, and golden dolphins surmounted the roof as protection against fires. Despite the protection these dolphins offered, the horrendous Long Sleeves Fire of 1657 destroyed this magnificent tower. The fire started with the burning in an exorcism ceremony of an accursed kimono at a Buddhist temple in *shitamachi,* a fire which then spread in the teeth of a gale and which turned the city into a roaring inferno. Today nothing but the base of the donjon remains, along with the story that all of the shogun's gold in the vaults beneath the tower melted, a hoard whose whereabouts is still a puzzle and a challenge for those who imagine that it remains within the Hon-maru grounds. The base to the tower can be mounted by means of a slope for a view of the Hon-maru grounds.

A small granary building, Kokumotsugura, is adjacent to the donjon base, and this ceremonial structure was re-erected in the 1990s for a portion of the services concerned with the enthronement of the Emperor Heisei. Other modern buildings are now located down a slope from Hon-maru, and these include the octagonal **Toka Music Hall** created in 1966 for the then empress' sixtieth birthday. It is in the shape of an imperial chrysanthemum petal, and the building by Kenji Imai shows the influence of Antonio Gaudí in its octagonal roof shaped in the form of a peach flower. As a result, the hall has been nicknamed the Peach Auditorium. Imai used traditional Japanese motifs in the mosaic decorations of the external walls of the structure, a somewhat garish-looking building. Adjacent is the Imperial Music Academy and the unattractive, fireproof Imperial Archives and Mausolea Department Building.

One can leave the castle grounds at this point through the Hirakawa-mon gate by taking the path from the donjon base that runs behind the Archives and Mausolea Building and ultimately to Takebashi Station of the Tozai Subway Line. Alternatively, as this tour does, one can continue on through the Kita-hane-bashi-mon gate into Kita-no-maru Park. If one wishes to leave the castle grounds at this time, the path to the exit leads down the slope to the Hirakawa-mon gate. This slope is known as the Bairin-zaka (Plum Grove Slope), a slope which it is said was planted with plum trees back in 1478 by Ota Dokan when he established his fortress here. Hirakawa-mon was the main gate to San-no-maru, which disappeared in the 1657 fire. The gate was a *masugata* "box" gate similar to Ote-mon. It was the gate used by the women of the shogun's residence on the few occasions when they left the castle grounds. Adjacent to it is the smaller Fujo-mon (Unclean Gate), through which those convicted of crimes within the castle or the bodies of the deceased were removed. A pleasant restored wooden bridge provides the exit over the castle moat.

Continuing from the Hon-maru area, the Kita-hane-bashi-mon (North Drawbridge Gate), leads into **Kita-no-maru.** In the 1400s Ota Dokan used this area for the training of his troops, and later under the Tokugawa shoguns it became a walled area for the residences of collateral families of the shogun and for some of his highest officials. After the great fire of 1657 the area was kept cleared as a fire break before the castle buildings. After the demise of the shogunate in 1868, the area was taken over by the military for barracks for the soldiers of the Imperial Guard, who were charged with protecting the Imperial Palace. Kita-no-maru became a public park in 1969 in celebration of the sixty-first birthday of the Showa Emperor, Hirohito.

Go down Kinokuni-zaka (Kinokuni Slope) to find on the right the National Archives and the **National Museum of Modern Art** by architect Yoshiro Taniguchi. The museum is open from 10:00 A.M. to 5:00 P.M. and until 8:00 P.M. on Fridays; it is closed on Mondays and during the New Year period of December 27 through January 4. Entry fee. The museum, which was founded in 1952 and was relocated here in 1969, exhibits paintings of Western and Japanese artists in changing exhibitions on the first two floors (an extra fee is sometimes charged for these show-ings). The third and fourth floors exhibit paintings by Japanese artists since 1868, items which change frequently since the collection exceeds three thousand paintings.

The Crafts Gallery of the National Museum of Modern Art is just a five-minute walk away. Continuing along the path which came from the Kinokuni Slope and crossing the highway, after a few minutes' walk one will find the Science Museum to the right while the Crafts Gallery is to the left. The **Crafts Gallery** is housed in a government-listed building which once served as the admin-istrative headquarters of the Imperial Guard. It is at this site that the unusual revolt by 215 of the emperor's soldiers occurred when they mutinied on August 23, 1878. They killed their officers and marched to the Akasaka Palace, where Emperor Meiji was then living, to protest the unfair division of rewards to those who had suppressed the Saigo Takamori revolt in Ueno Park and to demand a raise in pay. Severe punishment was meted out after the mutiny was put down, and, as a result of this insurrection, the military barracks were razed and the divisional headquarters was eventually located here.

This 1910 former military, gothic brick structure, in what has been kindly termed "Nineteenth Century Renaissance" architecture, is one of five remaining Meiji period brick buildings in Tokyo. Exhibits are shown on the second floor of the building, and they encompass all of the various techniques at which Japanese craftsmen have excelled: ceramics, bamboo, lacquer, metal, textiles, and other crafts. The hours for the gallery are the same as for the Modern Art Museum.

The **Science and Technology Museum** is the other museum in the Kita-no-maru Park, and it is open from 9:30 A.M. to 5:00 P.M. except on Mondays. Entry fee. It is closed from December 29 through January 3. The five-story pentagonally shaped museum is under the jurisdiction of the Japan Science Foundation, and its displays in fourteen sections, especially its working models and space-age exhibits, appeal greatly to children. The labels are primarily in Japanese. The museum covers many aspects of science from agriculture to nuclear science and from earthquakes to electricity—the latter topic being described by a robot who lectures to children about electricity. The museum also has a laboratory, a workroom, and a library.

Beyond the museum complex lies the massive **Budokan** (The Japan Martial Arts Hall), constructed in 1964 for the Olympics of that year. Reminiscent of the Horyu-ji Dream Hall south of Nara, but on a more massive scale, its octagonal roof is topped with a gold-leafed *giboshi*, an onion-shaped finial such as is often seen on the top of posts of rail fences at traditional Japanese temples. The building, which can seat 14,000 spectators, is used for sports events, concerts, and other large gatherings—its first use as a concert hall occurred in 1968 when the Beatles came to Japan.

Leave Kita-no-maru Park through the Tayasu-mon gate, a

former *masugata* gate, and on to Yasukuni-dori, slightly to the west of Kudanshita Station of the Toei Shinjuku and Tozai Subway lines. Yasukuni-dori here descends the **Kudanzaka** hill to the Jimbocho area to the right. At one time this hill was higher and steeper than it now is, but it lost its top half for part of the fill needed to cover the marshy land at its foot as Shogun Ieyasu expanded *shitamachi* below his castle. The hill received its name of *kudan* (nine steps) since it was so steep that it had to be cut in 1709 into nine sections for ease of mounting. The slope was further reduced in 1923 with the advent of the motor car. Strange as it may seem, there is a lighthouse, no longer used, at this point. Built in 1871, before much of the land of Tokyo Bay was filled in and before tall buildings were erected, this beacon could be observed by boats in Tokyo Bay. Originally the lighthouse was in the Yasukuni grounds, but it was later moved to the south side of Yasukuni-dori.

Toward the end of the Tokugawa period there were barracks for the military at the top of Kudan hill, but in 1869 it became the site for "A Shrine to which the Spirits of the Dead Are Invited." The shrine was intended to honor those who had died in the battles involved with the Meiji "Imperial Restoration" and the extinguishing of the Tokugawa shogunate. In traditional Japanese custom, the spirits of the dead are enshrined here and can be feasted and entertained, not unlike the Bon ceremonies of the Buddhist faith—a faith, ironically, which the Meiji leaders did not favor. The shrine was run by the army until 1945, thus it became the center of the most rabid nationalism. It still attracts right-wing militarists and nationalists today.

In 1879 the shrine became **Yasukuni Jinja** (Yasukuni Shrine), "The Shrine of Peace for the Nation," on a more organized basis. Here horse racing took place until 1898. Sumo matches and Noh plays also took place here. In fact, a Noh stage was constructed on the grounds in 1902. In 1882 a military exhibition hall was built, and today it houses exhibits which honor the various wars Japan became involved in after 1868, up to and including the Second

World War. While commemorating the dead of the war, as is the purpose of the shrine, the displays which range from the human torpedoes and even a Zero fighter and a steam engine from the "Bridge of the River Kwai" episode often seem to glorify the warlike in the Japanese past rather than succoring of the spirits of the war dead. The labels of the exhibits, in Japanese, still offer the warped militaristic view of Japan's aggressive actions in Asia between 1895 and 1945.

With the war against China in the 1890s and then the Russo-Japanese War of 1905, the shrine became a memorial site to the dead of all Japanese wars since 1853, when the Imperial Restoration began. As a result of the Japanese wars of the 1930s and 40s, there are now 2.5 million spirits that are honored at the shrine. Soldiers heading into battle traditionally parted with the words, "Let us meet at Yasukuni." There their spirits would be worshiped. As indicated above, the shrine has become a gathering place for the more militant of Japanese nationalists who still see Japan's wars of the 1930s and 40s as crusades to free Asia of Western imperialism. As a result, the visits by members of the government to this shrine have caused deep unrest among many victims of past Japanese wars, particularly since even those who were convicted of war crimes, such as General Tojo, are also enshrined here, an action taken surreptitiously by the Japanese government much to the outrage of other nations. Before 1945 the shrine was under military administration, but the American Occupation after 1945 had the shrine revert to non-governmental control.

The grounds are entered under the huge, steel First Torii. The torii's predecessor was melted in 1943 for use in armament production. Beyond it at an intersection of paths is the statue to Omura Masujiro (1824–69), the first minister of war after the Meiji Restoration. He was in charge of the Meiji forces which defeated the shogunate's supporters who held out in Ueno in 1868; just one year later he was assassinated. This statue in his honor was the first modern bronze statue in Japan when it was unveiled in 1888. Further along the path there is a stone torii and then the bronze Second Torii of 1887, and to its left is a place to wash one's hands before entering the inner shrine quarters. The path is lined with flowering cherry and gingko trees and monuments to military men of the past.

The Divine Gate of twelve pillars, with the imperial chrysanthemum of sixteen petals embossed on its doors, follows, the Shrine Offices being to the left and the Noh Theater to the right. At the end of the path is the *haiden,* the hall for worship of the spirits of the dead, and beyond that the sacred *honden* (main hall), where the spirits are enshrined. Between the Noh Theater and the Hall of Worship is the Festivals Section, while the Hall of Arrival is to the right of the honden. Behind the haiden is the Treasury with mementos of Japan's wars, as mentioned above. Further to the right-hand rear of the shrine are the attractive Divine Pond, teahouses, and a sumo ring.

The two major festivals of Yasukuni Shrine occur on April 21–23 and October 17–19. At these times, in the tradition of the past, Noh dances, Bugaku, (court dance and music), Kyogen farces, *biwa* music, folk music, sumo, kendo and other activities to please the spirits of the dead are offered. These are festive occasions as are all Japanese commemorative functions for the dead. At these times an imperial messenger presents imperial offerings at the shrine and reads the imperial message to the deities enshrined here. Commemorative services are also held each August 15, the day the Second World War ended for Japan. One other period of the year is particularly noted at this shrine, and that is the springtime blossoming of the many ornamental cherry trees on the grounds.

Returning to the large statue of Omura Masujiro and crossing Yasukuni-dori, one can walk down Yasukuni-dori to the street which runs along **Chidorigafuchi** (Plover Depths), a pond which existed before the castle was built and which was included within the moat structure of the castle grounds. It has its name from the supposed resemblance of this waterway to the wings of a plover in flight. Chidorigafuchi Water Park is lined with about ninety cherry trees, which in 1953 replaced the ones first planted here by Sir Ernest Satow (1843–1929), a British diplomat in the early Meiji period. (The original trees were uprooted in the course of the construction of the Shuto Expressway.)

The name "Water Park" refers not only to the moat but to the fact that one can rent rowboats for a pleasurable period on the waters of the park. Beyond the Fairmont Hotel and just before the Shuto Expressway in a small park on the right is the hexagonal pavilion with a light green roof which has served since 1959 as the Tomb of the Unknown Soldier, a sacred spot that commemorates the 90,000 unknown dead of Japan's wars. Under the roof is a symbolic, large stone sarcophagus. Each August 15, the anniversary of the end of the Second World War, the emperor makes his obeisance at this shrine. The shrine remembers all those who died, civilian or military, regardless of their religion (in contrast Yasukuni Shrine is a Shinto shrine), without the opprobrium which is connected with the Yasukuni Shrine for many non-nationalists and for those of other nations.

Continuing along the western side of the Imperial Palace grounds, one passes the handsome **British Embassy** in the Bancho district. In this sector the *hatamoto* (the seven thousand guardsmen) drawn from the retainers of the shogunal domains, were stationed in an area which stretched to Ichigaya. Six regiments of these warrior guards lived here, each in its own district, and the districts are still divided into six *bancho*, or blocks. After 1868 many of the Meiji nobility had their mansions here, and the area is still an upper-class residential district. Opposite the British Embassy, for example, is the modern Bancho House by the American architect Robert Stern, which is a combination office and apartment building.

This tour ends at the police-guarded **Hanzomon** gate to the Imperial Palace. This place was once home to Hattori Hanzo, the leader of the shogun's spies, those black-clad *ninja* of tradition who were adept at infiltration, assassination, and acts of derring-do which still fill Japanese cinema and television. The Hanzomon gate has a more pacific reputation in modern times since this is one of the entrances to the Fukiage area of the Imperial Palace private grounds. It was in this area that the Showa Emperor, Hirohito, had his botanical laboratory and rice paddy fields. The emperor was actually carrying on a tradition from the eighteenth century, for here the eighth shogun, Yoshimune (1716–45), had an herb garden and a plantation for plant research.

Just before the gate, on the left, is a small park which runs along the palace moat, and in it is a statue grouping of three nude young male figures. The park is a favored place during lunch time for workers from adjacent office buildings.

The Hanzomon Subway Station lies two short streets to the west of the Hanzomon entrance to the palace, and it can be taken to other connecting lines as one leaves this area.

TOUR

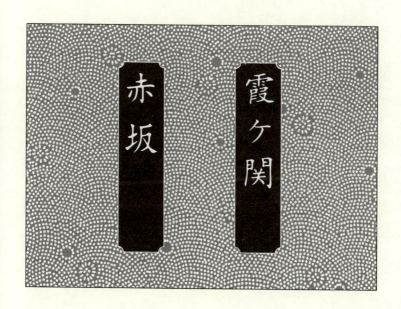

3

Kasumigaseki
and Akasaka

赤坂　　霞ケ関

A S THE capital of Japan, Tokyo has its legislative chambers and its massive bureaucratic offices as major aspects of contemporary life. Few countries are as controlled by their bureaucracy as is Japan, and most of Japan's government offices are clustered about the National Diet Building. The area geographically falls into two districts: Nagatacho, whose center is the Diet Building and the offices of political parties; and Kasumigaseki, where the governmental offices and ministries and the first skyscraper of modern Tokyo, the thirty-six-story Kasumigaseki Building, are located. Kasumigaseki derives its name from the *seki,* or fourteenth century guarded barrier that once existed in this quarter. It was poetically named the Kasumi barrier, the "Barrier of the Mists," a name that is perhaps appropriate even today for a government quarter.

Behind the political center of Tokyo and of Japan, situated on one of those fingers of hills which stretch into *shitamachi,* is the Sanno Hie Shrine, a Shinto shrine of great antiquity which served to protect the shogun's capital and perhaps still protects governmental affairs today. It was the locus of one of the three great celebrations that enlivened old Edo, a festive few days which are still enjoyed by modern Tokyo residents every other year when the festival brings a colorful procession and excitement to the city.

Below the Hie Shrine, in the flat land spreading from the Diet Building to Akasaka Mitsuke, is an area where the politicians and reporters, and today the minions of the television studios, continue to find places for relaxation, gossip, and the making of political deals. Much of this activity has always taken place in expensive restaurants on side streets off Sotobori-dori, the main street running through Akasaka and once the outer moat of the castle grounds. Here too are the luxurious New Otani and Akasaka Prince hotels with their striking architecture.

Hanzomon Station on the subway line of the same name is where this tour begins, and it starts where the previous tour ended. From the subway station to the main Shinjuku-dori street which runs from the palace grounds to the west, the most striking element in this part of Tokyo is the nine-story 1984 **Wacoal Kojimachi Building** of architect Kisho Kurokawa. As buildings go, it is not as tall and overpowering as some of the recent skyscrapers in the city, but its architectural design is striking. It has been described by some as an oversized sewing machine (not inappropriate considering the lingerie manufacturer whose main office this is). From a distance the design on its east side gives the appearance of having a baleful eye near the top of the building—or so it is claimed Emperor Showa regarded it, for the building peers over the palace grounds. Synthetic marble and aluminum bands cover the façade of the structure, and the canopy over its entrance has been described as a giant flying saucer. The lobby of the building is interestingly decorated with mosaics from China, Korea, and Japan, and the reception area on the ninth floor is striking with its high domed ceiling. Exhibits are frequently on display, and the building has an art deco theater and a café-lounge.

Turning to the right on Uchibori-dori (Inner Moat Street), which runs along the palace moat, one comes to the **National Theater** (Kokuritsu Gekijo). This 1983 edifice provided the nation with its first state-owned theater, a center which offers productions of traditional Japanese performing arts. The theater sits on a rise, and its reinforced concrete structure is built in the *azekura* (log cabin) style of the Shosoin treasury of Nara, that 1,300-year-old wooden storehouse which the exterior of this building imitates. The theater has two auditoriums, the larger one to the left, seating 1,764, is primarily for Kabuki productions and for Gagaku (court music). The smaller auditorium, to the right, has 630 seats and is meant for Bunraku, Kyogen (farce), and other traditional forms of Japanese dance, music, and theater. The L-shaped lobby contains displays pertaining to Japanese theater, ranging from scrolls concerned with everything from ancient performing arts to costumes. These may be viewed between 10:00 A.M. and 5:00 P.M. Adjacent is the Engei

Hall, a smaller more intimate theater seating three hundred, which offers Rakugo and other forms of traditional story telling or comedy.

Just beyond the National Theater is the 1974 **Supreme Court** of Japan (Saiko Saibansho), an austere white, granite building which was designed by Shinichi Okada, who had studied architecture at Yale University. Many people find the interior of the building to be somewhat overwhelming. The building has the appearance of a bunker where justice has hunkered down, a not-too-inviting structure. Perhaps in contrast to this less than graceful and almost windowless building, at the corner in front of the edifice is a piece of sculpture of three young nude female figures in bronze—an art form that would hardly have been accepted in the decades and centuries before 1950. They complement the statue of three nude male figures in the park alongside the moat just to the left of the point where Shinjuku-dori meets Uchibori-dori, across from the Wacoal Building.

Continuing along Uchibori-dori, at the crossroad on the right one approaches the Miyake-zaka slope that the overhead Shuto Expressway mounts. At this crossroad, abandon the moat and Uchibori-dori, which diverge to the left, and head under the Shuto Expressway into the street leading to the National Diet Building, passing the headquarters of the Socialist Party of Japan on the right. This area bore a more military outlook prior to 1945, for here after 1870 was located the War Ministry while the headquarters of the General Staff Officers sat where the Parliamentary Museum is now located. Behind these structures was the official residence of the Minister of War. For a period after 1945 this area held the office of the U.S. Occupation Chief of Staff. In the years since the Second World War these various military units have been replaced by more peaceful and democratic structures.

On the left along this street toward the Diet Building is the **Parliamentary Museum** (Kensei Kinenkan), which is open without charge from 9:30 A.M. to 4:30 P.M. (last entry at 3:30 P.M.) but is closed on Saturdays, Sundays, national holidays, the last day of each month, and from December 27 through January 4. The museum was established in 1972 to commemorate the establishment of the Diet a century earlier. The first floor (as the building is approached from Uchibori-dori) contains the 1960 Ozaki Memorial Hall (Ozaki Yukio Kinenkan), which commemorates Ozaki Yukio (1859–1954), who was a member of parliament starting with the session of the first Diet in 1890 and who served in the Diet for sixty-three years. A fearless opponent of the military in the 1920s and 1930s, he stood for parliamentary government at a time when it was being undermined by the Japanese military. He was also responsible for the gift in 1912 of the cherry trees which grace the parks of Washington, D.C. The adjacent main portion of the Parliamentary Museum offers a model of the Diet on the second floor which is accompanied by an audio-visual slide presentation in Japanese and English detailing the development of parliamentary democracy in Japan and the vicissitudes the building and democracy have faced through the years. Special exhibitions are presented from time to time.

Across the street from the Parliamentary Museum is the 1961 eight-story **National Diet Library** with more than two million books in its six above-ground floors and two below-ground levels. It is open daily without charge from 9:30 A.M. to 5:00 P.M. except Sundays, national holidays, and the last day of each month. The National Diet library has thirty branch libraries.

Ahead on the street we have been following lies the massive three-story **National Diet Building** (Kokkai Gijido) on the right. But first attention should be drawn to a small "temple" on the left in the park. On the hill below the Diet Building is a small classical Roman temple, which covers the Water Level Bench Mark Repository. It is from this marker that the height of the Japanese plains and mountains are measured. The marker is set at 80.3 feet above the level of the Sumida River. Between the temple and the Parliamentary Museum is a plaza with a long pool with fountains, and beside it are three metal shafts one hundred feet tall supporting a clock. This area is on a height above and overlooking the Sakurada-mon gate of the palace and the governmental offices below.

The National Diet Building stands on the site of the mansion of Lord Ii, the leading minister of the Tokugawa Shogun in the 1850s. With his guards, Lord Ii was cut down not far from here at the Sakurada-mon gate at the entrance to the castle grounds in 1860. A park or plaza, as mentioned above, stands before the Diet Building with a 164-foot-wide boulevard below it leading from the Sakurada-mon gate and the Sakurada-bori moat of the Imperial Palace where Lord Ii was slain. There is a garden on either side of this boulevard, one Western-style and one Japanese-style, both created in 1964.

The granite and marble Diet Building with a central clock tower rising 200 feet above the entry portals was begun in 1920, the architects being Yoshikuni Okuma and Kenkichi Yabashi, but it was not completed until 1937. From the front of the building, the House of Councillors, with 250 seats, is on the right while the House of Representatives, with 467 seats, is on the left. Before the Second World War, the House of Councillors was the House of Peers, the Peers being the newly created nobility of the post-1868 Meiji years. The building is not open to the public but it may be visited on the presentation of one's passport and a letter of introduction from a member of the Diet, which is to say that entry is seldom possible. Entry to the Visitors' Gallery when the Diet is in session may be obtained from one's embassy in advance of the date of visit. It is possible to enter the grounds alone by requesting permission from the office at the rear of the Diet Building. Visiting hours are generally from 9:00 A.M. to 5:00 P.M. (last entry at 4:30 P.M.) except for Saturdays, Sundays, and national holidays, depending on whether the Diet is in session.

To the south and east of the Diet Building are the many offices of the national government. Some thirty such offices lie to either side of Sakurada-dori, which runs southwest from the Sakurada-mon gate of the Imperial Palace. Further south is the thirty-six-story **Kasumigaseki Building,** Tokyo's first skyscraper, built in

1968. One reaches this structure by continuing along the street in front of the Diet Building and following that street as it bends slightly to the left. On the left one passes the Ministry of Foreign Affairs Building and the Ministry of Finance Building on the right. Turning to the right on Sakurada-dori and following this street as it bends to the right, one comes on to Sotobori-dori at Toranomon. The Kasumigaseki Building lies to the right. The observation platform atop the building may be visited from 10:00 A.M. to 9:30 P.M. daily. Entry fee. It offers one of the finer panoramic views of the city.

Toranomon (Tiger Gate) supposedly received its name when, in the distant past, a Korean diplomatic mission exhibited a large tiger in a cage at this former gateway at the Sotobori moat. This area of Sotobori-dori is in the lowland below two hills, land which was originally a marshland when Tokyo Bay extended close to the castle grounds. Here was a lake, Tame-ike, the name of the intersection along Sotobori-dori to the west today. Once a weir and a dam stood here so as to back up waters to keep the Sotobori moat about the castle filled. With time the lake shrank, and in 1910 it was finally drained to create Sotobori-dori, which here leads to Akasaka Mitsuke.

Continuing along Sotobori-dori, the Shuto Expressway crosses overhead at Roppongi-dori. An optional diversion, although somewhat lengthy, to the left on this walk can take one along Roppongi-dori to the Ark Hills development with the ANA Hotel Tokyo, a luxury hotel which even boasts a waterfall and a model Venetian gondola in its lobby. Here, too, is the Suntory Concert Hall seating two thousand people, a part of the Ark Hills development along with the hotel, restaurants, office space, and luxury apartments.

The more ambitious who take this side jaunt may wish to follow the street behind the ANA Hotel up to the Hotel Okura where the **Okura Museum** (Okura Shukokan) is located at its front entrance. (Open from 10:00 A.M. to 4:00 P.M. but closed on Mondays, national holidays, and from December 29 through

January 4. Entry fee.) This museum, whose art objects were collected by Baron Okura, became the first private museum to open in Tokyo when it made its debut in 1917. Okura was a Meiji period industrialist specializing in armaments who founded the Imperial Hotel and whose son founded the luxurious Okura Hotel. The museum was destroyed in the 1923 earthquake, but it was rebuilt in a Chinese style in 1928. The two floors of the museum display Baron Okura's collection of ancient art from India, China, Tibet, and Japan, and exquisite ceramics, sculptures, bronzes, costumes, and lacquer-ware from its many diverse holdings. Exhibits run for three to four months at a time.

From the hotel, the street before the Okura can be taken to the right, passing the large **United States Embassy** complex. In 1884 this property, assessed at $25,000, was given by the Japanese government as a perpetual gift of friendship with the United States. (Nonetheless, the United States six years later gave the Meiji government $16,000 for the land.) This 1976 structure was designed by Cesar Pelli, and the arrangement of windows on one side gives the appearance of the American flag in stone and glass. Continuing downhill to the Toranomon intersection with Sotobori-dori, a turn to the left brings one back to the point at the Shuto Expressway where this diversion began.

Ahead on Sotobori-dori, past the Sannoshita intersection, a roadway on the right leads up to the left to the **Sanno Hie Shrine** on the hill. The huge torii at the foot of the hill marks the beginning of a path within the confines of the shrine, a path which is lined with vermilion torii, which form a tunnel of red gateways to the shrine atop the hill. If the diversionary route to the Ark Hills complex and the Okura Museum has not been taken, on leaving the front of the Diet building and walking around the grounds of the Diet, at the major intersection at the rear one can see the prime minister's residence on the left. Crossing the street and heading toward the right, one passes the House of Representative Office Building Number One. The street between it and Building Number Two should be taken downhill to the left, and this brings one to the upper level of the Hie Shrine. (The two office buildings are of an uninspired modern architectural style.)

The Sanno Hie Shrine was created in the year 830 and was located in the outer reaches of the future city of Edo, but in 1478 Ota Dokan removed it to the castle grounds as a protector for his stronghold. In 1607 Tokugawa Ieyasu moved it to the hill to the west of the castle to the land on which the Supreme Court now stands so as to protect the castle from the southeast in the same manner that the Kan'ei-ji temple in Ueno protected the castle from the northeast. When the shrine burned to the ground in the Long Sleeves Fire of 1657, it was eventually rebuilt at its present site in the highly decorated *gongen* style favored by the Tokugawa. Its main façade faced the castle. Here it acted not only as a protector of the castle, but it served as well as the site for worship of the deity who protected the Tokugawa family. Each Tokugawa infant was ceremoniously brought to the shrine shortly after birth to be blessed by the shrine deity. The Hie Shrine was not surprisingly the largest Shinto shrine in Edo in Tokugawa days, and it was given its name from the fact that it is a branch of the Kyoto Hiyoshi (Hie) Shrine. The Sanno Festival is held at Hie Shrine, and it is still one of Tokyo's major celebrations.

The shrine was destroyed in the firebombings of 1945, and it was recreated in ferroconcrete in 1967. The deity of the shrine is Oyamakui-no-kami, the god of the Kyoto shrine on Mount Hiei who protected the city of Kyoto from the northeast, the point from which evil flows, and thus it serves here as the protector of the earlier castle and now the present palace, and perhaps since Meiji times the Diet Building and government offices as well. This is but one of three thousand Hie shrines throughout Japan. The messenger of the shrine deity is the monkey, thus monkey images can be found about the complex. One image of a female monkey holding its child (to the left of the main shrine building) is regarded as a symbol of maternal harmony, and thus the shrine has earned a reputation as being one which can grant fertility and then ensure safe childbirth to those who worship here. A shrine to the Shinto deity Inari is also on the grounds.

The main entrance to the shrine is on its eastern side, the side facing toward the hill on which the National Diet Building stands. A stone torii stands at the foot of the fifty-one steps that lead up to the roofed corridor which encloses the square before the *haiden* and *honden.* The entry gate is guarded on either side of the passageway into the shrine by the seated Shinto guardians Yadaijin and Sadaijin with their bow and arrows and sword. Before the *haiden,* a female monkey holding her infant is on the left while a male monkey is on the right. Both are clothed or draped with protective colorful cloth. To the right of the *haiden* and the corridors are a series of smaller shrine buildings, including *kura,* in which are stored shrine festive objects, and *mikoshi,* in which the spirits of the deities are taken in procession every other year. Roosters strut freely about the grounds.

The shrine museum at the top of the steps from Sotobori-dori is open every day but Tuesday and Friday from 10:00 A.M. to 4:00 P.M., and it holds many important swords once owned by the Tokugawa clan. The Sanno Festival (The Festival Without Equal) has always been one of the great festivals of Tokyo, and it takes place every other year from June 10 through 16 with a great procession on June 15. Some fifty *mikoshi* (sacred palanquins holding the god spirit), two imperial carriages, and four hundred participants in Heian period (784–1185) costume participate in the procession behind the most sacred *mikoshi,* which is drawn by oxen while shrine officials are on horseback.

On February 26, 1936, the shrine was the center of excitement. In that period, when the Japanese military was beginning to drift out of civilian control, some 1,400 soldiers set out to "restore power" to the emperor and to bring wealth to the people. They executed two former premiers and the inspector general of military training, seized government buildings, and set up their headquarters below the Hie Shrine. Four days later, with little support from the military, the government, or the emperor, they surrendered. Nineteen of the ringleaders were executed—but they are remembered by those with nationalistic and militarist bent on a memorial stone at their place of execution, which today faces the Shibuya Ward Office and the NHK Broadcasting Building in Shibuya.

On leaving the shrine, the hill which descends before it is lined with the aforementioned vermilion torii. The torii of this shrine are unique in that they have a triangular-shaped top rather than the normal slightly curved top bar these sacred gateways usually employ. (One can also descend the street which runs from the rear of the Diet Building to Sotobori-dori.)

On the descent of the hill to Sotobori-dori, there are a series of streets running parallel to Sotobori-dori to the west, streets noted for their restaurants. These streets took a new lease on life when the Kasumigaseki area became the seat of government after 1868. Then the **Akasaka** district developed restaurants to serve the new government quarters, some of these restaurants providing geisha entertainment. As the traditional Shimbashi geisha area grew more expensive and more exclusive, a new entertainment and geisha sector developed in this area between the hills not far from the Diet. (It also at one time had its seamier side with the "bath girls" or prostitutes who served visitors to Akasaka.) By the early 1900s the sector was in its heyday, supported by politicians, businessmen, and the new breed of journalists. In more recent times these individuals have been augmented by staff from the nearby TBS television studios. Tourists frequent the restaurants as well, but the *ryotei* (geisha restaurants) have declined greatly with the passage of time. They can still be ascertained by the huge limousines parked out front. The *ryotei* sit behind their high walls—restaurants only the most wealthy industrialists or bribed politicians can afford. The three streets, Hitotsugi-dori, Misuji-dori, and Tamachi-dori to the west of Sotobori-dori, are at the heart of this entertainment area. Misuji-dori is between Hitotsugi-dori and Tamachi-dori, and has some of the major *geisha* restaurants.

Back on Sotobori-dori and continuing toward the overhead expressway is Akasaka Mitsuke, that crossroad of streets, subway stations, and the overhead Shuto Expressway (once again encountered in another of its branches). The Ginza, Marunouchi, and Hanzomon Subway lines all have entrances here. Sotobori-dori which we have been following was, as has been indicated, the outer moat for the Tokugawa castle, and it was completed in 1636 by the third shogun, Tokugawa Iemitsu. The moats about the castle each had a *mitsuke* (a fortified gate) at the bridges which crossed the moat. As with the *masugata* gates at the Ote-mon and the Sakurada-mon entrances to the castle, each *mitsuke* had a fortified wall behind the gate, a wall which formed a "box" within which any trespasser or enemy could be ambushed. It is claimed that there were thirty-six of these *mitsuke* about the moats. The gate at Akasaka Mitsuke is said to have been one of the finest of these defensive units, and it guarded the road (the present Aoyama-dori) that led from the castle to Shibuya. The last remnants of this gate and the one at Sotobori-dori at Toranomon were removed by the Meiji government in 1873.

Today there is no gate in Akasaka Mitsuke (Red Hill Fortress Gate). A portion of the moat continues to exist, separating the lands of the Akasaka Detached Palace from the New Otani Hotel and running in part in front of the Akasaka Prince Hotel. On the left of the Akasaka Mitsuke intersection is the Suntory Building with the **Suntory Museum of Art** (Suntory Bijutsukan) on the eleventh floor. The museum is open from 10:00 A.M. to 5:00 P.M. (to 7:00 P.M. on Fridays) except on Mondays and the New Year holiday. Entry fee. This very fine museum has a main gallery, a reading room, and a tea ceremony room. Its collection specializes in the decorative arts of the Muromachi and Edo Periods (1336 to 1868), and it offers some seven exhibitions of a varied nature during the year, some borrowed from other museums and private collections. For a fee, tea may be enjoyed in the museum's traditional tearoom.

Across the expressway, the forty-story **Akasaka Prince Hotel** stands out prominently at this juncture. This starkly white build-ing shaped in the form of a folding fan in mirrored white glass and aluminum was designed by Kenzo Tange in 1983. It is worth entering the lobby to view the entire white interior, right down to a white baby grand piano. The 1983 building is quite different from the old 1928 wing behind it, a structure originally built as the residence of Prince Yi of Korea (when Korea was a Japanese colony), which in 1955 became the hotel's guest house. Today only the ballroom and a restaurant use this older portion of the hotel.

Returning to and crossing the Benkei Bridge which spans the moat brings one to the impressive **Hotel New Otani** and its traditional garden. The forty-story main structure was built in 1974, and then in 1991 a thirty-story New Otani Tower was added. Between the two units of the hotel, some 2,100 rooms are available for guests. The New Otani Art Museum can be found off the sixth-floor lobby of the original building: The gallery to the right offers paintings by noted Japanese artists while the gallery on the left shows the work of Western artists and particularly the *École de Paris* school. The lower floors of the hotel offer a variety of gift shops, coffee shops, and restaurants that can provide a break in the tour if one wishes. The gorgeous traditional outdoor gardens of the hotel are well worth a visit; they were once a portion of the estate of Kato Kiyomasa (1562–1611), the Lord of Kumamoto, and they are a fine example of a traditional Japanese garden. The garden can be entered from the corridor between the two buildings of the hotel, the door to the garden being next to the lounge.

Returning to the Suntory Building, a turn to the right on its far side brings one onto Aoyama-dori. Walking along this avenue, at the second street on the right is the **Myogon-ji** temple or Toyokawa Inari Shrine. This is one of those delightful anomalies of Japanese culture, for here is a Zen temple which has red lanterns such as are only found at Shinto shrines. There was a tradition for such a joint situation before 1868 when temples and shrines cohabited, but from that time on, temples and shrines were forcibly separated by the new Meiji government. Shinto had always been an unorganized folk faith (unorganized, not disorganized). The advent of Buddhism in the 600s provided a faith which was highly organized and structured, and in time Ryobu Shinto (Dual Shinto) developed whereby Shinto shrines were often run by Buddhist temples. There had always been a relationship between the two faiths (the Japanese are not as prone to sharp divisions between faiths as in the West) since in Japan each temple has a small shrine to the Shinto deity of the land which it occupies.

What is the occasion for this seemingly open confusion here at this temple-shrine? According to tradition, in the early 1200s Emperor Juntoku's third son Kanganzenji, who happened to be a Zen priest, was on a ship returning from China. In the midst of a terrible storm when all seemed lost, the son saw the image of the Buddhist deity Dakini (who also is known as the Shinto deity Inari) with a rice bale on his back, riding on a white fox. The ship did not founder, and the son carved an image of Dakini on his return to Japan. This carved figure of a deity who has both a Buddhist and a Shinto aspect is said to be the *hibutsu* (hidden image) at the altar of the temple. (It is pictured within the temple, even though the original may not be viewed.)

In the period from 1717 to 1736 there lived across the street from this temple a daimyo who served as a city magistrate. He had come from Toyokawa in the provinces, and he brought with him the image carved by the noble Zen monk, an image which he established in the branch shrine which he had built across from his residence. This daimyo, Ooka Tadasuke, was noted for his beneficent rule as a magistrate, and he is credited, among other charitable acts, with having created the first fire brigades to protect the whole city in times of danger.

Within the temple grounds there is the main hall of the temple, guarded in a rather unusual manner by red-bibbed foxes, images which normally grace many Shinto shrines but seldom appear before Buddhist temples. There is a hexagonally roofed shrine to the noble magistrate on the left side of the hall while to the right is a modern building, the Akasaka Tokyo Toyokawa Inari Kaikan, where one can have priests pray for whatever type of success one is imploring Dakini (Inari) to grant. Even in these modern days there is a bit of the supernatural in such requests, for the priest uses "the wind of wisdom" in reading the sutra, which may help in the granting of one's wishes. This "wind" insures that while the priest may chant only from the first and last page of an extensive sutra, when the intervening pages are being quickly flipped, the "wind of wisdom" sees to it that the entire reading is automatically efficacious. (The hall also provides space where shrine events can be held.)

Before the Kaikan is a statue of the Kodakara Kanzeon Bosatsu, a Kannon image holding a child in its arms. This Bodhisattva is prayed to for the birth of healthy children and for prosperity for the future family line. In addition to the shrine to the magistrate and the main Buddhist hall, Inari shrines can be found on the grounds, guarded by their fox images—to which some worshippers bring offerings from nearby restaurants. The approach to the main Inari shrine is lined with banners, given by worshippers as prayers for the granting of their wishes or for thanks for the successful fulfillment of their prayers. Along the path to the Inari shrine is the Migawari Jizo on the right, another example of the unusual situation where a Buddhist deity is worshipped in the approaches to this Shinto shrine. He is a favored deity since he takes upon himself the problems or troubles afflicting those who pray to him. To the left of the Inari shrine are images of the Seven Gods of Good Fortune. At the far end of this busy and self-contained temple-shrine is the Akasaka Tokyo Toyokawa Bunka Kaikan, a hall for wedding receptions, conventions, and other affairs both religious and secular.

Farther along Aoyama-dori on the right are the parklands of the **Akasaka Detached Palace.** Not too far within the grounds are the separate palace units of members of the Imperial family, the mansions of Emperor Showa's brothers, Prince Chichibu and Prince Mikasa and their families. While the palace cannot be seen on this walking tour, it is here described so that those interested in it can view it at another time. Also, for those who are interested, the Akasaka Detached Palace can best be seen by a seven minute walk from Yotsuya Station of the JR Sobu Line. The palace itself cannot be entered since it serves today as a State Guest House, but the gardens and fountains may be visited.

Before the end of the Tokugawa regime in 1868, the land that the Akasaka Palace occupies had belonged to the Kii branch of the Tokugawa family. Taken over by the Imperial Household Agency in 1868, it had to serve as the Emperor Meiji's residence from 1873 to 1888, when the buildings of the Imperial Palace were destroyed by fire. The Akasaka Palace was built for the emperor by public subscription, and it was completed in 1909 as the Togu Palace. The structure was created after the fashion of English, French, and German palaces in an attempt to be as Western as the West in imperial architecture. In part it was modeled after the Palace of Versailles in France in the vain attempt to create a Western residence for the emperor. The original on which the Akasaka Palace was modeled reflected a pre-French Revolution era, and so the palace hardly served as an example of the best of turn-of-the-century official dwellings.

To further complicate matters, an American architect's advice was also invited. The new palace had all the grandeur and many of the discomforts of European palaces of the past. There was, for example, but one bathroom, and it was in the basement. The emperor's bedroom was in one wing of the building while that of the empress was in another wing. This may not have made for the closest of marital bliss, but on the other hand, it was the custom of the emperor to drop his handkerchief each evening in front of one of the ladies-in-waiting (a euphemism if ever there was one), who was thereby invited to his wing.

The palace has seen changes through the years. Emperor Meiji, on his move to the Imperial Palace after 1888, gave the

Togu Palace to the crown prince for a residence. After the Second World War, it housed the National Diet Library until 1962. Next it was the headquarters for the 1964 Olympics in Japan. Then in 1974 the palace was redone so it could serve as the State Guest House for heads of state when they visit Japan. President Ford of the United States in 1974, Queen Elizabeth of Britain in 1975, world leaders attending the 1980 summit, and other heads of state have used the guest house. The various rooms are quite impressive: the Egyptian Room was the former Smoking Room of the original palace, while the Hall of the Feathered Robe (the former ballroom) has a painted ceiling inspired by the Noh play *The Feathered Robe.* The former dining room is now the Hall of Flowers and Birds. In addition to the above, the grounds also contain the Omiya Palace Park with mansions of the branches of the imperial family, including a residence for the crown prince.

Some three streets further along Aoyama-dori is the **Sogetsu Art Center,** a 1977 Kenzo Tange building of mirrored glass. The Sogetsu School of Flower Arranging was begun by Sofu Teshigahara, and the present head of the school is his son Hiroshi Teshigahara, who is also well known as the director of the film *Woman in the Dunes.* The lobby, a cascade of stone, has sculptures by Isamu Noguchi, and flower arrangements here are often on a very large scale. A small theater is on the lower level, a café on an upper level overlooks the lobby and the street, and the Sogetsu Art Museum is on the sixth floor, where flower arrangements by members of the school as well as other Japanese artists may be seen. Traveling exhibits of contemporary art are frequently on view. Lessons in the Sogetsu style of flower arrangement are possible for a fee. The Sogetsu Art Museum on the sixth floor is open from 10:00 A.M. to 5:00 P.M. with the exceptions of Saturdays, Sundays, national holidays, and the New Year holiday. Entry fee.

One can continue farther along Aoyama-dori to the **Meiji Shrine Outer Gardens,** but this is recommended only for those who wish to see the 1964 Olympic sports complex or the Meiji Picture Gallery, a rather heavy-handed glorification of the life of Emperor Meiji in eighty pictures (described below). If one does not continue to the picture gallery, a return to Akasaka Mitsuke brings one back to the various subway lines which lie below that intersection. (One can also reach the picture gallery and sports complex by taking the subway from Akasaka Mitsuke to Gaien-mae Station, which is close to the gallery.)

The twenty acres of the Meiji Shrine Outer Gardens are an extension in part of the former daimyo lands, which became the Akasaka Detached Palace. This portion of the land was developed into the 120-acre Aoyama Parade Ground for the military after 1868. Here in 1912 Emperor Meiji's funeral service was held, and in recent years a major portion of the area has become a sports grounds. On the left side of the Outer Gardens can be found those units which were the center of athletic events during

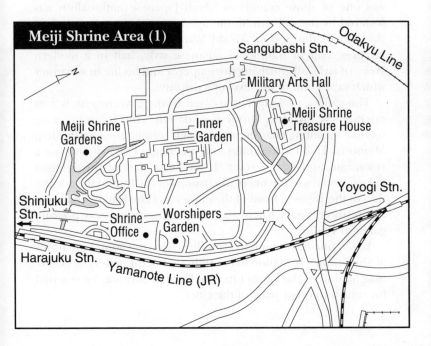

the 1964 Olympics: the National Stadium, which can seat 75,000, the two Jingu Baseball stadiums, which can accommodate 66,000 and 12,000 respectively, the Prince Chichibu Memorial Football Field, seating 20,000, the 5,300-seat Tokyo Gymnasium, and the Metropolitan Indoor Swimming Pool, which can accommodate 3,000 swimmers.

A long walk into the grounds along the gingko tree-lined roadway leads to the **Meiji Memorial Picture Gallery** (Seitoku Kinen Kaigakan), a building which in part resembles that of the National Diet except that its center portion is domed rather than having a tower. The gallery is open from 9:00 A.M. to 4:00 P.M. daily between April and October and from 9:00 A.M. to 3:00 P.M. between November and March. Entry fee. It is closed from December 20 to January 20.

Construction of the gallery was begun within three years of the emperor's death in 1912, but it was not completed until 1920. It was one of those centers at which Japanese nationalism was fostered by the militant Shinto agencies of government before the end of the Second World War. The hall contains eighty pictures, half in traditional Japanese style, half in a modern Western style, all glorifying the emperor and his life in a manner which raises him to the level of a divinity.

The gallery, no longer supported by the government, is now operated by the Meiji Shrine Foundation. Thus it has to create income by selling charms and through renting the nearby Meiji Memorial Hall for weddings and meetings. The hall also has a restaurant and beer terrace. It was once part of the Aoyama Palace, and it was the site of discussions of the Imperial Constitution of the 1890s in front of the emperor. (The Kinkei Lounge is the restored room where the Meiji Constitution was promulgated in 1890.)

When one has completed this diversion, the Sobu Line trains at Shinanomachi Station to the right rear of the gallery or Gaienmae Station of the Ginza Line on Aoyama-dori may be reached for return to other parts of the city.

TOUR

4

Tsukiji and Hama
Detached Palace Garden

IF TOKUGAWA Ieyasu were to return to Tokyo today, there is one area of his onetime capital that would utterly amaze him, and that is the Tsukiji area to the east of the Ginza. His astonishment would arise from the fact that this was still part of Tokyo Bay while he was alive. The very name of the sector is a giveaway as to the change which has taken place over the centuries since Tsukiji means "reclaimed land."

When Shogun Ieyasu had the hills of Kanda to the north of the castle leveled to fill in the Hibiya Inlet, the fill also helped to create solid land on the marshes of what became the Nihombashi and Ginza areas of old Edo. The creation of the Tsukiji sector began about 1650, but it was greatly enlarged after 1657, the result of one of those perennial "Flowers of Edo" which in the case of the Furisode Fire, the Long Sleeves Fire of that year, destroyed much of the city. The marshy sections to the west of the Ginza were thus filled in order to create additional land where some of the daimyo could build their mansions and where land could be granted to certain temples. (The filling in of Tokyo Bay continues. In the four decades after 1945, one-seventh of the bay was filled in so as to create an additional 87 square miles of dry land.)

A goodly portion of the land was granted to the heirs of Okudaira Nobumasa (1555–1615), politics and marriage being involved with this grant. Nobumasa had been an ally of Ieyasu, and, in one of the many battles before Ieyasu became supreme, the enemies of Nobumasa killed his wife in revenge for his defection to Ieyasu's side. To atone for the loss Nobumasa had sustained, Ieyasu therefore granted Nobumasa his eldest daughter in marriage. In time Ieyasu even adopted his grandson from this marriage, giving him the new family name of Matsudaira. A descendant, Matsudaira Sadanobu (1758–1829), was one of the great Tokugawa administrators, and it was his family, living in the Tsukiji area, who would unwittingly help in the founding of modern Japanese studies of the West.

Even before the Matsudaira family set foot on their newly

created land, there were others of a less powerful group who were living on one of the small islands, later much enlarged, at the point where the Sumida River flows into the bay. Here on the island of Tsukuda-jima, Ieyasu's son Hidetada settled a group of fishermen from the Osaka area with a twofold purpose to suit his needs, one culinary and one political. Those purposes will be revealed when the fishermen's island is explored.

This walking tour begins at the **Kabuki-za** theater which sits above Higashi Ginza Station of the Hibiya and the Toei Asakusa Subway lines at the corner of Harumi-dori and Showa-dori. Kabuki as a form of entertainment was a problem for the shoguns from Kabuki's earliest beginning and throughout the Tokugawa's rule. Kabuki had its beginnings in 1603 when a woman involved in sacred dances at the great shrine of Izumo brought her dancers to Kyoto. There they began their dances, now secularized, and these gradually grew into plotless tales, many of which involved young men and prostitutes in the bathhouses. Some of her associates were quite experienced in this realm, and the rowdiness which resulted from these skits, for that is all they were, led in 1629 to the shogunate banning female performers in Kabuki drama.

The women's places were taken from 1630 to 1652 by attractive young men, some of whom were so sexually appealing to the Buddhist priests and samurai who attended these performances that they sometimes fell into brawls for a certain actor's favors. Thus the shogunate banned this form of young men's Kabuki, but not until after the current shogun had expired, since he too found the young men of Kabuki attractive. Thereafter the actors had to be mature males who took both the male and female parts in the dramas, as they still do today.

Kabuki had its beginnings in Edo in the Yoshiwara "licensed quarter" at Ningyocho (see Tour 6). Periodically a streak of puritanism would emanate from the shogunate, and in 1841 Kabuki was banished from the Hamacho (Ningyocho) Yoshiwara district to a new Yoshiwara area beyond the Asakusa Shrine, and there Kabuki remained while the Tokugawa were in power. In 1872, four years after the fall of the Tokugawa, the Morita-za Kabuki theater moved from Yoshiwara to the area around the present Shintomicho Subway Station and took the name Shintomi-za. Here Kabuki was quite successful under an innovative management which brought new life to this stage form. The theater had come to the Tsukiji area since it was able to obtain land cheaply after the great fire which had destroyed the Ginza district in 1872. The land the theater purchased had belonged to the defunct Shimabara "licensed" quarters which the Meiji government had permitted to become established on this recently filled ground.

The Shintomi-za lasted just four years before it burned in 1876, but it was rebuilt and re-opened in 1878, and it was here that former President Ulysses S. Grant was entertained on his trip to Japan. The new theater made use of bright gas lights for its evening performances, and there was an attempt to raise the level of Kabuki drama over the coarseness which had developed in its Yoshiwara days. Soon the Shintomi-za attracted other theaters to the district, one of them being the Kabuki-za, and this new arrival became the great competitor to the Shintomi-za after its establishment in 1889. The 1923 earthquake destroyed the Shintomi-za, but this theatrical district soon obtained a legitimate theater which arose nearby in 1925 and which offered modern Western plays. It came to an end when it was destroyed in 1945 by air raids.

The Kabuki-za remained, despite earthquakes and wartime bombing. It was a much larger theater than the Shintomi-za, and it was to become the center for Kabuki in Tokyo. In its new home, Kabuki was becoming a more elevated form of theater than it had been in Yoshiwara. Moreover, various theatrical techniques had been developing that were to make Kabuki a more dramatic and more spectacular form of entertainment. As early as 1758 the revolving stage had appeared in Kabuki to provide for a quick changing of sets. Trap doors in the stage could make for unexpected appearances or sudden disappearances. Black-hooded stage-hands changed scenery or props; their being all in black meant that they were not "seen," an artifice easily accepted by the public. The *hanamichi* (flower path) was found to be useful, for this runway extending into the audience permitted actors to enter and exit easily. It also became a favorite place for actors to strike one of those frozen and exaggerated poses which Tokyo audiences still adore. The use of the *shamisen* softened, while drums and wooden clappers heightened, dramatic moments in the drama. Costumes became ever more gorgeous and flamboyant, and a completely stylized form of acting developed, thereby creating an art form of its own.

The Kabuki-za was damaged in the 1923 earthquake but was rebuilt in a modified Momoyama style so as to give it its distinctive exterior look. Damaged in the 1945 air raids on Tokyo, it was reconstructed in 1950 and it can now seat up to 2,600 spectators. Performances are presented at 11:00 A.M. and 4:30 P.M. throughout the year with the exception of August and September. During intermissions, food can be obtained since performances usually last some five hours.

As it happened, in 1925, another Kabuki house arrived when the Shimbashi Embujo theater, two streets south from the Kabuki-za, opened its doors. Aside from Kabuki, for years Shimbashi geisha offered their Azuma Odori, the spring and autumn dance plays, in the Shimbashi Embujo theater. In 1982 the Nissan New Building was erected on the site of the Shimbashi Embujo theater, incorporating a replacement theater of the same name into it. Seating 1,428 theatergoers, the Shimbashi Embujo offers Kabuki, Buto (traditional dance), plays from the Meiji era, as well as modern plays.

Walking east along Harumi-dori (away from the downtown Ginza district), after some five streets one arrives at Shin Ohashi-dori. On the left is the **Tsukiji Hongan-ji** temple, an unusual-looking structure reminiscent of the architecture of India. The temple is a branch of the Jodo Shinshu sect of Buddhism, a onetime militarily powerful religious group. In their Osaka headquarters in the mid-1500s they were able to stand off Oda Nobunaga and his troops when he was the leading general as well as the civil ruler of Japan. In the 1590s Toyotomi Hideyoshi, Nobunaga's successor and Tokugawa Ieyasu's predecessor, disarmed the sect and offered it a location in Kyoto for their new headquarters. There they settled in what was, and is, a most luxurious site. When Ieyasu came to power in 1603, he still feared the arrogance of the sect, and because of this he split the Hongan-ji temple and the Jodo Shinshu sect into two groups, the Nishi (West) Hongan-ji and the Higashi (East) Hongan-ji temple. Since he was also the head of the newly established Higashi splinter group, he placed a disaffected relative of the leader of the main branch of the faith as abbot in charge of these dissidents. Divide and conquer, Ieyasu found, was better than a head-on approach when faced with potential opponents, religious or secular.

A subsidiary temple of the original sect moved to Edo in 1617 and was settled in Hamacho, the original Yoshiwara district. After its destruction in the Long Sleeves Fire of 1657, the temple was offered a site in the newly created Tsukiji area, and as a result the Tsukiji Hongan-ji temple came into being. The 1923 earthquake marked the ninth time the temple was destroyed by fire, and thus the decision was made at this time to rebuild in stone. In the period of its greatest strength, the Tsukiji Hongan-ji had more than fifty sub-temples around it, a few of which survive hither-and-yon in the Tsukiji district today.

Buddhism began in India, and so in the 1935 rebuilding of the temple, Ito Chuta, the temple architect, wished to show the tie of Japanese Buddhism to its early heritage by creating a temple which reflects the traditional architecture of India. This temple of the Jodo Shinshu sect, in a classical Indian style of architecture, can seat 1,000 worshippers and as the central temple of the sect in the Tokyo area it supervises more than 600 other temples in the Kanto region. Standing 114 feet tall and covering 70,600 square feet, it is one of the largest Buddhist temples in Japan. The temple offers daily services, supports a Sunday school, and at 10:30 A.M. on Sunday mornings it offers services in English and in Japanese for those interested in the Shinshu faith, which reveres the Amida Buddha. Within the *hondo* (main hall), the front of the worship hall offers a golden façade, its transoms above the golden altar being intricately carved, while the altar area is embellished with golden furnishings. A modern-day temple, it offers soft seats for worshipers while a large organ is on hand to provide music during religious services.

Five short streets to the north along Shin Ohashi-dori, to the right on leaving the temple, lead to Shintomicho Subway Station. (The subway entrance is on the west side of Shin Ohashi-dori.) Here it is easiest to take the train one station to the east to Tsukishima on the island of this name. It was indicated above that in 1615 the recently established Tokugawa shogunate had several motives in bringing fishermen to this location. To begin with, the fishermen of Tsukuda in the Osaka area had assisted Ieyasu before 1603 and were due a reward. They were therefore brought to these reclaimed mud flats at the entrance to the bay of Edo, an area which would grow as the bay was continuously filled in.

Tsukudajima (Island of Cultivated Rice Fields) originally consisted of two mud flats at the mouth of the Sumida River. In the early 1600s they were developed into two islands, the northern one named Ishikawa-jima since it was granted to Ishikawa Hachizaemon, the controller of the shogun's ships. The southern island became Tsukuda-jima, named for the fishermen's original home near Osaka. It was not until 1872 that the two islands were joined to become one, and then in 1893 reclaimed mud flats to their south created the present large **Tsukishima** island. The old fishermen's quarter has a branch of the Sumida River on its western side while a narrow canal still exists on its northern and eastern side. Its southern side has had its waterway filled in, and it has been replaced by the elevated highway leading to the bridge to Tsukiji.

The shogunate's appreciation for past favors was not the essence of this move, however. These fishermen were skilled in their trade, and they supplied the whitebait from the bay which garnished the shogunate's tables. They fished in the dark of the night, burning firewood in metal baskets at the stern of their boats so as to attract the fish. Then, as excellent navigators, they offered another service for the shogunate: they could report sightings of any strange boats in the bay and thus better protect Edo and the shogunate against any hostile forces. (A later shogun in 1715 brought skilled gardeners to Edo from Kii province. Not only could they garden, but they were adept at entering the gardens of dissident daimyos by night and carrying out the shogun's less than charitable missions.)

One of the attractions of the island for Tokyo residents through the years has been the odor of soy sauce permeating the air on Tsukuda-jima, for the fishermen developed a culinary delight by simmering fish in seaweed and soy sauce. Preserved in this boiled-down sauce along with salt, *tsukudani* became a much-desired delicacy. The island was known as well for a less happy association, for in the 1790s Matsudaira Sadanobu used the island for a detention center for *ronin* (samurai who had lost their lord and thus their employment) and vagrants. These individuals had become a political problem for the shogunate since they were often at the heart of brawls and riots. In a sense, what was being attempted was a halfway house where vagrants could be taught a trade. Later, for the fifteen years after 1870, a prison was established here, one which was later moved to Sugamo in the Ikebukuro area.

Three things are of interest on this island: the Sumiyoshi Shrine; the old houses of the fishing village, which are all too quickly disappearing; and the River City 21 project, which has been created in a former industrial area.

We begin with **River City 21.** It has been indicated that once there were two islands, Ishikawa-jima and Tsukuda-jima, both of which are now joined. The former Ishikawa-jima is the northern half of the present island. Here the shogunate's Master of Ships had his land in the seventeenth century, and here in 1854 the Mito branch of the Tokugawa built a modern shipyard. It became the first shipyard to launch a Western-style ship in 1876, and this small shipbuilding factory became the predecessor to Ishikawajima Harima Heavy Industries, now relocated to the east of this area.

Beginning in the 1980s, the factory and warehouse sites were cleared, and a new River City 21 appeared. This fascinating complex of high-rise apartments and office buildings is set in parklike landscaped areas with a river promenade on three sides. Its architecture is strikingly modern, and therefore this tour should begin at exit number four of Tsukishima Station. This brings one to Kiyosumi-dori, and one should walk to the north away from the overhead highway. After a few short streets one reaches the new complex on the left, just before the bridge which crosses over the Sumida River into the Fukagawa district of Tokyo. Steps or a ramp can be mounted to the park which encircles the River City 21 buildings on three sides, a riverside promenade below at the water's edge. Condominiums for 7,500 inhabitants are available for leasing (to avoid price speculation) in these forty-story-tall buildings. A park, Tsukuda Koen, lies in front of these high-rise structures, and a lighthouse remains on its western side as a memorial to the beacon of the mid-nineteenth century, which once guided ships into the port of Edo. The new complex sits on a raised site above the dangers of tidal floods, whereas the older section of the island, closer to the subway line and main east-west street, are protected by high flood walls. A small canal separates River City 21 from the former Tsukuda fisherman's area, and thus a sluice in the river front with a red gate serves to control the waters of the Sumida River from flooding the canal at times of high water.

In their home near Osaka, the fishermen had worshiped the deity of the great **Sumiyoshi Shrine.** That shrine had been created by Empress Jingo, who was deeply indebted to Sumiyoshi, the god of the sea. It seems that when the Empress, then quite pregnant but determined to conquer Korea, made war against that country, Sumiyoshi had served as the pilot of her ship. When a huge storm threatened the survival of the ship and passengers, the legend goes, the god had a school of large fish support the boat in the high seas.

Thus those involved with the sea are always beholden to Sumiyoshi, the deity of safety at sea. As a result, there are some two thousand branches of the Osaka main shrine throughout Japan, of which this small shrine is a representative. A large copper-plated torii provides an entrance to the shrine with its unpainted and aged wooden buildings, and down the residential street beyond this first torii is a second stone torii. Behind it to the right is a traditional fountain for the cleansing of hands and mouth before approaching the *haiden* and the *honden* of the shrine. Both these buildings have copper-plated roofs with the traditional *chigi* beams to hold them in place. Thus the architecture of the shrine is typical of all Sumiyoshi shrines. The two units are joined by a roofed corridor or room.

Smaller shrine units lie before the *haiden* on the left and right side while to the left of the *honden* is an unusual brick *kura* (storage building) standing in front of and adjoining a traditional white plastered *kura*. The large inscribed Katsuozuka stone on the grounds, behind the purification fountain, is a memorial to the fish which are caught each year for the *tsukudani* delicacy, and services are held here in their memory annually. A *kagura* stage for religious dances is on the right side of the grounds. Aside from the usual stone lanterns, a pair of *koma-inu* (Korean lion-dogs) stand guard on either side of the path behind the stone torii. *Kura* to store the portable shrines are also on the grounds.

The Sumiyoshi Festival, which occurs on the first weekend in August every third year, is always a fascinating event. Then the octagonal *mikoshi* (portable shrine) holding the god spirit is paraded through the streets behind a huge, golden lion's head. Traditionally the *mikoshi* was brought to the river where it was partially immersed as a part of the exciting procession, but since 1962 the flood walls built to protect the island preclude this part of the festivities. Instead the *mikoshi* is now paraded on a barge and is doused with water as part of the festival, the offering of water to the deities being seen as religiously efficacious.

Since the shogun had brought the fishermen from Osaka to Edo, they attempted to show their appreciation to him by having their shrine face toward the shogun's castle, and on festival days huge banners were raised so as to attract the attention of the denizens of the castle. Another festival related to Buddhist beliefs rather than to those of Shinto occurs each July 13, 14, and 15 from 7:00 to 9:00 P.M. when the residents of the area dance the traditional *bon odori*, which is a part of the Buddhist festivity to honor the spirits of the deceased who return to this world for a few brief days each summer. Of interest also are the number of traditional wooden homes that still exist near the shrine. These buildings were fortunate enough to be spared in the 1923 earthquake and fire and then the 1945 fire bombings. The narrow streets and alleyways still retain some of the original fishermen's houses. However, many have been modernized or replaced entirely, so that the flavor of the old fishermen's quarter is gradually being lost. In addition, the old lighthouse which once guided ships to port now stands dwarfed by the very tall high-rise apartments, a monument to times past.

Returning to the elevated highway street under which the Yurakucho Subway Line runs, one has to climb a set of stairs up to the bridge which can be taken back to the west to the Tsukiji area mainland. Until 1964 the only access to this island was by means of a ferry which had existed from 1645 to 1964, for neither a bridge nor the later subway reached the island from Tsukiji, although the island had been connected by a bridge to Fukagawa to the north since early in the 1900s. At the western end of the more recent bridge is a memorial stone recalling the ferry which traversed the river for so many centuries. In the early 1990s another novel bridge connected Tsukuda island with the mainland, its single inverted-Y-shaped tower supporting the roadway over the river by means of cables.

The Sumida River, a stream for pleasure boats with restaurants along the banks in centuries past, became less than desirable as the twentieth century advanced. Commercial and industrial sites took away the pleasurable aspects of the waterway, and then the high flood waters coursing in from the bay in the later 1940s led to the construction of the tall floodwalls which effectively cut out any view of the waterway from riverside restaurants. In the last decades of the twentieth century this despoiling of the river is being reversed as new, modern buildings, many of them high-rise units, are appearing along the banks of the Sumida. Attempts are being made as well to create promenades on the river side of the flood walls from the Tsukiji area up through Asakusa so as to return the waterfront to public enjoyment once more.

Once across the bridge, one is in an area which belonged to the Matsudaira lords. The whole sector was part of the retirement estate of Matsudaira Sadanobu in the 1700s, an area ennobled by the huge palace-residence of this important family. While nothing remains of the estate today, a very large model of a Matsudaira palace with its outbuildings can be seen in a large model at the Edo-Tokyo Museum (*see* Tour 7). Today the area has changed tremendously, but historic markers are encountered as the walk continues to remind one of the rich history of this district.

Here on Sadanobu's estate began one of those actions which was to transform Japanese medicine, an action which is in part remembered by memorial stones in the neighborhood. Japanese medicine had always relied upon Chinese learning for its basic beliefs, but beginning in the 1770s this was to change drastically. There was the realization by a handful of Japanese physicians that much could be learned from a number of Western sources: first, from the few Dutch medical books available to them, then by the advice in the early 1800s of a Dutch physician named Philipp Franz von Siebold, and eventually at the end of the nineteenth century, from St. Luke's Hospital, a hospital which still exists.

In 1770, Maeno Ryotaku, a physician and a retainer of the Matsudaira, journeyed to Nagasaki where he was able to obtain a copy of a Dutch book on anatomy, *Ontleedkundige Tafelen*. Ryotaku had studied under Aoki Kon'yo, one of the early students of Dutch learning in Japan, and thus he knew of this Dutch anatomy text. The only type of foreign books available in Japan were those in Dutch, often surreptitiously available from the Dutch station at Dejima in Nagasaki due to the shogunal ban on anything foreign. Thus Ryotaku, who had learned a smattering of Dutch, developed a curiosity for greater European learning. (His mentor was nicknamed Doctor Potato by his contemporaries since he had introduced the sweet potato to the diet as an edible staple.) With another physician friend, Sugita Gempaku, Ryotaku had the opportunity to perform an autopsy on an executed criminal, and they were amazed to find that the anatomical plates in the Dutch book were, in fact, a true representation of the human internal organs.

By 1774 Ryotaku had translated the Dutch work and thus set Japanese medicine in new directions over the next century. With his appetite for more "esoteric" Western knowledge, he mastered the Dutch language and went on to translate works on geography, military matters, and astronomy. This interest in Dutch learning was to expand among a group of Edo scholars, and thus the nineteenth century saw a gradual broadening of Japanese views. In 1826 Philipp Franz von Siebold was the first foreigner to teach modern European medical practices in Japan, and the revolution in the knowledge of modern medicine gathered steam.

In 1858 another retainer of the Matsudaira clan, Fukuzawa Yukichi (1835–1901), was asked to open a school of Western learning on the clan property in Tsukiji. His students followed Dutch studies at first, but they then moved to studies in English. Within a decade his school became the forerunner of Keio University, which today is south of Tsukiji in the Mita area of Tokyo.

With the demise of the Tokugawa shogunate, the daimyo moved back to their estates and abandoned their Edo holdings, which in many cases were seized by the Meiji government. The Tsukiji area was not much in demand since it was isolated by various canals from the Ginza, and its space became known as the Navy Meadow since a naval installation existed here between 1858 and 1888. The Meiji government after 1868 was not happy with the unequal treaties forced upon Japan under the Tokugawas, and if Japan had to have foreigners in its midst, what better place to put them than in the comparatively isolated Tsukiji sector which had been abandoned by the daimyo. To entice the foreigners to this somewhat out-of-the-way area, the government held out certain inducements.

To begin with, they built a three-story hotel of 200 rooms. Since the foreigners ungraciously preferred to live in Yokohama, the hotel had to be sold to a Japanese entrepreneur four years after it was built. This grand if unsuccessful hostelry burned to the ground in 1872. Wooden houses of a vaguely Western nature were built for the foreigners who served in the legations and in the missionary enterprises which developed in Tsukiji. The American legation was settled here as well, and remained here until the extra-territorial status ended in 1899 and an embassy was set up in Toranomon.

For the benefit of the foreigners, the Meiji government even established a New Shimabara, or red-light district, in the Shintomicho district, that area which one day would be occupied by the first Kabuki theater. Shimabara was the licensed red-light district in Kyoto, and here in Tokyo was created the New Shimabara brothel with eighty-four teahouses where one made an appointment to meet the more respectable geisha. It is claimed that there were 1,700 courtesans in 130 brothels aside from the 200 geisha (21 of them male) in 200 establishments. Unfortunately the government did not realize that the few foreigners who were settling in the Tsukiji area were mostly Protestant missionaries, and thus the government's gracious accommodation found few foreign takers. The New Shimabara folded in 1870 within one year of its creation. So much for the first major enterprise of the Meiji government.

At this time missionaries, teachers, and missionary physicians began to appear in Tsukiji. One such Presbyterian missionary from Scotland from 1874 to 1887, Henry Faulds, opened a hospital close to the river. He noted that the illiterate among the Japanese used the print of their thumb for identification on documents. The scholarly paper he wrote concerning this discovery, which he later submitted to the British journal *Nature* in 1880, led in time to the use by police of fingerprints as a source of identification for criminals in the West. Schools as well as medical facilities were established by Western missionaries in this area, and these were to eventuate in Rikkyo University (now in Ikebukuro) and Aoyama Gakuin University (now in the Aoyama–Omotesando area).

The abolition of the unequal treaties led to a move by foreigners out of the Tsukiji area after 1900, and the earthquake of 1923 brought to an end the residential phase of this sector. One great reminder of this phase today is St. Luke's Hospital, whose initial buildings were replaced in 1933 and which have undergone modernization and expansion since the 1980s. St. Luke's was initiated in 1902 by Dr. Rudolf Teusler from Virginia, an Episcopal missionary. Unlike other Western-style hospitals in Tokyo, its records were kept in English rather than German, the Meiji government having wisely turned to German medical schools and hospitals as a model for medical Westernization. The 1932 building which eventually arose was designed with colorful tile decorations by an American architect in the art nouveau style, and its tower was topped with a cross. An inscription at one of the entrances to the hospital notes the fact that the hospital was an endeavor of Christianity in Japan. New buildings had to be created in the 1990s to meet the needs of modern medicine, and they occupy a major portion of Tsukiji just beyond the end of the Tsukuda Ohashi bridge, thereby creating a luxurious area in which two skyscraper units offer residence apartments for St. Luke's Hospital as well as a hotel, shops, and offices.

After crossing the bridge from Tsukuda-jima, the first major cross street should be taken to the left. At the beginning of the second street is a small granite memorial to Henry Faulds indicating that "Dr. Henry Faulds, pioneer in fingerprint identification, lived here from 1874 to 1884." A small bubbling fountain behind the stone sends water coursing down a tiny channel along the sidewalk. The original American legation sat on the left in this second block from the bridge, the site now covered by the twin high-rise buildings mentioned above. The area on the west of these twin towers was the location of the foreigners' settlement. Ahead on this street which parallels the river, in the **Akatsuki Koen** park, is a bust to Philipp Franz von Siebold (1796–1866) who came to Edo as early as 1826 and here gave lessons in medicine and surgery. A plaque dated June 18, 1988, next to the bust of Siebold explains that the memorial was presented to Chuo Ward by Leiden University of the Netherlands and by the Isaac Alfred Ailion Foundation in cooperation with the *Asahi Shimbun* newspaper. The park has lovely fountains and a delightful children's playground.

Going back one street to the end of the block on which the twin towers mentioned above are located and turning to the left (away from the river), one comes upon a tiny triangular plot named the **Nihon Kindai Bunka Kotohajime no Chi** (The Cradle of Modern Japanese Culture). Two memorial stones erected in 1958 stand in commemoration of those Japanese who lived or worked here and brought Western knowledge to Japan. The larger stone to the rear, depicting an illustration from an anatomy book, is to Maeno Ryotaku and Sugita Gempaku and their associate Nakagawa Jun'an, who translated the first Dutch textbook on anatomy between 1771 and 1774. The second stone is to Fukuzawa Yukichi, whose 1858 private classes for the Matsudaira clan were to lead in time to the formation of Keio University; inscribed in the stone book are Fukuzawa's words "Heaven created no man above another—nor below." (This egalitarian sentiment no doubt was a part of the reason in 1901 that the Meiji government would not permit Fukuzawa and his wife to be buried in the graveyard of Fukuzawa's family temple, which was too near the Imperial Palace. This spiteful action has been remedied since 1950 by the moving of their remains to the family temple graveyard.) Another stone commemorates the fact that "Here Dutch Studies Began."

The buildings of St. Luke's Hospital, begun by Dr. Rudolf Teusler in 1901, cover much of this area. Teusler not only introduced American medical approaches to health care, but he was concerned that his hospital offer medical care to all classes of society and not just the former samurai or Meiji official class. Opposite the entrance to St. Luke's in times past was the location of the residence of Lord Asano, the unfortunate daimyo whose followers gained notoriety after his death as "The Forty-Seven Ronin." On his disgrace, his lands were transferred to the Matsudaira clan.

Continuing along the street running to the south from the memorials, one finds at the end of the street a plaque which delineates the foreign quarters as they once existed. Crossing Harumi-dori one comes in time to the small **Namiyoke Shinto Shrine** with its dragon head on display. Nearby are many small shops, some 600 it is claimed, which offer a most interesting assortment of baskets, knives, and other utilitarian goods not to be found in the stylish shops of the Ginza to the west. It should be noted that many of these stores close about 1:00 P.M. Here and there in this district one finds numerous small Jodo Shinshu temples, offshoots of the great Tsukiji Hongan-ji temple just a few streets away.

We have arrived at the **Tsukiji Central Wholesale Markets,** known among foreigners primarily as the fish market of Tokyo. It is, however, a central market which handles all kinds of produce with the exception of rice. (It is difficult to imagine that this area was once the exquisite garden of the Matsudaira lords.) From the beginnings of Edo in the early 1600s, the city's fish market lay to the north along the Nihombashi River at the far side of the bridge of that name. There the many white plastered storehouses and the fish market reigned supreme. The 1923 earthquake and fire, however, destroyed the area, and the move of the market was begun to its present site, a site which became official in 1935 as new buildings were erected.

With the change in forms of shipping and packaging of bulk foodstuffs, the 1935 market has proved less than efficient. Plans have been suggested for moving the market elsewhere to the south, but in 1991 a twelve-year renovation program was begun. The revamped three-story market will have multistory skyscrapers around it, the market itself will be doubled in size, and adequate parking for all the vehicles flooding into the area each morning will be provided. Whereas much of the produce, particularly fish, came by boats in the past, today frozen bulk foods arrive by air and are then transported here by trucks from Narita Airport, which can boast that it is Japan's leading fish port. It is estimated that 90 percent of the fish now arrives overland rather than by sea to the market's docks, bringing salmon from Canada and Chile, shrimp from Thailand, sea urchin roe from Maine (U.S.A.), and tuna from Spain. So many fish have died to satisfy the Japanese palate that a monument has been raised outside the market to memorialize the fish who have given up their lives.

The market, the largest fish market in Asia, is owned and under the control of the metropolitan government. The figures of this market—the number of stalls, employees, and wholesalers—are staggering. It is estimated that there are some 1,677 wholesale shops which employ 15,000 workers. Work begins at 2:00 A.M., and the auctions themselves start at 5:00 A.M. About 3,000 barrows take the fish from the auction to the buyers' quarters. It is said that 60,000 individuals are within the market each day, 30,000 of them wholesalers and retailers. (Foreign workers have been on the increase as Japanese workers find this labor less to their liking.) While the most exciting time to visit the market is when the auctions begin at 5:00 A.M., it can be difficult getting there at this hour. If one arises this early, wear boots, since the flow of water for the sake of cleanliness in the markets can pose a problem for those not dressed for the type of work which goes on here. Perhaps a better time for a visit is from 8:30 A.M. to 9:30 A.M. before the market begins to wind down for the day. As late as 1:00 P.M. the market is still active as the work day comes to an end.

On leaving the front gate of the market (to the west), one is opposite the plant and offices of the *Asahi Shimbun* newspaper. Guided tours can be arranged. A ten-minute walk to the south along the street in front of the market, a street which gradually curves to the right, brings one to the entrance to the **Hama Detached Palace** grounds. The Hama Palace grounds originally belonged to a Matsudaira lord who filled in a portion of the bay to create wharves and warehouses to hold the rice brought in from his Nagoya estates. This rice was sold to offset the expense of maintaining the clan's Edo mansion. The Matsudaira daimyo eventually gave the land to the sixth Tokugawa shogun, Ienobu, who in 1709 erected a villa and created gardens filled with pavilions, pine trees, cherry trees, and duck ponds. Unlike the previous shogun, who forbade the killing of any animals, Ienobu loved duck hunting, and thus there were three duck ponds on the grounds. The large pond in the garden was a tidal pond whose waters were continually cleansed by the flow of the tides. A floodgate still controls the filling and cleansing of the ponds by the tide.

At the end of the Tokugawa shogunate the grounds were taken over by the Meiji Foreign Ministry. The shogunal villa burned but was restored in 1869 when a brick building with a veranda was built to house guests of State. It was here that the former U.S. president Grant and his wife stayed on their visit to Japan in 1879. Emperor Meiji had his first carriage ride to the Detached Palace for his visit to Grant, and the emperor and the president held conversations through interpreters in a pavilion, a "floating" teahouse set in the midst of one of the ponds. This official guest house did not prove to be a success, however, and guests were soon put up in the new Rokumeikan opposite Hibiya Park. With ownership transferred to the Imperial Household Agency, the grounds continued to be used for outdoor parties for Meiji nobles and for receptions for foreign guests. The original brick guest house was removed.

The Hama Detached Palace passed to the city of Tokyo after 1945 and was turned into a public park the next year. (Open from 9:00 A.M. to 4:30 P.M., closed Mondays and the end of December. Entry fee.) Stands for snacks and a midday repast are available on the grounds of the garden. The sixty-acre Hama Detached Palace park holds a lovely tidal pond which is spanned by staggered bridges shaded by wisteria-covered trellises. Of the three ponds in the garden, two are now fenced in as nature and duck preserves. Pines bordering the shores of the ponds and cherry trees which flower in the spring add charm to the garden. The pavilion on an island in the middle of the larger pond, in whose predecessor the emperor and the president met in 1879, has been rebuilt with its veranda "floating" on the pond. A path along the northern side of the park leads to a pier where a water bus may be taken up the Sumida River to the Azumabashi bridge or to Asakusa. The boats sail from 9:50 A.M. to dusk and the full trip takes thirty-five minutes. The waterway at the Hama Detached Garden at which the boat docks is enclosed with flood walls with flood gates which can be closed in times of exceedingly high tides. Where once the park faced the bay, today it confronts one of the large man-made islands which has lengthened the Sumida River. The river now flows in front of the park.

On leaving the park, continue walking along the street from the Tsukiji Market toward **Shimbashi.** Along the way on the right, one cannot help but notice the Nakagin Capsule Tower Building of Kisho Kurokawa of 1972. The building consists of 140 boxes cantilevered from two concrete towers which contain the elevators and stairs. Meant to serve as small offices or intimate apartments for out-of-towners who want a part-time residence in Tokyo, they come complete with bed, desk, and telephone. On the left is the former Shiodome freight yard of Japan Railways, one of the expanding areas for offices and apartments in downtown Tokyo and for a new elevated rail line which crosses the bay.

It was here at Shimbashi that the first steam locomotive appeared in 1872 when it pulled into the new Shimbashi terminal of the Yokohama line. The eighteen-mile distance was covered in fifty-three minutes. The station, destroyed by the 1923 earthquake, was built on the site of the mansion of the daimyo of Tatsuno, at which the forty-seven ronin stopped to refresh themselves that snowy December night when en route to their assassination of Lord Kira (see Tour 7 and Tour 11). The original starting point of the 1872 railroad and a bit of rail have been kept as a memorial to the beginning of modern transportation in Japan, while a 1945 steam locomotive has been preserved in front of the station to commemorate the 1972 centennial of rail transport in Japan.

The Shimbashi district beyond the west exit from the station became one of the most popular geisha quarters after 1868, for here the nouveaux riches and the new politicians of the Meiji era could relax and be entertained. The geisha of Yoshiwara looked down upon this quarter and its customers, seeing these new governmental patrons of geisha *divertissement* as rather uncouth provincials and the geisha of a distinctly inferior nature. Unfortunately for Yoshiwara, the 1923 earthquake pretty much finished off that traditional "licensed quarter" since the Great Kanto Earthquake came not too many years after a major fire had hit the Yoshiwara district. As a result, Shimbashi geisha and the *ryotei* restaurants in which they served both businessmen and politicians flourished. The period after 1945 was a difficult time for the geisha as for everyone else, and the geisha district gradually faded from the scene. At the end of the twentieth century some 150 geisha are still employed in the district, and they may occasionally be seen in the early evening heading to one of the thirty to forty *ryotei* still in existence. Sometimes these geisha arrive in rickshaws, probably pulled by university students in need of extra money, for rickshaws have long since passed from general use. The district is now filled with small restaurants, drinking establishments, and other shops.

This tour ends at the transportation means of one's choice, for the Toei Asakusa and the Ginza Subway lines have stations at Shimbashi as does the Yamanote Line.

TOUR

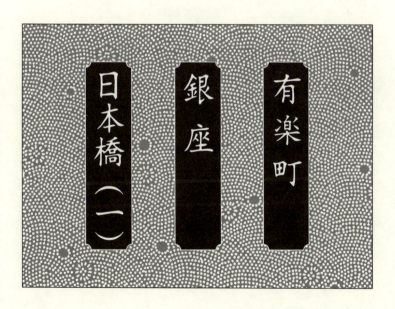

❀ 5 ❀

Yurakucho, Ginza, and Nihombashi (1)

日本橋（一）　銀座　有楽町

THE NAMES of the original commercial center of old Edo and modern Tokyo, Ginza, Yurakucho, and Nihombashi, are rather flexible descriptions for the areas they encompass. Chuo-dori, Central Avenue, is the traditional heart of the Ginza district, and often foreigners have used the term "Ginza" as though that were the name of Chuo-dori. Although Chuo-dori extends to the north beyond the limits of this tour, we shall be concerned with that portion of the street which lies between the Nihombashi bridge to the north and the Shimbashi Station to the south. Thus each segment ought to be defined and described.

Ginza means "Silver Mint," for it was in this area in the early 1600s that the Tokugawa shoguns had their mint for the production of silver (*gin*) coins. A stone monument in a flower planter of low evergreens at the edge of the sidewalk near the Itoya Stationery store in Ginza 2-chome commemorates the birthplace of the *gin-za*, the place of silver casting. Yurakucho is the western quarter of the Ginza area, the elevated Yamanote and the Japan Railway tracks serving as a boundary for the district on its western side. Nihombashi was the heart of *shitamachi* ("low city") in Edo times, and even into Meiji days it was the commercial and financial center of the city. Nihombashi for this tour is that portion of the district which lies to the south of the Nihombashi River; in Tour 6 the other part of Nihombashi will be combined with the adjacent Ningyocho, into which it merges geographically.

The three districts really form a unit, and they will be treated here in the popular tourist sense which designates all three areas as "the Ginza." This tour thus begins at Nihombashi bridge, and then proceeds down the eight portions of the Ginza from 1-chome through 8-chome, deviating to the side occasionally for places of interest (a *chome* is a grouping of city blocks). We begin at Nihombashi Station of the various subway lines serving the area, and we can start our walk at Nihombashi bridge itself. The Ginza subway line runs the length of this walk with stations at

Kyobashi, the Ginza Crossing, and Shimbashi. Thus one can break the tour at any of these points and can pick up the route at a later time if one desires.

In one sense Nihombashi is where any visit to Tokyo should begin. In that wonderful woodblock *Print No. 1* of his *Fifty-Three Stages of the Tokaido,* Hiroshige shows the arched, wooden bridge which first spanned the Nihombashi River in 1603. Across the bridge in the print comes a daimyo's procession, the lance bearers holding their covered weapons aloft, the retinue follow-ing behind. In the foreground appear fishmongers, workers who enlivened the riverfront for the next 300 years, here hastily making way for a procession they dare not block out of fear for their lives. In the background are the roofs of the *kura,* the warehouses along the river, while fire-towers with their alarm bells raise their ladder-like structures above distant buildings.

Nihombashi was the center of this exciting and boisterous community. The Tokaido, the great "Eastern Road" of Japan in the period from 1600 to the late 1800s, began at Nihombashi bridge in Edo. This road was the most important connection between the imperial capital of the emperor at Kyoto and the seat of the shogun in Edo, the latter a civil leader who ruled in the name of the emperor, giving the emperor the obeisance tradition required while at the same time ignoring him politically as a powerless figurehead. From 1604, a milepost on the Nihombashi bridge marked the beginning of those mileposts that counted off the 292 miles between the nation's two seats of governance. The black pole on the bridge which was the zero marker began the count of the distance not only to Kyoto but to all the towns on the other highways from Edo. Four great roads took off from this point leading to Ueno, Nikko, and the Nakasendo road through the mountains to Kyoto as well as the more heavily used Tokaido to Kyoto. Kyobashi to the south was the first bridge to be crossed on the way to Kyoto, but most of the rivers en route had to be forded, many times with difficulty.

Nihombashi bridge served a number of purposes aside from

its means of access between the north and south portions of Edo. At the south end of the bridge felons were exposed in fetters, and adulterers and priests guilty of sexual offenses were among those so treated before they were led off to their deaths. Those guilty of murder were placed in a hole with but their neck and head protruding. Two saws were available for anyone who wished to cut off their heads, which in the long run the authorities would accomplish more quickly. Their severed heads were then mounted on a pike at the end of the bridge as a warning to any potential wrongdoers.

An official notice board stood at the bridge so that the will of the shogunate could be made plain. The announcement in 1702 of the fate of the Forty-Seven Ronin (see Tour 7 and 11) was so distasteful to citizens that the notice was ripped down almost as soon as it was put in place. There was the "lost child stone" whereby the announcement regarding a child who was lost was posted on one side while notices of children who had been found were placed on the opposite side. In 1711 an improvement to the bridge brought the placement of the Toki-no-kane, a bell which sounded the hours of the day based on the lunar calendar with its twelve horary signs. (Hours varied in length by summer or winter daylight in old Edo.)

We begin at **Nihombashi** bridge, albeit certainly not Ieyasu's 1603 arched, wooden structure whose raised middle section permitted boats to pass beneath it. In 1806 the bridge collapsed as hundreds fled to the south from a fire in the Echigoya warehouse, one of a number of times in which the bridge was destroyed. At the beginning of the twentieth century any replacement for this or other bridges would require the capability of carrying the traffic which trams and then automobiles engendered. Thus in 1911 a modern stone and metal bridge of some charm, 161 feet long by 89 feet wide, was erected.

Four bronze Chinese lions stand on either side of the bridge at the northern and southern edges, while four seated unicorns rest on either side of two bronze obelisk-like light standards on the central balustrades on either side of the bridge. A copper plaque in the pavement at the center of the bridge, rather than the original black pole, today marks the point from which all distances are measured from Tokyo. Time heals all wounds, and in 1911 Tokugawa Yoshinobu, the fifteenth and last of the Tokugawa shoguns, was invited back to Tokyo from his exile in Shizuoka for the first time since 1868 to inscribe the name of the bridge Nihombashi (Bridge of Japan) on the new structure. His calligraphic inscription of the bridge's traditional name appears in stone. A plaque on the western side of the southern portion of the bridge shows the appearance of the original wooden bridge.

At the northeast side of the bridge is a commemorative statue of Princess Otohime-sama, the Daughter of the Dragon King. The tale of Otohime-sama is the Japanese equivalent of the American story of Rip van Winkle. Urashima Taro, smitten by the princess's beauty, is said to have followed this daughter of the Dragon King to her home beneath the sea. They married, but when he later left her to return to his village, he found that years undersea were equal to centuries on land, and thus he was a stranger in the world to which he returned.

In 1964, in preparation for the Olympics of that year, an elevated highway was completed over the Nihombashi River, and it crosses above the bridge to the detriment of the attractiveness of this 1911 structure. In 1991, on the eightieth birthday of the present Nihombashi bridge, a small terrace with benches was created at the south side of the bridge, and steps were built down to a terrace where one can obtain a better view of the 1911 structure. The terrace on the east side has a wall of water enhancing the small landing.

Stretching south from the Nihombashi bridge is that portion of Chuo-dori that is generally known as the Ginza. The first major cross street is Eitai-dori, and on the left, in **Nihombashi 1-chome,** is the Tokyu Department Store, a shop founded in 1662 that has developed into a major merchandising enterprise with numerous branches. Under the original name of Shirokiya, it was the scene of a tragic fire in which many of its female employees died. In the second level basement of the modern store is the "magic well" which, it is claimed, emitted an image of Kannon in the early 1700s. Opposite it is the Tokyo Daido Life Insurance Building, a thin building created by Kisho Kurokawa in 1978. The narrow arcade running through the building has its shop windows arranged in a staggered fashion along the walkway and the waterway which traverses this long, narrow interior thorough-fare. The ceiling lies nine floors above the promenade. Adjacent is Haibara, which has been selling fine papers since the eighteenth century in a shop which resembles an old-time storage building.

Two blocks further along Chuo-dori in **Nihombashi 2-chome** is Maruzen on the right, one of Tokyo's premier bookstores. Maruzen has an unusual history in that it first opened in 1869, right after the Meiji era began, and its intent was to bring Western writings to Japan so as to assist in the modernization of the nation. Books in languages other than Japanese can be found on the second floor while the fourth floor has a sales center for Japanese crafts, A later development has been the opening of a Burberry's clothing shop in the basement (closed Sundays and during the New Year period). Across the way is Takashimaya, another of the major department stores, with an exhibition gallery and restaurants on the upper floors, a fine kimono department, food sales in the basement, and, as with all such stores, a roof garden that offers bonsai, goldfish, and amusement rides in season for children (closed Wednesdays). There is even a small Shinto shrine here.

Four minor streets beyond Takashimaya is the wide Yaesu-dori. Across the street on the left side of Chuo-dori is the **Bridgestone Art Gallery** with the collection of Shojiro Ishibashi on the second floor of the Bridgestone Building. (Ishibashi means "stone bridge," and thus the name of the company and gallery.) While the art of the French impressionists as well as modern Japanese paintings intrigued Ishibashi, he did not neglect to collect some Greek and modern sculpture as well. The museum is open from 10:00 A.M. to 5:30 P.M. weekdays but opens at 11:00 A.M. on Saturdays; it is closed on Mondays. It is also closed on Sundays in July and August and from December 28 through January 4. Entry fee. The collection includes paintings by Rembrandt, Picasso, Rouault, Utrillo, and Modigliani among others, together with sculptures by Rodin, Moore, and Giacometti. Ishibashi also collected the works of post-Meiji Japanese artists who painted in the Western style, such as Fujita.

Yaesu-dori, the broad street which intersects Chuo-dori, leads to the right to Tokyo Central Station, and beneath the street is an underground arcade of shops leading to the station. Above ground, where Yaesu-dori meets Sotobori-dori is the Yaesu entrance to Tokyo Central Station. This is the "missing" entrance which took so long to create due to the dispute over where the Sotobori moat (now Sotobori-dori) should be bridged to permit entrance to the station from the east.

The name of **Yaesu** for the district is a reflection of Tokugawa Ieyasu's day. Will Adams, the shipwrecked English sailor who served Ieyasu so well as a naval advisor, had a fellow officer of his wrecked ship as a companion in Edo, Jan Joosten Loodensteijn. A Dutch seaman, Jan Joosten acted as Ieyasu's agent for trade with Southeast Asia. His residence was at the Babasaki Moat in front of the castle, then still an inlet of Edo Bay (in the area of today's Hibiya Park), where he lived with his Japanese wife. In 1929 the area called "Yaesu" after Jan Joosten's name ("Jan Joosten" becoming "Yayoosu" and thence "Yaesu" in seventeenth-century Japanese mouths) became part of Marunouchi. Thus for a while the name Yaesu disappeared, but in 1954 the name became current again, this time a bit further to the north and on the opposite side of Tokyo Central Station as the area was renamed Yaesu. Joosten is reported to have died at sea near Indonesia in an attempt to return to Holland.

In front of the Yaesu side of Tokyo Central Station is the Daimaru Department Store (closed Wednesdays). Daimaru offers the amazing variety of goods which one comes to expect in Japanese department stores, but it also provides those services no American or European enterprise would offer. It cashes travelers' checks on the main floor, makes quick repairs or presses clothes for the traveler on the fourth floor, and has set up a putting green for golfers on the fifth floor.

Four short streets to the south on Sotobori-dori is the Yaesu Book Center, an eight-story building whose lower four floors are filled with books. It includes a coffee shop and a library where, for a small fee, one may rest and read. The Center is open Monday through Saturday from 10:00 A.M. to 7:00 P.M. Two streets further down Sotobori-dori there is a cross street which is the first one to run to the east past the main line railroad tracks and Tokyo Central Station. Turning to the right on this street one is at the site of the Kenzo Tange 1957 city hall, which replaced the earlier city administrative building described in Tour 1. As with its predecessor, Tange's city hall is now but a memory, for it was torn down in 1991 when the new city hall, also by Tange, opened in Shinjuku. In its place the city has created the Tokyo International Forum by the Argentine-born American architect Raphael Vinely, a convention and cultural center to enhance the life of Tokyo's residents and visitors. Its active program is listed in English-language newspapers, and information concerning the program can be obtained at the Tourist Information Center on Harumi-dori.

Here one can turn to regain Chuo-dori and the Kyobashi Station of the **Ginza.** The streets further along Chuo-dori are at the heart of the Ginza district. Having arrived at the Ginza, it is appropriate to look at the development of this portion of the city which was one of the first to attempt to move into the new world of Western architecture in the 1870s. What is generally considered as "Ginza," as previously mentioned, is Chuo-dori from Kyobashi to Shimbashi, although the district really extends up to the Nihombashi River. When the district was modernized after the 1872 fire, it only extended from Kyobashi to the Harumi-dori crossing. Kyobashi was the first bridge over the beginning of the Tokaido road to Kyoto, and thus its name "Kyo" indicates its relationship to the ultimate destination of the road in Kyoto. It was a bridge (*hashi*), now gone, over one of the outlets of the moats of Edo Castle.

Each block in the Ginza district is numbered, the 1-chome block being the first square unit after Kyobashi (and the overhead expressway) between Sotobori-dori on the west and Showa-dori on the east. Ginza 4-chome ends at the Harumi-dori intersection. With the expansion of the Ginza district in time, there are now eight *chome* which reach down to Shimbashi. Chuo-dori becomes a pedestrian's delight on Saturdays from 3:00 to 6:00 P.M. and on Sundays from noon to 6:00 P.M., for then all traffic is banned from the street, and it becomes a place where one can enjoy the traditional *Gin-bura* or "Ginza stroll," which has been popular for over one hundred years.

The silver mint (*gin-za*) which Ieyasu established here in 1612 in the second *chome* after Kyobashi was later moved to the Nihombashi district after some financial indiscretions on the part of the mint operator, but the name of Ginza remained. In 1872 Tokyo suffered another of its "Flowers of Edo," and this whole portion of the city disappeared in flames, some 3,000 houses being lost in the Ginza and Tsukiji districts. By coincidence, on September 13, 1872, the first train from Yokohama arrived at Shimbashi Station further down this road to the Tokaido, a highway to Kyoto which the railroad would soon put out of business. The new railroad terminus at Shimbashi was to bring new life to the Ginza area in the years after the fire, for, until the railroad was extended to Tokyo Central Station, Shimbashi was the front door to the new capital of Japan.

After the 1872 fire, the way was thus cleared for a new beginning, and the Meiji government made the most of it. Here in this still moated area, for the old defensive canals were not yet filled in, would arise the first modern (that is, European-style) portion of Tokyo with two-story red-brick buildings and paved sidewalks. The transformation took ten years, but before 1874 had passed there were eighty-five gas lights illuminating the street at night. Within two years the lights were extended to Asakusa to the north and the palace to the west. Even the Kabuki-za theater illuminated its performances by gas light in 1877; within ten years these lights would be replaced by electricity. In 1881 horse-drawn trams appeared, making their way along Chuo-dori to Asakusa, to be eventually replaced in 1903 by the new electric trams.

The creation of this modern "European" city was placed in the hands of an English planner. In the next three years after the last embers of the 1872 fire had died, one thousand fireproof, red-brick buildings were erected in the Kyobashi area. At the time there were just a few such buildings in the entire city. Wooden houses still dominated. The streets were lined with cherry, maple, and willow trees; in the long run, only the willows lasted. Unfortunately this modern street was not a great success at first. Ventilation was poor in the new brick buildings, which tended to hold the dampness of the summer seasons. It took pressure by the government to have the new buildings made more amenable.

Success did come, but slowly, and by 1894 the Hattori Building at Harumi-dori and Chuo-dori had begun to change the area. Its clock tower became a rendezvous spot, and what had been a newspaper building was now to become a major store of quality products under the name of Wako. The building originally bore the name of Kintaro Hattori, a twenty-two-year-old watchmaker who opened a shop on the Ginza. By 1881 his watches were so well made that they were given as gifts by the Imperial Household. He named his watches Seiko meaning "precision," a name and a reputation they have maintained.

Traffic, of course, increased with the advent of the automobile, and in 1921 it was decided that the roadway had to be widened—unfortunately at the expense of the trees which had graced the street. Modernization can have its pitfalls. The new 1923 roadway was paved with wooden blocks which were held in place by an asphalt binder; it was a setback when the asphalt caught fire and the roadway burned.

The 1923 Great Kanto Earthquake saw the demise of the last of the two-story red-brick buildings, and by 1930 the Ginza was ready once more for a new beginning as larger buildings arose. The Ginza now reached down to Shimbashi, and a new subway was built under Chuo-dori, reaching to Asakusa. (Ninety percent of all of Tokyo's subways, however, have been created since 1945.) A wider street was created to the east of Chuo-dori after the earthquake, running from Shimbashi to Ueno, but the newly created Showa-dori never replaced the Ginza as an exciting commercial street of shops. A new Hattori building, now re-named Wako by its new owners, replaced the original structure in 1932, and its clock remains a focal point at the main Ginza crossing. It was designed by Hiroshi Watanabe, who also is responsible for the Dai-Ichi Insurance Building on Hibiya-dori and the National Museum Building in Ueno. Then came the war and U.S. military occupation, and Wako and the Matsuya Department Store became post exchanges for the American military for several years.

Ginza's department stores, beer halls (à la Czech, Slovak, and German), restaurants, coffee shops, and bars all created a lively center for the city. Department stores made the street the focus of women who, while they do make purchases, also enjoy the simple art of *depato meguri* (browsing in the department stores), to view the latest in fashions, to visit the exhibitions these stores generously mount in special halls, and to have lunch in one of their many restaurants.

This portion of the tour of the Ginza begins at Ginza 1-chome and then proceeds down Chuo-dori to Ginza 8-chome near Shimbashi. Thus we start at the overhead Tokyo Expressway, where the Ginza district begins. The first locations of interest are in Ginza 2-chome where the **Tokyo Central Museum of Art** and Itoya are on the east side of the street. The Tokyo Central Museum of Art exhibits modern art and changes its exhibits every two weeks. It is open from 10:00 A.M. to 6:00 P.M. (closed Mondays), entry fee. Within the building are coffee shops and restaurants. Itoya primarily offers office supplies and stationery, but it is noted for its crafts and hobby department as well as for its selection of fine Japanese papers. It also has an exhibition gallery and a tea room. A memorial stone in a planter at the curb marks the site of the silver mint which closed in 1790 to be re-opened in 1800 north of the Nihombashi River. The Kagami Crystal Shop, one of the very fine glass makers of Japan, is on the west side of Chuo-dori.

The Matsuya Department Store and Printemps (on Sotobori-dori) are in Ginza 3-chome. Also in Ginza 3-chome on the east-west street to the east of Showa-dori is the Magazine World Building which can be recognized by its external pink and silver tiled façade. This is the headquarters of a publishing house which specializes in magazines for young people, a purpose which can be surmised from the figures of Popeye and Olive Oyl at the main entrance. At the top of the main staircase is the World Magazine Library where one can browse through magazines from all over the world.

In Ginza 4-chome is Mikimoto Kokichi's shop for the sale of his cultured pearls. In 1883 Mikimoto discovered that it was possible to force oysters to create "cultured" pearls if a bit of irritant were placed within their shells. His success led to the opening of his shop in the Ginza in 1899, and it continues, having added an exhibition area to its premises. At the corner of Harumi-dori and Chuo-dori is Wako (the Tiffany or Asprey of the Ginza), owned by the makers of Seiko watches and selling the finest of luxury articles. It too has an exhibition hall.

Across the street, still in Ginza 4-chome, is the Mitsukoshi Ginza Department Store (which brings us to the "Times Square" crossing of the district). As with all department stores in Tokyo, the roof of the building offers a roof garden where plants (particularly bonsai) are sold, a children's playground exists, and, as always, there is a Shinto shrine so that the proper respect can be paid to the deity of business. Mitsukoshi Ginza also has a Jizo image on its roof, albeit Jizo is normally found in the Buddhist pantheon. This Jizo was found during excavations of a canal about 1870 as the Ginza was being modernized, and it was placed in a small hall in Ginza 4-chome. The image disappeared in the 1945 air raids, but it was later found in the rubble. In 1965 it was given a home on the roof of Mitsukoshi where this protector of children, pregnant women, and the dead can be revered. Mitsukoshi is a good store for souvenirs to take home. Adjacent is Kintaro, an interesting toy shop which attracts adults as well as children.

Crossing Harumi-dori brings one to Ginza 5-chome and the Japanese Saké Center on Harumi-dori to the east. The center offers information on all aspects of saké as well as where to buy a favored brand. It is popular because samples of saké are offered. The Kabuki-za (covered in Tour 4) is in Ginza 5-chome as well.

The Matsuzakaya Department Store is in Ginza 6-chome, and a few blocks to the east is the Tokyo Onsen, a public spa for those desiring a sauna or the benefits of hot springs (manmade springs in this case). The block of Ginza 7-chome offers not only the Sapporo Beer Hall, but the Pilsen and the Lion Beer halls, the former in the design of a pub while the latter has a 1934 imitation Frank Lloyd Wright interior. The Toto Pavilion with all of its porcelain bathtubs and other related items on display, Yamaha Hall with its pianos, and Shiseido which has added boutique shops to its cosmetic products are all in Ginza 7-chome as well. The strangely named Pocket Park is here too, a small building which houses an architecture studio and a ten-year-retrospective collection of architectural magazines. It is open from Thursday through Tuesday from 10:30 A.M. to 7:00 P.M.

Crossing the street into Ginza 8-chome brings us to the end of the Ginza district, but here is the Shiseido Parlor which offers the weary a convenient coffee shop noted for its ice cream. This *chome* also boasts the architecturally unusual **Shizuoka Press** building. Virtually alongside the elevated railroad tracks is the Shizuoka

Press and Broadcasting Building which was designed by Kenzo Tange in 1967. This unusual structure consists of four asymmetrical boxes which are appended to a 187-foot-tall black shaft, the top of which is sliced off at an angle. It is one of the most striking items on the Tokyo skyline for visitors arriving by Bullet Train (*shinkansen*).

Many restaurants and small bars can be found throughout the Ginza district in the streets between Sotobori-dori and Chuo-dori. Their neon signs make the area an illuminated wonderland at night. Many of the bars with their "hostesses" delight to detach the visitor from his money through the extravagant costs of the beverages consumed, so caution is the byword. The area is also a center for karaoke for those who cannot restrain the desire to show off.

At Shimbashi the elevated train line should be taken one stop to the north to Yurakucho Station. **"Yurakucho"** is a name with a history. When Shogun Tokugawa Ieyasu first began his castle in Edo, he filled in the Hibiya Inlet of the bay of Edo and at the same time created a series of moats around his castle. Sotobori (Outside Moat) on the east of the castle ran roughly to the east of the elevated Yamanote line in the area behind the present Imperial Hotel and down past Tokyo Central Station. Oda Urakusai was one of the first to move into this area, and he built his residence and a teahouse alongside the Sotobori moat. The teahouse was created in the natural, light, and asymmetrical *sukiya* style, an unostentatious approach, for Oda was a devotee of the great tea master Sen-no-Rikyu of Kyoto.

Both Oda and his teahouse style were to become place-names in this area in time. A bridge over the moat near the teahouse became known as Sukiyabashi (The Sukiya Bridge). This bridge lasted until the 1960s when the Sotobori moat was finally filled in. That name still lives on at the Harumi-dori and Sotobori-dori crossing even though neither bridge nor the water it crossed exist any longer. The moat itself is remembered in those areas encircling the castle by the street which retains the name of the moat:

Sotobori-dori. Thus Oda Urakusai's name became attached to that portion of Edo where his mansion and teahouse had been, and it still exists as Yurakucho, the "Quarter Where Pleasure Can Be Had." The pleasure for this seventeenth-century amateur of the tea ceremony was a spiritual pleasure, and not the more sensual pleasures for which the area became noted in the last half of the twentieth century.

The meaning of Yurakucho was but a foretaste of what the centuries would bring to this quarter. After the Second World War, Yurakucho provided pleasures of a more dubious nature. Not too far away, at Chuo-dori and Harumi-dori, the U.S. military took over certain department stores to serve as post exchanges where American troops could buy items not available on the local impoverished post-war markets. Many of these items found their way into the black market which flourished under the elevated tracks in the Yurakucho Station area. At a time when jobs were not plentiful and when food was equally scarce, small stalls also sprang up under the elevated tracks where items of questionable ownership could be purchased and where yakitori could be obtained. The area became a hangout for young Japanese girls (nicknamed *pan pan* girls) willing to be picked up by American soldiers. The nearby Nichigeki Theater became notorious, for it not only provided recent motion pictures, but it offered revues with a line of chorus girls, and even striptease shows. As a result, after 1945 the area truly became a "Quarter Where Pleasure Can Be Had."

The post-war improvement of the Japanese economy, the departure of the occupying troops, the closing of the post exchanges, and then in 1960 the filling in of the Sotobori moat in favor of an expressway changed the area once more. Today a few yakitori stalls survive, but the old Nichigeki Theater is no more. Between the elevated railway and Sotobori-dori at Harumi-dori is the **Mullion** complex or Yurakucho Center which has helped to revive the Ginza area when it started to lose some of its glamour to Shinjuku and Shibuya. The fourteen-story Mullion complex (with four floors underground, three of them for parking) houses the modern Hankyu and Seibu Department stores (both closed on Thursday), separated by a pedestrian walkway. The most noted element of the complex is the clock on the front of the building facing Harumi-dori. On the hour, between 10:00 A.M. and 9:00 P.M., the face of the clock moves up, a group of figures move forward from the interior of the clock, and they then move to a musical accompaniment. Seven theaters lie within the building, one of which is a revived and more respectable Nichigeki, and the glistening elevators and hanging illuminations make the Yurakucho Center an intriguing and busy location. Down Sotobori-dori, to the north of the Mullion complex, is Printemps, a branch of the Parisian Au Printemps department store (closed Wednesday).

Behind the Yurakucho elevated station is the Sogo Department Store with its Yomiuri Hall and a department where one can buy tickets to the games of the Yomiuri Giants as well as another department that sells souvenirs of the team.

In the side streets to the south of the Sukiyabashi crossing between the overhead expressway and Chuo-dori there are a few hundred art galleries offering many styles of paintings to prospective collectors. Aside from these commercial galleries, a major museum of an especially desired Japanese art form can be found behind the Imperial Hotel on the east side of the elevated railway and the raised highway. This is the **Riccar Art Museum** (Riccar Bijutsukan) on the seventh floor of the Riccar Building. The museum is home to five thousand ukiyo-e woodblock prints, which were the collection of the late Shinji Hiraki, the onetime president of the now defunct Riccar Company. The work of Hokusai, Utamaro, and other masters of eighteenth- and nineteenth-century woodblock prints are on exhibition. The collection is rotated monthly. One room of the museum illustrates the technique of woodblock printmaking, and a library on the subject is open to the public. The museum is open from 11:00 A.M. to 6:00 P.M. daily (closed Monday), entry fee.

East on Harumi-dori from the Mullion complex and the Sukiyabashi crossing, one of Tokyo's 1,250 *koban* (small police stations) can be seen. Most *koban* are utilitarian affairs, but the one here at Harumi-dori with its pointed roof is a more unusual unit. Before 1945, each *koban* kept a register of those who lived within the district, which was one way the police state that was Japan kept control of its subjects. Today the units are there to assist local citizens, particularly the elderly, to give directions (especially because of the somewhat confusing address system in Tokyo), and to provide whatever other help is needed by the public.

Past the **Sukiyabashi** intersection, on the right is the 1966 Sony Building, a showcase for Sony products. Further along the street is Jena, one of the major foreign language bookstores in Tokyo. It fills four floors with books on all subjects. At the corner of Harumi-dori and Chuo-dori is one of the eye-catching attractions of the Ginza: the 1963 San-ai Building, a twelve-story glass cylinder whose floor divisions are illuminated with fluorescent lights. As a result, it is one of the many nighttime attractions in the area.

We have now made a complete circuit of the Ginza district, and here at the intersection of Harumi-dori and Chuo-dori we have a choice of many shops and restaurants. Also, several subway lines intersect here. Thus a choice can be made as to whether to return to one's hotel or to further explore this shopper's paradise.

△ Tokyo Metropolitan Government Offices.

▷ Hozomon gate at
Senso-ji, Asakusa.

▽ Kokugikan, the sumo
stadium at Ryogoku.

△ Kaminari-mon, Asakusa.

◁ Niimi Building, Kappabashi.

▽ Edo-Tokyo Museum.

Korakuen Garden. ⟶

Statues of Jizo at Zojo-ji. ⟶

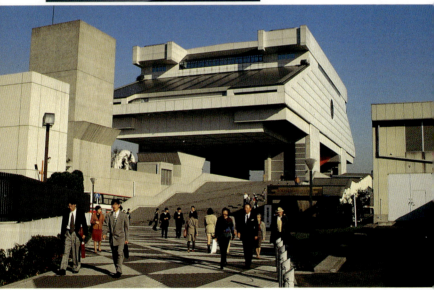

△ National Diet Building, Kasumigaseki.

TOUR

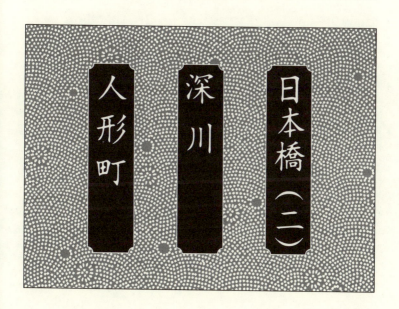

6

Nihombashi (2), Fukagawa, and Ningyocho

日本橋（二）

深川

人形町

TOUR 6 begins at the Nihombashi bridge because it represents the heart of *shitamachi* (literally "low city"), the city of artisans and merchants during Tokyo's centuries. In this tour we are concerned with that *shitamachi* which strove to make a living and which served the daimyo and their retainers around the castle and in the High City on the raised land to the west of the Tokugawa castle. In time it was to become the entertainment and then the commercial and finally the financial section of old Edo, aspects which are retained in this portion of Tokyo today. *Shitamachi* began in that filled-in land in the Nihombashi and Ningyocho areas of Edo north of the Nihombashi River, and, after the Long Sleeves Fire of 1657, it spread across the Sumida River into Fukagawa as industries were moved across the river and as bridges at last began to be built.

Nihombashi was the center of the commercial life of Edo. It was also the heart of the male-dominated *shitamachi*. In the early years, Nihombashi grew as Edo grew—explosively. What began as a small village in 1590 was to grow to a half-million population some forty years later and to number more than a million inhabitants before it was ninety years old. This swampy area at the head of Edo (Tokyo) Bay benefited from the landfill operations begun by Tokugawa Ieyasu in the early 1600s, making possible the Nihombashi and Ningyocho areas for housing and commercial enterprises. Ieyasu encouraged immigration into his new military and civil capital, for producers of everyday wares and distributors of foodstuffs were needed by his court and by the three hundred daimyo and their retinues. The craftsmen, tradesmen, fishermen, and merchants (many from the Ise region) who flocked to Edo created a lively population of commoners whose hard lives were all too frequently disrupted by the "Flowers of Edo," which burned down their warrens ("homes" is too luxurious a term) and their livelihoods. Between 1603, when Tokugawa Ieyasu became shogun in his new Edo headquarters, and 1868, when the Tokugawa rule ended, Edo had suffered ninety-seven major conflagrations.

This tour begins at **Nihombashi,** which was the center of this exciting and boisterous community. Then along the south side of the river the route will move to the Kabuto-cho district and then by subway to Fukagawa, that area of *shitamachi* across the Sumida River which blossomed after the Long Sleeves Fire of 1657. We'll return from Fukagawa, with its intriguing museum of old Edo, to Ningyocho, the early licensed quarter where Yoshiwara first began, to explore this former district of pleasure before returning once more to Nihombashi.

The banks of the river on either side of the bridge were busy places, for here were the quays where vessels were unloaded. Also, the *kura* in which goods were stored were located along the waterway. From 1628 to 1923 the north bank of the river between the bridge and today's Showa-dori was the location of the city's fish market, a flourishing enterprise which supplied one of the main sources of the city's food. Fishing vessels sailed into the bay of Edo and, if too large, transferred their catches to smaller boats which would then come up the Sumida River and into the Nihombashi River to the stalls where fish was sold. To the market stalls came the representatives of the shogun to requisition the best of the day's catch, making their selection before any other sales could begin. Delivery of the fresh fish was then made to the shogun's castle along the canals or moats which led to the stronghold on the hill above the Hibiya flats. The fish market was an unsightly place. Dead fish and the spoils of gutted fish lay all about. It is not surprising that cholera often raged in the city. A marker on the north side of the river today provides a remembrance of the 300 years during which the fish market was located here until forced to move after the 1923 earthquake.

To the north of the river were the many shops that supplied the daily needs of the city. Dried bonito and seaweed were available here in the 1600s because of the proximity to the fish stalls, and these items are still available in some shops on the north side of the river today. This district, too, would develop those stores which in later years blossomed into large department stores, for trade was to pick up greatly after 1635, when the shogunate required the three hundred daimyo and their entourages to make the biennial procession from their home districts to Edo for a two-year stay. This requirement of "alternate residence" by the daimyo provided an additional populace which could be served by the fishermen, farmers, and tradespeople.

In the southeastern part of Nihombashi, in Hatchobori, were the lumberyards. The selling of lumber was a trade which engendered great wealth for active entrepreneurs because the constant fires of Edo necessitated constant rebuilding. One of the more noted lumber magnates was Kinokuniya Bunzaemon who had his rich villa to the north and east of the Nihombashi River, an area which adjoined Ningyocho with its Kabuki theater, its Bunraku puppet plays, and its licensed quarters of courtesans. Ningyocho was the red-light district of Edo, particularly that area called Yoshiwara (Field of Reeds), since it had only recently been swamp land. Bunzaemon was a generous spender in this quarter, since Buddhism teaches that life is brief and Shinto encourages the enjoyment of life. Thus money was to be enjoyed, and Bunzaemon dispensed his wealth lavishly among the courtesans in the Ningyocho entertainment area. No doubt there must be a moral here, for it is said that he died penniless due to his extravagant ways in Yoshiwara.

The lumberyards were moved from Nihombashi across the river to Fukagawa after the devastating 1657 fire, for their stock provided an ever-present danger to the welfare of the city. (Fukagawa residents therefore took a preventative measure by creating the Akiba Shrine where protective amulets to the deity of fire were mass-produced and sold.) Fukagawa thus became an extension of the *shitamachi* reached by ferry, for the Tokugawas would not permit the Sumida River to be spanned lest it provide too easy access for any potentially unfriendly forces. Trade necessitated shrines and temples, and some of these were relocated from Edo to Fukagawa after 1657. Not surprisingly an unlicensed "licensed quarter" followed quite soon thereafter, a section of Fukagawa which in Meiji times became the licensed Susaki quarter.

We begin at the Nihombashi Station of either the Ginza or Tozai subway line, stations which connect at Chuo-dori and Eitai-dori. The Tokyu Department Store is at this intersection and we start the tour by walking along the side of the store toward Showa-dori. Turning left behind the Tokyu store, one sees the Taimei Kan restaurant on the right at the end of one block. It is an early Western restaurant whose proprietor created the **Kite Museum,** which is on the fifth floor. The museum's collection consists of more than 2,000 traditional kites, and these are not just for children. Adults not only collect kites, but often enjoy kite battles in which extremely large kites, constructed from the finest of strong paper, are flown by teams which move as well as restrain the heavy ropes controlling the kites. The "battle" occurs when the ropes holding the kites are covered with powdered glass. This enables the operators of the kites to maneuver their ropes to cut the ropes of their opponents. A downed kite belongs to those who brought it to the ground. The museum is open from 11:00 A.M. to 5:00 P.M. daily (except Sundays, national holidays, mid-August, and the New Year holiday), entry fee.

On leaving the Kite Museum, Showa-dori should be taken to the north toward the river and the overhead expressway over the Nihombashi River. Turn to the right at the street parallel the river and pass the expressway interchange to get to **Kabuto Shrine** (The War Helmet Shrine), just on the other side of the overhead expressway. In the eleventh century the emperor dispatched one of his most trusted warriors to the eastern part of the country to subdue the "barbarians" from Hokkaido and eastern Japan who were preventing the spread of imperial power into this unsettled area of the country. The warrior paused here at Nihombashi River to pray to the dragon god of the river for success in battle, and on his successful defeat of the barbarians, he buried his golden helmet (*kabuto*) in homage to the god who had answered his prayers. A Shinto shrine to the dragon god still exists here.

Just south of the shrine is the **Tokyo Stock Exchange,** which first opened in 1878. It became a lone hold-out in what had been the financial section of Tokyo once the Mitsubishi group enticed many of Japan's leading corporations to the Marunouchi area after the First World War. After the Second World War, a new exchange building was constructed at this site, and in the plaza before the present 1985 building is the sculpture *Homage to the Sun.* An exhibition center offers information on the working of the exchange while a Hand Signals Robot illustrates the signaling techniques used by the 1,800 workers on the floor of the exchange. The actual pandemonium of buying and selling in the exchange can be seen from a glass-walled viewing area set aside for visitors from 9:00 to 11:00 A.M. and from 1:00 to 3:00 P.M., after application at the reception desk (when the exchange is in session).

Follow the overhead expressway to the south and turn to the left at Eitai-dori, beyond the overhead Shuto Expressway, to arrive at the black Yamatane Securities Building which is on the left at the second street. Within, on the eighth and ninth floors, is the **Yamatane Museum of Art,** which specializes in Japanese paintings since 1868 that have been executed in the traditional manner. Changing exhibitions every two months provide an opportunity to rotate the collections. A Japanese tea ceremony room is located on the eighth floor as is an interior garden and a library. The museum is open from 10:00 A.M. to 5:00 P.M. (except on Mondays), entry fee.

At the corner on Eitai-dori, the Tozai Subway Line may be taken from Kayabacho Station to the next station to the east, Monzen Nakacho Station in **Fukagawa.** Fukagawa was a swamp in 1657 at the time of the Long Sleeves Fire, which destroyed so much of Edo, particularly the Nihombashi and Hatchobori districts across the Sumida River to the west. The fire gave an impetus to the reclamation of this low-lying land across the river so that the lumberyards could be relocated here, a river's width away from the city should fire break out again. The few fishing villages in this swampy area thus became a center of the lumber trade with its storage yards and docks.

Fukagawa was to see fire and flood on more than one occasion. The 1923 earthquake destroyed much of the area, and the nights of March 9 and 10 in 1945 saw almost half of Tokyo destroyed by American bombers. Out of the 70,000 deaths which resulted on those two nights, one-third occurred in Fukagawa. Floods have always been a problem for this low-lying district, and the flood walls erected during the twentieth century have protected the area from some of the backup of water from the bay during typhoons and other times of high water.

The lumberyards and warehouses brought men to work across the Sumida at a time when there were no bridges to the rest of Edo. As a result, an "unlicensed" quarter beyond the jurisdiction of the Edo magistrates developed to serve the workers. There were times when fires in Yoshiwara drove the courtesans out of that licensed quarter, and thus there would be an influx into Fukagawa. The fact that a shrine and a temple arose in Fukagawa led to the establishment of shops along the way which were patronized by pilgrims or worshipers, and thus teahouses which stood among these shops added girls to their staff. Soon arrangements could be made at these teahouses for the "geisha of the seven hills" or "hill place," as the red-light sector of Fukagawa was nicknamed. Unhappily, these geisha were not of the accomplished sort and were in most instances little more than prostitutes. This "unlicensed" aspect of the quarter was to disappear entirely after the 1958 anti-prostitution law became effective.

On leaving the subway station from the front of the train, one sees a street to the right that leads to the **Fudo-do** temple, a red torii heralding the temple and shrine to come. The street itself becomes the site of the temple market on the first, fifteenth, and twenty-eighth day of each month. At the top of the street is the Fudo-do, the Fudo Hall; just before it on the right is the small Eitai-ji temple which once existed within the grounds of the Tomioka Hachiman Shrine farther along the way. In the iconoclastic Meiji Period when temples were separated from the shrines with which they were often associated, Eitai-ji was reduced to the small unit which still exists, a peculiar cupola topping its one building. Beyond Eitai-ji, a stone torii at the entrance to the Fudo-do has a large incense burner at the head of the steps to the temple, and a roofed ablution basin on the left is supplied with water which issues from the mouths of three rearing dragons. To one side, three fountains pour into a stone basin, which has a gong that can be sounded by pulling on its rope.

The temple is a branch of the famed Fudo temple at Narita and thus has a Fudo as its main image with his fierce-looking face and a large tooth protruding from either side of his mouth. He carries a rope with which to bind evildoers, and he carries a sword to smite evil. On either side of the figure of Fudo are multi-armed deities. A *ranma* (transom) before the altar is carved in the form of a dragon, and here also is an unusual item worth noting, a *haraigushi*, the sacred wand used in purifying ceremonies by Shinto priests.

The *goma* rite is the important ceremony in the Fudo-do, and it occurs five times a day, at 9:00 A.M., 11:00 A.M., 1:00 P.M., 3:00 P.M., and 5:00 P.M. *Goma* sticks are cedar sticks on which one can write one's name, age, address, and a wish. At the set time the priests place the sticks, one at a time, into the sacred fire, chanting sutras to a drumbeat. The burning of the *goma* stick makes the wish come true, according to lore. Priests will also bless items over the fire, just as they will bless vehicles brought to the temple, although those ceremonies are usually offered by Shinto shrines rather than Buddhist temples. The temple itself was brought here from near Narita to replace the previous hall which burned in 1945. One room at the rear is used for sutra copying by devotees of the temple while another room serves as a small museum for the Fudo-do.

On leaving the Fudo-do and returning to the main street, Eitai-dori, one is traversing the area which served as the "licensed" district in the past. Turning left at Eitai-dori and continuing for two streets, one finds the bronze-plated torii at the entrance to the path to the **Tomioka Hachiman-gu** on the left. This shrine which attracted people to Fukagawa was originally called the Fukagawa Hachiman-gu, but it is now known as the Tomioka Hachiman-gu. The shrine was established in 1627, and it was famous in Edo times for the fact that sumo bouts were held here from 1684 on. As with all shrines, the grounds are entered through a torii. To the right are large stones commemorating noted sumo wrestlers. The middle stone lists the names of those who have achieved the rank of *ozeki*, the second highest rank in sumo. Stones to either side provide the statistics any devotee of sumo would want to know: the wrestler's height and size of his hands and feet.

A building on the left holds the shrine's two huge portable *mikoshi* (shrine palanquins) used during festivals to take the symbols of the deity in a public procession. Two buildings, the *haiden* (prayer hall) and the *honden* (spirit hall) with copper-tiled roofs that were rebuilt in 1968, lie at the end of the path. Behind the buildings is a hall with mementos of the trades which once enriched Fukagawa: the rafters of lumber and the makers of saké. Beyond the shrine to the right is an exceedingly large stone known as the Yokozuna Stone since it has inscribed upon it the names of those who reach the highest of sumo honors, the status of *yokozuna*. A tiny shrine to the right honors the Shinto goddess Benten while to the left and behind the treasury is a shrine to Ebisu. The shrine festival takes place every third year (1995, 1998, etc.), when fifty very large *mikoshi* are paraded through the streets. The three-day festival begins on a weekend in mid-August, and since this can be one of the hotter days of summer, much water is thrown on the shrine and the husky bearers as they jostle their way along the procession route.

On leaving the shrine, a turn to the right takes one under the Shuto Expressway and to a major street, where a left turn is made at the traffic light. Another turn to the right at a series of small temples puts one on a main north-south road, Kiyosumi-dori, which will lead, in a fifteen-minute walk, to the 1986 **Fukagawa Edo Folk Museum.** Just beyond this intersection, on the right, is a square vermilion building in a courtyard. It is a temple to Emma, the King of Hell, and his fearful image overpowers this small hall.

Farther along Kiyosumi-dori, the Fukagawa Edo Folk Museum, which is open daily from 10:00 A.M. to 5:00 P.M., entry fee, will eventually appear on the right about three-quarters of the way along the walled Kiyosumi Garden on the left side of the Kiyosumi-dori. Two temple posts at the entrance to the side street are an indication that the museum lies a block or two beyond. (Just before the museum is the Reigan-ji, a temple which retains one of the six Jizo images, nine feet tall, which once marked the borders of Edo at main roads leading into the city.) The museum is in a tall, windowless, white brick building. On entering the museum and having paid the entry fee, it is worthwhile to purchase the English-language guidebook, which explains the purpose of the museum and elucidates the various sights within the complex.

A room off the lobby is filled with life-sized figures (drawn on heavy plastic sheets) of the residents of Fukagawa during the Edo centuries, including a fortune teller, a flower vendor, a hairdresser, and other Edo citizens. From this room one enters onto a balcony overlooking a huge exhibition hall in which a portion of Edo lies below. Here are the wooden houses of the seventeenth and eighteenth century, the fireproof *kura* in which merchants stored their valuables, riverside taverns, a shop selling vegetables, and a watch tower where the alarm could be sounded should fire break out. The cycle of the day passes before one, for slowly the lights dim as the temple bell rings nightfall; with the coming of dawn a rooster crows, and the cries of the wandering vendors can be heard as the city awakens. The variety of homes, from those of the tenement dwellers to those of the well-to-do merchants, can be entered and the objects of everyday life are present as though life were still going on in these narrow quarters of the Saga-cho district in 1840, the era portrayed in this lifelike museum. A side hall shows the changes which overcame this small area of Fukagawa, dioramas of the outbreak of fire and the subsequent destruction, then the process of rebuilding the community once more. Video units offer fine brief films on the crafts and life of the earlier period in Fukagawa life. Many of these crafts are still created today.

Saga-cho was rebuilt after the 1923 earthquake and 1945 bombings, but two events still recall former times. On the first Sunday in October, there is the Saga-cho Power Contest when the strength of local citizens is evidenced in a contest to see who can hold a 132-pound rice bag over his head the longest. There is also the October *kakunori* event (Timberyard Log Rolling), where two men carrying a *kago* on their shoulders balance themselves on rolling logs in the water, trying to remain upright as they traverse a "road" of bobbing logs.

Back at the main road, a turn to the right and then to the left at the next intersection will bring one to the entrance to the **Kiyosumi Garden.** The garden once was part of the villa of Kinokuniya Bunzaemon, whom we encountered as a wealthy timber merchant in the Hatchobori sector of Nihombashi. In his more affluent days in 1688, this garden was designed as a stroll garden with its lake, its teahouse, and its stone lanterns. The garden was to fall on unhappy times as the years passed, but in 1878 Yataro Iwasaki, the founder of the house of Mitsubishi, purchased the land and had the lake and the garden restored and re-landscaped. Fifty-five rare rocks from all over Japan were gathered to enhance the garden and the villa that Iwasaki had created.

The garden eventually became a place of leisure for the employees of Iwasaki's enterprises. The earthquake of 1923 extensively damaged the garden and its building, and thus the site was turned over to the city as a gift in 1924. Restored to its former beauty and with a traditional house built at the edge of the lake, the garden is open from 9:00 A.M. to 4:30 P.M., free entry. The lakeside building is a reproduction of the unit which was built by the government in 1909 to entertain General Kitchener of Britain on his visit to Japan. (This park was the site of the funeral pavilion of the Emperor Taisho in the mid-1920s.) If one has purchased sandwiches or a *bento* en route, these can be enjoyed in this garden.

The street beyond the entrance to the garden should be followed to the left alongside the Kiyosumi Park. Turn to the right onto the north-south street and then cross Kiyosubashi-dori (the bridge of that name over the Sumida River is one street to the left). At the second street on the right is the Kitanoumi Sumo Stable, while at the intersection beyond, on the southwest corner, is the Taiho Sumo Stable. "Stable" may seem a peculiar term to use in conjunction with sumo, but this is the term for the places where the sumo wrestlers train and live. Additional units lie further to the north near the sumo stadium. We'll cover those on a later tour in this guidebook. Continuing on the main street we have been following, cross over the Onagigawa canal via the Mannenbashi bridge (*mannen* means "one thousand years"—as in the wish "May you live one thousand years").

Across the bridge and to the left, between the north-south street we are on and the Sumida River to the east, is the Basho-an, the site of the house in which the poet Basho was living when on March 27, 1689, he set out for his wanderings which resulted in his *The Narrow Road to the Deep North*. The land on which Basho's small house stood belonged to the villa of Sugiyama Sampu, another of the lumber tycoons of the late 1600s. On these grounds in which Basho resided for ten years, banana trees (*basho*) grew. Basho humorously took his name from his neighbors' references to him as "the old man of the banana trees." All that remains today is a concrete torii, a stone monument, and a small Inari shrine. Symbolically it has meaning, but it is a meager reminder of the great poet who resided here.

One-half mile further along the main street we have been

following, after three streets on the right, is a three-story white building on the left. This is the 1981 **Basho Memorial Hall.** The Hall is primarily of interest to those who read Japanese since the memorabilia connected with Basho are described only in Japanese. It contains examples of Basho's haiku and his letters as well as exhibiting travel clothes from Basho's days.

The north-south street we have been on reaches Shin Ohashi-dori with the Shin Ohashi bridge on the left. A turn to the right after one long block brings one to Morishita Subway Station where a train can be taken to the west to the Hamacho Station for the Ningyocho section of Tokyo. **Ningyocho** ("Doll Town" or "Puppet Town," as the area was named) reflected the location here of the Bunraku puppet theaters and the doll makers. Ningyocho once was a primary pleasure district of Edo until a wave of puritanism emanated from the shogunate and forced the theaters to the north in 1840.

As with much of Edo, the area was a swamp before Ieyasu began his project of filling in the low-lying lands to the east of his castle. In 1617 the area was selected as the "licensed quarter" for the town, sufficiently far away from the castle and residences of the daimyo, yet in the midst of the growing *shitamachi* of the commoners who needed an outlet in their work-weary lives. The new pleasure district was named Yoshiwara (Plain of Reeds), an indication of the nature of the terrain. Aside from the pleasures of what was basically a red-light district, two important Kabuki theaters were established: the Nakamura-za and the Ichimura-za. Also, Bunraku puppet theaters were established. Kabuki and Bunraku came from Kyoto and Osaka, respectively, once Edo's licensed quarters opened.

Ningyocho had its problems. The 1657 Long Sleeves Fire destroyed the area, and Yoshiwara was moved farther north (beyond the great temple at Asakusa), where a cult of pleasure was to develop about the cultured geisha. That is not to say that Yoshiwara did not have its common prostitutes, but Yoshiwara had restaurants and other forms of pleasure as well. The Kabuki and puppet theaters moved to the north in 1841 as a result of the shogunate's bout of moralism, but the puppet craftsmen and doll makers remained in the area. With the overthrow of the shogunate in 1868, theaters and restaurants were to return to the area once more, and in the Meiji and Taisho eras, up to the 1923 earthquake, the area began to flourish as an entertainment district again.

The new post-1868 entertainment area centered about the Hamacho district next to the Sumida River, the point where one exits the subway from Fukagawa. Many of the Meiji military officials had their residences near the Sumida River, but Ningyocho itself remained a working district of traders and craftsmen. In the midst of this new modern pleasure district, the Meiji-za theater with 1,770 seats opened in 1893 for the new audience composed of the middle class and military. The theater offered a newer, less formal form of Kabuki, and it was the first theater in Tokyo which was illuminated by electricity. In Hamacho were the *machiai* (assignation houses) where geisha of the district could be summoned to entertain the well-to-do new governing and middle class. Thus an elegant geisha world developed in the *ryotei* (traditional restaurants) with a view overlooking the river. At the end of the twentieth century, eleven *ryotei* and fifty-five geisha still provide an ambiance of another era in Hamacho, although the view of the Sumida River is gone because of the concrete flood wall and the elevated Shuto Expressway.

From the subway, the stairway leads to Hamacho Park, created after the devastation of the 1923 earthquake. The 1893 ferroconcrete Meiji-za theater survived the 1923 earthquake, but a new disaster struck in 1945. Ningyocho was fortunate in the terrible firestorms which broke out in the 1945 spring air raids on the city, for a shift of the wind took the fire away from the district. However, thousands seeking refuge in the theater were steamed alive by the intense heat created by a tornado of flames.

Leaving Hamacho Park by the street which heads into town from the middle of the park, one street along on the right at the end of the park one finds the Meiji-za in a new high-rise structure where it continues to offer a lively form of Kabuki which is noted for its fast pace and special effects. Amazake-Yokocho is the street being traversed, and it takes its name from a semi-alcoholic drink made from the lees of saké; it was considered non-volatile enough that it could be drunk by *ama* (Buddhist nuns). Amazake-Yokocho was the heart of the Ningyocho pleasure district from 1868 through 1923; previously it had been the southernmost limit of the original Yoshiwara. One street along the way is the **Kurita Museum,** which holds a portion of the Imari and Nabeshima-ware collection of Kurita Hideo. These fine ceramics were made in the kilns of Arita in Kyushu from 1651 to 1720, and they are prized by connoisseurs of fine porcelains. The museum is open from 10:00 A.M. to 5:00 P.M. Closed on Mondays, entry fee. One leaves one's shoes before the large golden Kannon on the first floor, pays the entry fee in the office on the left on the second floor, and then takes the small elevator to the fifth floor. The collections are shown on the fifth and the fourth floors.

At the fifth intersection along Amazake-dori, a turn to the left on the major shopping street heads one toward the **Suiten-gu** shrine. (A turn to the right would bring one to the subway entrance to the Hibiya Line Ningyocho Station where a plaque indicates that this was once the site of the Kakigara-cho Ginza where the silver mint had remained until 1868.) Crossing Shin Ohashi-dori, the shrine is ahead on the left. The Suiten-gu, the Celestial Palace in the Sea, is known for its relationship to pregnancy and childbirth. Its origins go back to the Battle of Dan-no-ura in 1185 when the child-Emperor Antoku, his mother, and his grandmother-nurse leaped into the sea from their vessel to escape capture by the Minamoto forces pursuing them. The mother was saved but the child and his nurse-grandmother drowned, and thus this shrine is in honor of the boy and his mother, the Empress Kenrei Mon'in. The mother is revered here as the deity who protects safe childbirth while the boy emperor is the patron of travelers. The shrine is a branch of the Suiten-gu shrine in Kyushu which was erected by the Arima, the daimyo of Kurume in Kyushu, and this branch was originally created on the grounds of Count Arima's former mansion on the Arima estate in the Shiba district south of Edo. The shrine was moved to Ningyocho in 1672, and a town grew up around it.

Stairs lead up to the raised level on which the shrine and its ancillary buildings are grouped. A bronze, plated torii stands well before the main building and two bronze lanterns decorated with dragons and water symbols stand just before it. The main building is a modern structure of white plaster with a copper-tiled roof. To the right of the main unit is a bronze statue of a dog with its newborn pup. Round projections on the surface of the base of the sculpture on which the images sit, as well as the images of the dogs, are frequently rubbed by visiting women since these are talismans which can bring about an easy birth. A four-pronged anchor also sits next to the stairs leading up to the shrine, a reminder of the fate of the young emperor who was drowned at sea.

The shrine is an exceedingly popular one, for here women come to pray for a safe and easy delivery in childbirth, and charms may be purchased to these ends. The fifth day of each month is a festival and market day, and the shrine is most crowded on these days as well as on the day of the dog in the zodiac calendar—since dogs deliver their offspring so easily. Thus the charms for easy delivery are made of papier-mâché in the form of dogs (*inu-hariko*). On these occasions women come to pray or to purchase *haraobi,* a white cotton belly-band that is blessed at the shrine by priests. The bands are sold at a stall between the torii and the shrine building. (It is said that the bands were originally made out of cloth from the red and white bell-pull which is pulled to attract the attention of the shrine deity.) These bands are intended to help in safe childbearing if worn from the fifth month of pregnancy on.

The connection with childbirth and children and the original location of the puppet theater in Ningyocho led to many doll makers and doll shops being centered in this district. Dolls even have affected local sweet foods, for one of the delicacies found in shops is the *ningyo-yaki,* a soft-baked confection in the shape of a doll made from wheat with sweet bean paste in its center. Confections sold in the form of Suitengu charms can also be purchased in the area.

On leaving the shrine, a little farther down the street is the entrance to Suiten-gu-mae Subway Station where a train goes to Mitsukoshi-mae Station, the next stop on the line. As the station name indicates, the stop is in front of the **Mitsukoshi Department Store** (*mae* means "in front of"). The store, which has always been considered the finest and most luxurious department store in Tokyo, had its humble origins as a dry goods store in 1673, a branch of the Kyoto Echigoya, a kimono shop. Mitsui Takatoshi, the owner of the shop, was an innovator in merchandising. He was the first to display his goods rather than bringing items out one at a time for examination by a customer. He also sold at set prices, doing away with the time-consuming haggling over prices. Moreover, he sold for cash only rather than offering credit, which was sometimes difficult to collect. The shop was also the first one to employ women as salesclerks. From a modest beginning the family enterprise grew not only to include the Mitsukoshi Department store (the successor to the Echigoya), but branched out into banking (the Mitsui Bank), real estate (Mitsui and Company), and other commercial and industrial enterprises.

In 1908 Mitsukoshi built a Western-style, three-story building, modeled to a great extent after the Harrods Department Store of London (indicating a fascination with English merchandise and merchandising which is still in evidence today). In 1914 a five-story building with an escalator was created, and in 1935 the present structure came into being. English and other imported goods can be found throughout the store, the third floor even having a replica of Fortnum and Mason's tea room in London, where high tea is served. The Mitsukoshi Theater is on the sixth floor, and the Mitsukoshi Culture Center and Mitsukoshi Royal

Theater are adjacent. The store is open every day but Monday from 10:00 A.M. to 6:00 P.M.

Behind Mitsukoshi and one block to the north is the Bank of Japan. Here originally was the gold mint of the Tokugawa shoguns, set up in 1601. In 1790 when the silver mint was suspended because of irregularities in its handling, the silver and copper mints were moved here as well. From 1890 to 1896 the Bank of Japan building was under construction at this location, a project of Tatsuno Kingo, one of the four Japanese architecture students of Josiah Conder and later, a student of William Burges. This was the first building in the new-to-Japan Western style of architecture, and it was inspired by the example of the neo-classical Berlin National Bank in Germany. A **Currency Museum** is located in the annex of the bank, offering a fascinating display of money from many nations and going back to ancient Roman and Chinese currencies. The heart of the collection is a retrospective of all the coinage of Japan. The museum is open from 9:30 A.M. to 4:30 P.M. except on Saturday, Sunday, national holidays, and December 29 through January 4. Reservations must be made in advance for a visit to the museum by calling (03) 3279-1111 and asking for the "Currency Museum." An English-language brochure is available, and exhibits are labeled in Japanese and in English.

There is one last site of note near Mitsukoshi, and that is William Adams' onetime Edo residence, at 1-16 Nihombashi. In Muromachi 1-chome there is a plaque that was unveiled on July 28, 1930, which reads:

> In memory of William Adams, known as Miura Anjin, the first Englishman to settle in Japan, coming as a pilot on board the *Charity* in 1600, who resided in a mansion on this spot, who instructed Ieyasu, the first Tokugawa shogun, in gunnery, geography, mathematics, etc., rendering a valuable service in foreign affairs, and who married a Japanese lady, Miss Magone, and died May 16, 1620, at age 45 years.

Anjin is "pilot" in Japanese. Adams was a pilot on the Dutch ship *Liefde* (Charity) and a shipmate of Jan Joosten, who has been mentioned in conjunction with the Yaesu district nearby. Until 1932 this area where Adams lived was known as Anjin-cho after its noted resident. The monument to Adams is found on the second street on the right after crossing the Nihombashi bridge and then two streets after turning to the right. In a small set-back section before a small wooden fence is the memorial stone quoted above. Adams built an 80- and then a 120-ton ship for Ieyasu. He was given the daughter of a neighborhood magistrate, Tenma-cho, as his wife, for he was never permitted to leave Japan to rejoin his wife and family in Kent, England. He and his Japanese wife are buried in the cemetery in Yokosuka where he was given an estate near the bay and harbor.

The Nihombashi bridge and the various Nihombashi subway stations are at hand for continuing to one's next destination.

TOUR
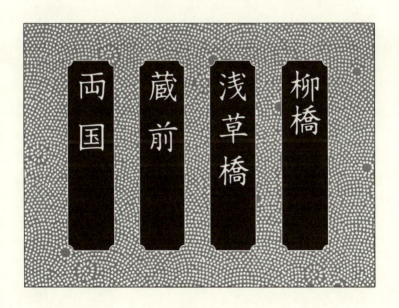

7

Yanagibashi, Asakusabashi, Kuramae, and Ryogoku

両国　蔵前　浅草橋　柳橋

A HISTORY of old Edo and then of Meiji Tokyo could almost be recorded by the movement of the various pleasure quarters, licit and illicit. In Meiji days (1868–1912) the two most respectable geisha sectors of the city were in Shimbashi and Yanagibashi (the New Bridge and the Willow Tree Bridge districts). Shimbashi was the more recent of these two geisha areas, for it had its great days after 1868 with the establishment of Imperial rule in Tokyo. It still continues, albeit on a much smaller scale today. Yanagibashi, on the other hand, flourished during the last one hundred years before the Tokugawa rule came to an end in 1868, and then it managed to hold its own through the First World War before it faded from the scene.

At Yanagibashi, which crossed the Kanda River just before the waterway joined the Sumida River, boats arrived from Edo downstream. An unlicensed quarter soon sprang up around the bridge, and the geishas entertained not only in restaurants but on house-boats along the Kanda River, the waterway which was the outermost moat around the castle. The delights of Yanagibashi were favored by native Tokyoites and the natives looked down on the brash newcomers who came to Tokyo after it became the capital and who patronized the pleasures of Shimbashi. Inevitably the attractions of the Yanagibashi geisha languished as times changed, and today its riverside restaurants are hard put to continue since flood walls have blocked the view of the river for one- and two-story buildings. (Walls fifteen to twenty-eight feet above water level enclose the river for fifteen miles inland as protection against high waters surging in from Tokyo Bay during storms. The Kanda and Nihombashi rivers have also had to be protected for this reason.) Thus a bridge remains at Yanagibashi and the street leading to it from the Asakusabashi bridge is appropriately enough lined with willow trees as it leads to the bridge. The traditional Yanagibashi geisha area where the Kanda River enters the Sumida River is now little more than a memory, and the pleasure boats on which geishas entertained have undergone a significant change. This tour will end at this site with a reflection on taking one's pleasure on the Kanda and Sumida rivers.

This tour begins at the JR Asakusabashi Station or the Toei Asakusa Subway Station. There are numerous wholesale districts in Tokyo, but the shops along Edo-dori, which runs between the Asakusabashi and the Kuramae subway stations of the Toei Asakusa subway line, are the centers for wholesalers of fireworks, toys, dolls, and Christmas and New Year decorations. Maps of Tokyo often distinguish two sections of these wholesale shops, which lie not only along Edo-dori but can be found in the narrow streets behind this avenue. The first section, between Asakusabashi and the Kuramae bridge, is referred to as Doll Town, while the section beyond the Kuramae bridge is referred to as Toy Town. Both portions of the overall district, with their specialized shops, can be enjoyable to explore on foot.

Kuramaebashi (The Bridge in Front of the Kura) received its name from the Edo days when a row of *kura* (granary storage buildings) stood along the river where rice received as tax money was stored. After exploring the wholesale toy and holiday decorations district, one can cross the Kuramaebashi bridge to the far side of the Sumida River. The original bridge across the Sumida River was a wooden one, and a bronze plaque on the right, just before the bridge is crossed, commemorates it with a drawing and a text (in Japanese). Below, between the flood wall and the river, a new promenade was built in the latter part of the twentieth century to return the river front to pedestrians once more. In this range of the promenade, the flood wall has been given a new facing so that it resembles the walls of the *kura* which once stood along the riverbank.

Across the bridge, where a promenade exists on the far bank as well, the sector between the river and Kiyosumi-dori (which is the main north-south street) offers a number of sites of interest. South of the bridge, on the right, is the Doai Kinen Byoin, the memorial hospital built with American funds after the Great Kanto Earthquake of 1923; it stands between the Earthquake

Memorial Hall and the road which crosses the bridge. Just beyond the hospital, a path on the right leads into the **Earthquake Memorial Park** with its museum and its memorial hall, called the Tokyo-to-Ireido (The Tokyo Metropolitan Hall for the Earthquake and War Victims).

In 1923 the site of the Memorial Hall was open ground since the Army Clothing Depot had been moved to a newer site. When the earthquake struck at one minute before noon on September 1, when cooking fires were lit in kitchens all over Tokyo, people fled from their damaged homes, which were now threatened by the spreading fires that followed the massive temblor. Many in East Tokyo raced with their household goods to this vacant area on the east bank of the Sumida River. Flying sparks set these household goods on fire, and the whirlwind inferno generated by the heat of the burning houses in this eastern district caused the deaths of an estimated 40,000 people within this open area. More than 100,000 died in the entire city. There were 1,700 aftershocks over the next three days (and three-fourths of the city was badly damaged or destroyed in the earthquake), but by the fourth day incense was being burned at the site of this holocaust in memory of the dead. Incense still burns here today.

Seven years after the earthquake, a three-story, concrete memorial hall topped by a pagoda was erected on the site, and within are large urns containing the ashes of those who died. The hall has pews and an "altar" up front while pictures of the disaster line the side walls. On September 1, 1951, the name of the Memorial Hall was changed to reflect that other catastrophe which afflicted this part of Tokyo in 1945, and it's now known as the Tokyo Memorial for Two Great Disasters. The expanded name of the Hall now includes a remembrance of those 100,000 or more who died during the bombing raids on Tokyo in March 1945. A two-story hall on the left-hand side of the path leading into the Memorial Park has along its exterior the Yokoami Open Gallery of melted metal machinery to attest to the ferocious heat generated by the fiery 1923 whirlwind which engulfed this area.

Within the hall, the first floor displays artifacts and illustrative materials of the earthquake and its fiery aftermath. The generous gift of blankets and clothing from the United States and France is also memorialized. On the second floor, paintings of the destroyed buildings in the city hang on the walls while a relief model of the city in 1923 shows the devastated areas.

Memorial services are held for the dead of the two disasters twice a year: on September 1 for the 1923 victims and on March 10 for those of 1945. There is yet another memorial on the grounds, a stone which commemorates the death of 2,000 Koreans who were killed in the panic immediately after the earthquake because of unfounded rumors that Koreans were responsible for the fires which followed the quake. These rumors led to brutal attacks and the deaths of resident Koreans, many of whom were murdered by merciless Japanese mobs.

Continuing along the south side of the Memorial Hall, a path toward the river leads to the **Yasuda Garden** with its large tidal pond. The garden had once been part of the estate of Zenjiro Yasuda, a financial magnate of the Meiji era. He was assassinated in 1921 and the land reverted as a gift to the city of Tokyo. Destroyed in the 1923 earthquake, the garden has since been rebuilt, and the Ryogoku Public Hall now sits to one side of the park nearest the river. A large pond, encircled by greenery and with stone bridges over water courses, as well as a small, vermilion, arched bridge (recreated in concrete) provide a restful setting.

On leaving the Yasuda Garden by way of the narrow street leading to the Sumo Hall which lies ahead, a turn to the left at the end of the street leads to the **Edo-Tokyo Museum,** one of the most fascinating museums in Tokyo. The museum is open from 10:00 A.M. to 6:00 P.M. (to 9:00 P.M. on Fridays) but is closed on Mondays unless Mondays is a national holiday, in which case it is closed the following day; it is also closed from December 28 to January 4; entry fee, free to pre-school children and adults over 65. Opened in 1993, this huge building standing on four huge posts offers a panorama of life during the four hundred years of Edo/Tokyo since Tokugawa Ieyasu chose the high ground at the head of Tokyo Bay for his castle. Was it by chance or by intent that this 203-foot-tall museum approximates the same height as Ieyasu's castle?

The ticket offices are on the first floor and on the Edo-Tokyo Plaza. Escalators to the museum rise from the raised platform above which the museum stands on its four huge supports. These escalators (or adjacent elevators) take one to the sixth floor, from where the tour begins and from where one can look down on the re-created buildings and the displays on the floor below. A reconstruction of the original Nihombashi wooden bridge is crossed to bring one to the beginning of the exhibition area. This mezzanine level offers the early history of the city while the main floor below it takes the story of Edo into the years of early Tokyo and up to the 1964 Olympics. The exhibition area encompasses the fifth and sixth floor of the structure, the ceiling over the exhibition hall being eighty-five feet above the floor.

A full-scale reconstruction of the nineteenth-century Nakamura Kabuki theater can be seen as well as one of the earliest modern buildings of the Meiji era. The exhibits range from documents and artifacts of daily life over a three-hundred-year period, even to one of the earliest compact cars produced by Subaru. Various portions of the museum offer audio-video displays to explore in depth areas of the city's history. Perhaps most fascinating is the fourth floor of the building, where the materials which many museums are forced to keep in closed storage space are available for viewing. Climate controlled and secure storage/exhibition cases display the thousands of artifacts which bring to life the culture of Tokyo's people and past. An auditorium for 450, a gift shop on the first floor, and two coffee shops on the first and seventh floors, a Japanese restaurant and a Western restaurant, and a library concerned with the history of Edo-Tokyo on the seventh floor are among the amenities of this gigantic museum. There is even a stall on the outdoor plaza level where one can purchase *bento* lunch boxes which can be enjoyed on the Edo-Tokyo Plaza.

For many Japanese, however, there is one hall on this side of the Sumida River which is of the greatest interest, and that is the **Kokugikan** (The Hall of the National Sport), the national center for sumo tournaments. Sumo has found a home for many years along the Sumida River: Sumo matches were held to the south in Fukagawa at the Tomioka Hachiman-gu shrine in the late 1600s, later at the Eko-in temple from 1833 to 1909 (due south of the present sumo building at Keiyo-dori), and then in a sumo hall next to the temple until war-time damage ruined this hall.

In 1984 a new sumo tournament hall and a sumo museum in a five-story ferroconcrete building was constructed on the east side of the Sumida River just to the north of Ryogoku Station on the JR Sobu Line. On leaving the Edo-Tokyo Museum, the Sumo Hall is directly behind the museum and its entrance is on the river side of the hall. The new hall can seat up to 10,000 spectators. The sumo ring with its round dirt mound (*dohyo*) and roof can be removed, the latter electronically, on those occasions when the hall is used for activities other than sumo. The Sumo Museum inside the main entrance is devoted to the history of sumo wrestling, and it is open from 9:30 A.M. to 4:30 P.M. without charge. It is closed on weekends and national holidays, and it is only available to ticket holders during sumo matches. (Sumo tournaments are held here for fifteen days in January, May, and September.)

Leaving the Sumo Hall and walking under the overhead rail line, to the south of Ryogoku Station, one comes to the area of the *heya,* (stables) in which sumo wrestlers train and live. More than a dozen *heya* are run by retired sumo wrestlers who have purchased the right to run such establishments from the Sumo Association. Between the rail line and the overhead Shuto Expressway to the south are a number of the shops serving the sumo world, particularly those selling clothes and footwear for men of the largest sizes. Walk under the overhead rail line, and where the main street splits, take the left-hand roadway. The street ends at Keiyo-dori, and across the street is the post-1945 Eko-in temple behind its very modern gateway.

Keiyo-dori is the main east-west street in this area since the Ryogokubashi bridge over the Sumida (to the right) connects this sector with most of Tokyo. The Tokugawas, as has been indicated previously, were opposed to any bridges over the Sumida in their desire to keep hostile forces at bay. Unhappily, in the 1657 Long Sleeves Fire people were trapped at the river's western edge during that inferno, and over 100,000 perished because there was no way across the Sumida to safety. The Ryogokubashi, the first bridge to cross the river, was built in 1659.

Here at Keiyo-dori is the **Eko-in** temple. Although Eko-in was destroyed in 1923 and then again in 1945, it has been rebuilt in a modern but not outstanding architectural form. The temple was noted for two events in particular. It was here that the ashes of those who died in the 1657 fire were interred, a grand ceremony at the interment in honor of the dead being held by orders of the shogun. Located in this area of sumo stables, it is obvious that the temple had to have a relationship with sumo. When the sumo tournaments were moved from the Tomioka Hachiman-gu shrine in the south in 1833, the Eko-in became the site of the matches until 1909. After 1909 the Kokugikan, the sumo stadium next door to the temple, became the location at which the matches were held until the building was damaged in 1945 and razed thereafter. A large memorial stone, to the left of the path leading to the main hall of the temple and known as the Stone of Strength, commemorates this location as the former home of sumo.

The Eko-in became a burial ground or a memorial place for many others, including animals, who have their spirits honored at the Bato Kannon (Horse-headed Kannon), honoring the spirits of dead animals. The spirits of still-born children and aborted fetuses are also remembered here: in the area to the left of the temple hall, up against the rear fence are rows of tiny Jizo figures, some with bibs, some holding pinwheels in memory of the unborn. Unfortunately, the modern temple structure is not one of great distinction.

On leaving Eko-in, a turn to the left and then to the left again takes one along the street behind the temple. Just before the second cross street on the left is all that remains of Lord Kira's onetime splendid estate. Kira was the daimyo who was to instruct Lord Asano in the subtleties of shogunal court etiquette at the beginning of the 1700s. He did not train his pupil properly, since his honorarium, he felt, did not suit his status. In fact, he became derisive of his pupil. As a result, Lord Asano performed inadequately at a shogunal audience. In a rage, Asano drew his sword to attack Kira even though it was a penal offense to uncover a sword in the castle. The penalty for such an action required ceremonial suicide. So begins the tale of The Forty-seven Ronin, which comes to its conclusion for visitors to modern Tokyo at the Sengaku-ji temple described in Tour 11.

The subsequent event is worth recounting: On the snowy night of December 15, 1702, forty-seven of Asano's followers obtained revenge for their master's death by storming Lord Kira's mansion here to the east of the Sumida River. A very small park sits on the site of Kira's villa, a white tile and plaster wall protecting the small enclosure. In the left-hand corner is the "head washing well" where Kira's decapitated head was washed by his assailants before bringing it to their master's grave. There is a small Inari shrine in the little park dedicated to Kira's retainers who died in the attack, and the story of the attack is portrayed here in reproductions of woodblock prints of scenes from the famous Kabuki play *Chushingura* that has immortalized the event.

Turning to the left at the corner of the memorial site and returning the one street to Keiyo-dori where another left turn is taken, one proceeds to the Ryogokubashi bridge over the Sumida River. On the far side of the bridge, a right turn on the first "zebra"-striped crosswalk leads into a short willow-tree-lined street to Yanagibashi. To the right the Kanda River flows into the

Sumida River, and here was once the noted Yanagibashi geisha quarters and the point at which one could take boats to the Yoshiwara and where geisha entertained on pleasure boats. Today pleasure craft still tie up here to provide a pleasant evening of food and drink for those seeking diversion from busy Tokyo life.

The Kanda River can be followed via the short streets to Edo-dori, where a few streets to the right lie the JR Asakusabashi Station and the Asakusabashi Station on the Toei Asakusa Subway Line. These can take one back to the center of the city.

TOUR

8

Asakusa, Senso-ji, Kappabashi, Yoshiwara, and Tsubouchi Theater Museum

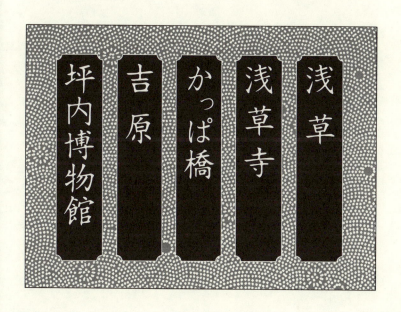

ASAKUSA was for two centuries the most exciting and dynamic area of old Edo and early Tokyo. Its early importance as a religious center can even be pinpointed to an exact date—March 18, 628—when two fishermen brothers, Hamanari and Takenari Hinokuma, caught a small, gilt-bronze image in their fishing net. According to tradition, they threw this unwanted object back into the river two times, but it kept reappearing in their net. So unusual an event seemed auspicious, and thus they took the image to their overlord, Haji-no-Nakatomo, who enshrined it in his house and built a hall for it in 645. Thus the Asakusa Kannon temple is the oldest temple in Tokyo. This two-inch gold image of Kannon has remained a *hibutsu* (a hidden image) within the temple since its earliest days because it is said to be too holy to gaze upon.

Scholars have speculated as to the origin of such an image, and a possible clue appeared after the 1945 firebombing when the remains of the *hondo* (main hall) were excavated prior to its rebuilding. Tiles and religious implements of the 600s and 700s were found. Could it be that the image was of Korean origin since images of this early time came primarily from the continent? Further speculation arises as to whether the image may have been tossed into the river by the Mononobe adherents who resisted the incursion of the new Buddhist faith in the late 500s— for just such a reaction had taken place earlier in the Osaka region when the Mononobe had acted in this manner and cast the earliest Buddhist images into the Naniwa River. The fact that the image was found after the Mononobe had been defeated and Buddhism was being encouraged by the court gives this supposition some validity. At any rate, it is said that a great golden dragon danced its way from heaven to earth upon the discovery of this tiny Kannon, an auspicious sign if ever there was one.

The **Senso-ji** temple (which is the temple's correct name, although it is usually referred to as the Asakusa Kannon Temple) has been rebuilt many times. The famous ninth-century priest Ennin is credited with building a new Kannon Hall for the temple in 864. Another rebuilding occurred in the 900s, and then an additional remake of the hall occurred in the 1100s at the request of Shogun Minamoto-no-Yoritomo. Naturally Tokugawa Ieyasu put his imprint on the temple with a new hall when Edo became his headquarters, and in 1620, two years after his death, the initial memorial to this shogun was erected on the temple grounds. When this memorial shrine burned, it was rebuilt in the Edo Castle grounds, and later this earliest of Tosho-gu shrines was relocated to Ueno Park, where it stands today.

The Ginza subway line ends at Asakusa Station at the junction of Asakusa-dori and Edo-dori at the Sumida River. One should walk down Asakusa-dori on its north side to the Kaminari-mon gateway, which is one street to the west. The Asakusa Tourist Information Center is on the south side of Asakusa-dori across from the Kaminari-mon gateway. (On leaving the subway station, across the Sumida River one sees the 1989 Super Dry Hall by the French architect Philippe Starck. Some see the Asahi Brewery Building as being beer-glass shaped, but all viewers remark upon the strange golden object which tops it.)

The *hondo* of the Asakusa Temple lies a good distance beyond the initial gateway to the temple complex. The vermilion **Kaminari-mon** (Thunder Gate) to the temple gets its name from the two deities who stand guard on either side of the gateway. Raijin, the deity of thunder, is on the left, while Fujin, the deity of wind, is on the right. They stand here at the beginning of the long path to the temple as protectors of the Kannon and thus act as a barrier keeping evil forces away. A large, red, paper lantern (which is eleven feet in size, weighs 1,482 pounds, and is illuminated from within at night) hangs from the center of the gateway roof. It seems strange that the Kaminari-mon, so important an element at the entrance to the temple grounds, was not recreated until 1955 after its destruction by fire in 1865. No doubt the Meiji antagonism to Buddhism after 1868 had its effect here and discouraged the restoration of the gate. The heads of the two deities are original, having been saved at the time of the fire, but the bodies are modern. In 1978, on the 1,350 anniversary of the appearance of the Kannon image in the fishermen's net, a new pair of guardian images were donated to stand in the rear niches of the gate. A male on one side and a female on the other side, these images do not quite have the attractive nature of the ones at the front of the gateway.

Beyond the Kaminari-mon stretches **Nakamise-dori** (Inside

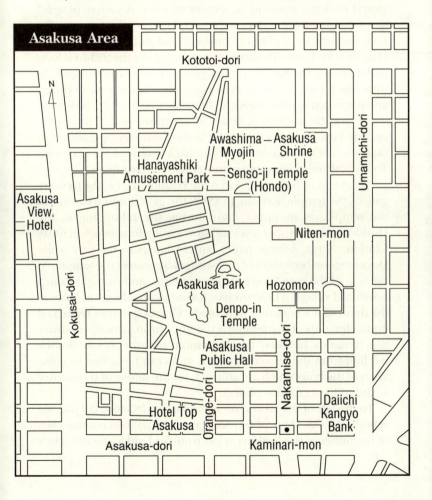

Asakusa Area

Kototoi-dori

N

Umamichi-dori

Awashima — Asakusa
Myojin   Shrine
Hanayashiki
Amusement Park — Senso-ji Temple
                (Hondo)

Asakusa
View
Hotel

Niten-mon

Kokusai-dori

Asakusa Park   Hozomon

Denpo-in
Temple

Nakamise-dori

Asakusa
Public Hall

Orange-dori

Hotel Top
Asakusa   Daiichi
                           Kangyo
                           Bank

Asakusa-dori   Kaminari-mon

Shops Street) within the temple grounds. Stalls have lined this pathway for centuries, but in 1885 the Meiji authorities had the stalls replaced by brick buildings from which the small shop-keepers operate. Such modernization no doubt had another motive, given the Meiji rulers' antipathy toward Buddhism. A number of Buddhist sub-temples behind the stalls disappeared in the modernization. Today moveable roof coverings can be closed over the street in inclement weather. A variety of small items ranging from *senbei* (rice crackers), to combs, paper crafts, toys, and articles of clothing can be found along Nakamise-dori. One hundred and fifty shops are ranged along the 984-foot-long path between the Kaminari-mon gate and the Hozomon gate. As with much else in Tokyo, even Nakamise-dori was modernized and upgraded in other ways with time. Missing from the Nakamise scene are the archery galleries of centuries past. These were presided over by attractive young women sufficiently made up so that one knew the purpose of the back rooms of the galleries. Today Nakamise is far more proper than in past times.

At the end of Nakamise-dori is the **Hozomon** gate, the treasury gate of the temple. Redone in 1964, the gate stored treasures of the temple on its upper floor during the rebuilding of the Hondo, and the upper level still stores some fourteenth century Chinese sutras. A large paper lantern hangs in the gate while Deva kings on both sides of the passageway protect the temple. At the rear of the gate hang two gigantic straw sandals, a gift from a provincial village. These oversized sandals are almost as large as the deities for whom they were made. One of the most remarked upon elements of the temple is the huge bronze incense burner which stands between the Hozomon and the *hondo*. Smoke swirling from the burning incense sticks can be wafted to those areas of the body which are afflicted, for the smoke of this burner is said to have curative powers.

To the left of the Hozomon is the 5-story, 183-foot-tall pagoda rebuilt in 1973. Made of ferroconcrete, the pagoda contains bits of the bones of the Buddha, a gift from Sri Lanka, the relics in a golden container hanging from the ceiling on the uppermost floor. The pagoda is open to the public on three occasions each year: February 15, the anniversary of the Buddha's death; April 8, the anniversary of the Buddha's birth; and December 8, the date of his enlightenment. A temple office is located within a portion of the pagoda through the door on the left.

To the right of the Hozomon and slightly back toward the rear of the Nakamise shops stand two large bronze images of Bodhisattvas, a 1687 gift of a rice merchant in honor of his deceased master. Before the images is a memorial to a man who killed many people and who asked to be buried at this spot so that his corpse would suffer the penalty of being walked upon forever by temple visitors. Beyond, in the southeast corner of the temple grounds, is a small hill, the **Benten-yama** (Benten Mound), with a small, red shrine (rebuilt in 1983) on top of it. This shrine is dedicated to the Shinto goddess Benten. The small hill is thought to be an ancient burial mound of the Kofun Period (c. A.D. 250–538), and a small bell upon it once rang the hours of the day. The bell now is rung each day at 6:00 A.M. to signal the opening of the temple grounds, and it is rung one hundred and eight times at the end of each year at midnight to symbolize the one hundred and eight shortcomings mankind is heir to.

Part way down the Nakamise an opening leads to a side street with additional shops. Here behind the Nakamise stalls on this side street is a building which displays one of the one hundred portable shrines, which are paraded at festival times.

The *hondo* looms beyond the Hozomon gate. This 113-foot-long by 107-foot-deep building was rebuilt in ferroconcrete as a protection against fire and earthquake after its destruction by fire on March 10, 1945. Since the hall is of concrete, it is permissible to enter wearing shoes. The sacred image of the Kannon is kept within the inner portions of the hall, and here monks chant sutras three times a day before the image case of the Kannon. To the left of the case holding the Kannon is an image of Aizen-Myo-o, while to the right is one of Fudo-Myo-o. Votive plaques, *ema,* are hung on the interior walls, works of the 1700s and 1800s. Having been removed before the air raids of 1945, the fifty paintings have been preserved. Eight are on view. The temple is also known as the Kinryuzan Sensoji, the Golden Dragon Mountain Asakusa Temple, due to the legend of the descent of the dragon on the finding of the small golden Kannon. Therefore, a dragon has been painted on the ceiling of the *hondo,* the work of Kawabata Ryushi. The angels and lotus flowers surrounding it are by Domoto Insho.

To the right rear of the *hondo* is the Asakusa Shrine to the two fishermen brothers, Hamanari and Takenari Hinokuma, and to their master, Haji-no-Nakatomo. Thus the shrine is also known as the Shrine of the Three Guardians (Sanja-sama). The shrine was built at the orders of Tokugawa Iemitsu in 1649. A stone torii stands at its entrance with protective *koma-inu* (lion-dogs) just beyond. Such shrines have a *haiden,* which stands before the *honden.* In this case the *honden* holds the spirits of the two brothers who found the Kannon image and their master who enshrined the image. A corridor in the form of a room, the Ishi-no-ma, connects the *haiden* and *honden.* The ceiling of the *haiden* is unusual in that it is embellished with painted flowers. Commemorative stones on the grounds of the shrine honor notable figures of the Tokyo theater, for the adjacent main street to the west was for many decades the center of entertainment in the Asakusa district.

To the right of the shrine at the entrance to a commercial street is the 1618 Niten-mon gate which leads into the temple grounds from the east. It originally stood before the temple's Toshogu shrine to Ieyasu, but the Meiji authorities moved it so as to have it in the area of the Shinto shrine on the grounds.

To the west (left) of the *hondo* is the **Awashima Myojin** shrine for the guardian deity of women, who looks after female ailments. Legend has it that the sixth daughter of the ninth century statesman Sugawara-no-Michizane had served as a *miko,* (priestess) at the Sumiyoshi Shrine in Sakai (Osaka). Since shrines could not be defiled by blood, when she fell ill in "her lower parts," she was set adrift in a boat on the Inland Sea. The small boat landed at Awashima in today's Wakayama Prefecture, and there she prayed for women with similar problems. A cult developed around the former priestess, and shrines proliferated throughout Japan. Women often bring dolls to such shrines so that the dolls can bear the ailments of the donor. The dolls are later burned in time in a religious service to make the prayers for relief of the ailment come true.

Religious custom in Japan permits for both the spread and enrichment of the powers of deities, so the Awashima Shrine now also protects the art of sewing as well as the health of women. Thus on the eighth of February each year, women bring their worn-out needles to the shrine. These are placed in a bean curd in the shrine where they can be blessed and properly disposed of. (The Asakusa Awashima Shrine stands on the site of the 1620 Tosho-gu shrine to Ieyasu.) Next to the shrine on the left is a very small hexagonal hall once covering a temple well but later dedicated to the Buddhist deity Jizo. This particular Jizo is a most accommodating one, for not only can one ask him for help, but one can set the date on which this help is to be made manifest. West of the *hondo* is also a small hall to Yakushi, the Buddhist deity of healing. Recently, additional halls and memorial stones have been created to the left of the Awashima shrine.

The **Denpo-in** is the residence of the abbot of the temple, and, although one cannot enter the priestly quarters, it is possible to visit the lovely garden surrounding the residence between 10:00 A.M. and 3:00 P.M. Permission is obtained by applying at the temple office in the pagoda, the second office on the left (after removing one's shoes). The Denpo-in was once the site of the *honbo* (the residence for the priests) and the present structure for the abbot's use was erected in 1777. The residence has an entrance hall, a Lion's Room where the shogun's courier was received, a reception room, and a kitchen.

The entrance to the garden is on the south side of the

complex, opposite the Asakusa Public Hall (where an exhibition of old Asakusa is mounted on the upper floors). The bell at the entryway of the garden is from 1387 and is one of the oldest bells in the city. The garden, of a stroll-garden type, was originally laid out in the early 1600s, and it is attributed to the great garden master, Kobori Enshu. A large pond in the shape of the Chinese character for "heart" is enhanced by colorful carp and turtles. A small teahouse from the 1780s was brought from Nagoya, and it is said to be a copy of a no longer extant teahouse designed by the great tea master of Kyoto, Sen-no-Rikyu.

Behind the Denpo-in is the Chinzo-do, a small unit dedicated to the spirits of aborted children. Thus bibs on the Jizo images, the 1,000 crane colorful paper decorations, and colorful pin-wheels are offered to the spirits of the unborn.

The Senso-ji Hospital, behind the *hondo,* is but one of a number of charitable endeavors of the temple. In addition, the temple runs a kindergarten which has its entrance at the side of Nakamise in the Denpo-in grounds. In 1958 the temple opened the Senso-ji Social Welfare Center to give marriage and educational counseling and to offer lectures to assist young women and housewives.

The temple enjoys a number of festivals throughout the year, and among these are:

March 18 Kinryu-no-mai (The Golden Dragon Dance), celebrating the great golden dragon said to have descended from heaven when the golden Kannon was found. Eight, strong, young men hold a golden dragon and make it dance through the streets.

May 17–18 or **the nearest weekend** Sanja Matsuri, a festival in honor of the three men enshrined in the Asakusa Shrine. There is a parade of over one hundred *mikoshi,* the three *mikoshi* belonging to the shrine leading the procession. Those carrying the heavy *mikoshi* imbibe a sufficient amount of strong beverages to ensure a reckless and exciting parade.

July 9–10 A visit to the temple on the tenth is equivalent to 40,000 visits. There is a sale of Chinese lantern plants at some 500 stalls. Holding the cherry within the "lantern" in one's mouth was said to ward off the plague. The festival now has branched out into the sale of bonsai, other plants, and ornaments for the garden.

October 18 A repeat of the March 18 festival.

December 17–19 Hagoita Ichi, a festival when New Years decorations are sold. *Hagoita* (battledores and shuttlecocks), the former richly decorated with the faces of Kabuki actors, are available for the New Year festival battledore sport.

The Asakusa district around the Kannon temple grew into one of the most active commercial and entertainment districts of Edo. Its development came in part from the location of the temple and from its stalls selling a variety of items along Nakamise-dori. Then in one of the bursts of puritanical zeal, the shogunate banned the "licensed district" in Ningyocho in 1657 and banished the Yoshiwara red-light district to the empty fields beyond the Asakusa Kannon temple. Boats now brought pilgrims to the pleasure houses of Yoshiwara, stopping at Asakusa from where, after sufficient refreshment, they could continue on to Yoshiwara. Thus around this convenient stopping place other *divertissements* grew up in time.

In 1841 another burst of purity befell the shogunate, and this time Kabuki and Bunraku were also banished to Yoshiwara, stopping somewhat short of that location and thus settling to the west of the Asakusa Kannon. Kabuki developed its *aragoto* style which delighted the citizens of Edo. This brash, overstated style would often climax in exaggerated, long poses, to the delight of the audience. It was far different from the more courtly type of Kabuki enjoyed in Kyoto. Here, just to the west of the temple, Kabuki remained until 1872 when it began its move back to the Ginza/Tsukiji area.

Rokku, the Sixth District, between Kokusai-dori on the west

and the temple on the east, became a center for all forms of *divertissement* because the shogunate designated it a restricted area where elements of entertainment it did not approve of were allowed to flourish. The shogunate was Confucianist enough to wish decorum to reign, but it was also pragmatic enough to realize that an emotional outlet was needed by the citizens of *shitamachi,* and thus it alternately permitted and then banned certain amusements which the working class enjoyed. With the advent of the Meiji government and an attempt at Westernization, a park was created in 1876 to the west of the temple on land taken from the temple. Two ornamental lakes, trees, and greenery were seen as an antidote to piety to the east and rowdiness to the west.

The U.S. Occupation after 1945 returned the parkland to the temple, and it has now been built over. On its site is the Senso-ji Hospital, the Hanayashiki Amusement Park, which has rides that delight children, and other structures.

Once one has visited the Denpo-in gardens, any of the streets leading back toward Asakusa-dori will bring one to the covered gallery street of **Shin Nakamise.** Shin Nakamise is crossed by narrow Sushiya-dori and by the major north-south Kokusai-dori, and these two streets held many of the theaters of the area. The first theater in the modern sense opened in 1886 in Rokku, and by 1903 the first movie house—Electricity Hall—had made its debut and lasted until 1976, when it disappeared. Asakusa had "archery stalls," as previously described, vaudeville houses, variety theaters, acrobatic acts, opera, revues, cabarets, bars, striptease theaters, restaurants—all the varieties of modern entertainment. In 1890 the octagonal Twelve Stories, the tallest skyscraper in Tokyo, which even boasted an elevator, was built. It lasted until 1923 when it lost its top four stories in the earthquake and had to be demolished. (After the Second World War, the Jinten Tower, a half-size copy of the Twelve Stories, was erected at the end of the street in which the Kaminari-mon gate stands.) In 1927 the first subway line from the Ginza to Asakusa opened.

Until 1940 Asakusa was *the* place for entertainment, but now the entertainment scene has faded and moved elsewhere. Even the International Theater (Kokusai Gekijo), with its line of dancing girls, has gone. The 1945 bombing raids did inestimable damage to the district, and other newer areas of entertainment, Shinjuku and Roppongi, now attract the younger crowd. Television has made a difference as well. Traces of the past can still be seen in part on the street with theaters to the east of Kokusai-dori, but it is a pale reflection of a former exciting time.

Down Kokusai-dori to Asakusa-dori (the street which runs in front of the Kaminari-mon entrance to Nakamise-dori), between Tawaramachi Station (which is at Kokusai-dori and Asakusa-dori) and Inaricho Station on the Ginza Subway Line, is another wholesale district. This one is devoted to Buddhist and Shinto shrine furniture and ritual implements. After the Long Sleeves Fire of 1657 many of the temples were moved from the heart of Edo to Asakusa, which became a new center for temples and shrines and the shops which supplied them and their worshipers. The Asakusa Hongan-ji temple was founded here just to the north of Asakusa-dori and east of Kappabashi-dori. This temple was used by the shogunate to lodge envoys coming from Korea, and in the 1894 war with China the temple was used to house Chinese prisoners of war. (See comments concerning the Nishi Hongan-ji temple in Tsukiji in Tour 4 for background.)

At the third street to the west of Tawaramachi Station on Asakusa-dori is the intersection with **Kappabashi-dori.** The intersection cannot be easily missed, for atop the Niimi Building on the corner is the thirty-nine-foot tall head of a chef with his tall white, pleated hat. Along Kappabashi to the north of Asakusa-dori are two hundred shops selling *sanpuru,* plastic samples of food. Here the foods one sees in restaurant windows and display cases are available from wholesalers, souvenirs most visitors cannot resist.

The tour of Asakusa can end here and the subway can be taken back to the Ginza from either Tawaramachi or Inaricho Station.

But perhaps a little more should be said about Yoshiwara even though there are but one or two sites which still exist of this onetime pleasure quarter to the north of the district just visited.

Yoshiwara was the pleasure quarter for three hundred years, a factor of life which the shogunate had to accept when men in Edo outnumbered women by two to one, a situation which lasted until late in the nineteenth century. Thus female prostitution was licensed so as to exert some government control over the situation. There was male prostitution as well, since homosexuality was also an accepted fact of life as well as a continuing attraction for both priests and samurai. Male prostitutes could usually be found around the temples. Female prostitution was centered in Yoshiwara to the north of the Asakusa temple from 1657, when it was moved here from Ningyocho by shogunal order, until 1957 when the Diet outlawed prostitution.

The 20-acre Yoshiwara was entirely surrounded by walls and a ditch, with but one entrance on its south side. This kept the women from escaping from the quarter, and it also kept patrons from leaving without honoring payment for services rendered. The gate was closed at night and not opened again until morning. The district was reached by boat from Yanagibashi to a landing just a short walk from the entrance to the "Five Streets" within the cloistered sector. The Ditch of Black Teeth (married women and courtesans blackened their teeth, an ancient custom meant to enhance female attractiveness) was crossed over by a drawbridge, and then the O-mon (the Great Gate) brought one into Yoshiwara. If one were modest or wished to go into Yoshiwara incognito, there were always shops available outside the enclave which sold large straw hats to mask one's self.

Yoshiwara was not only an area for sexual gratification, but it was a cultural center as well, a place where all classes could meet in a society which was hierarchical and rigid in its social stratifications. There were restaurants, some of which served as intermediaries to direct clients to assignations. There were the *ageya*, rendezvous teahouses where the higher class of geisha, the *tayu*, met their clients. There was a distinction between these geisha, who were accomplished, musical, and witty and who provided social and cultural entertainment, and the *yujo*, whose primary attraction was sex.

The central street had *ageya* where the *tayu* met her clients. The society of this demi-monde was strictly regulated. *Tayu* wore their obi tied in front, an indication of their exalted status. In time the geisha culture developed, and *tayu* and geisha were a great cut above the common prostitutes on view behind lattice screens in the back streets of Yoshiwara. It is estimated that two to three thousand women were in Yoshiwara, but in times of famine, when women were desperate or when parents sold off unwanted daughters, this walled enclave could hold up to ten thousand women. Overcrowding and a lowering of standards gradually drove the better class of geisha elsewhere, and so Shimbashi began to flourish as the Meiji period went on. The fire of 1911 seriously damaged Yoshiwara, and then in 1923 the earthquake completely destroyed it. About two hundred brothels and teahouses were destroyed and several hundred women were incinerated in the fires. Today the area has lost whatever glamour it may once have had, and "soaplands," massage parlors, and love hotels are all that is left to recall that other era. Yet here at the end of the twentieth century it is claimed that there are two hundred soaplands and 2,500 women employed in the trade in the Asakusa area.

One sad reminder of Yoshiwara's past is the **Jokan-ji** temple in the Minowa area not far from Minowa Station. Known as the Dump Temple, or the Disposal Temple, here more than eleven thousand girls who averaged not more than twenty-two years of age were buried in a common grave. These were the unfortunate women of the Yoshiwara, disposable wares who lie in unmarked graves. By 1900 the law permitted women who did not wish to remain within Yoshiwara to leave the enclave. That same year the Salvation Army arrived in Tokyo, and published a tract called *Triumphant Voice* encouraging the denizens of Yoshiwara to flee and offering them help. The amusing side effect of the Army's efforts was the increase in sales of the tract as the brothel owners tried to buy up all the copies.

If one ends the tour at Jokan-ji, Minowa Station on the Hibiya Subway Line is close at hand. Those who wish to partake of a diversion which has virtually disappeared from the Tokyo scene can take a ride on the last tramline (the *chin chin densha* as it is commonly called) still in existence in Tokyo. Minowa Station is under Showa-dori. Walking from the station to the north and continuing under the overhead elevated rail line, the tramline lies to the right at the end of a covered market. The 7.3-mile line wanders across Tokyo to its terminus at Waseda.

En route to the end of the line, one can stop at Oji Station to visit the **Paper Museum,** which is but a few minutes from the station. Here one can see a selection of paper, including Egyptian papyrus and early Chinese types, paper-making techniques, and exhibits of the various items made from paper during the years of Japanese seclusion under the Tokugawas. The museum is open from 9:30 A.M. to 4:30 P.M. except for Mondays and national holidays, entry fee.

The tramline comes to an end next to Waseda University. Interested parties may wish to visit the **Waseda University Tsubouchi Memorial Theater Museum** (Waseda Daigaku Tsubouchi-hakase Kinen Engeki Hakubutsukan). In a building modeled after the Fortune Theater of Shakespeare's London, its porch shaped like an Elizabethan stage, is a museum which is a memorial to Dr. Tsubouchi Shoyo, the university professor who translated Shakespeare into Japanese. The museum has an exceedingly rich collection of memorabilia of Asian, European, and American theater. More than fifty thousand theatrical prints, models of stages, and theatrical masks can be viewed and studied from 9:00 A.M. to 4:00 P.M. on weekdays and from 9:00 A.M. to 2:00 P.M. on Saturdays. The museum is open from Monday through Saturday from 9:00 A.M. to 5:00 P.M. and remains open until 7:00 P.M. on Tuesdays and Fridays. It is also open from 10:00 A.M. to 5:00

P.M. on some Sundays, but it closes on national holidays, August 1 to mid-September, October 21, at the end of the year and the New Year period. Tours in English may be arranged in advance.

Across the campus of Waseda University is Waseda Station on the Tozai Subway Line, just fifteen minutes on foot from the Tsubouchi Museum. Here a train can be taken back into the heart of the city.

TOUR

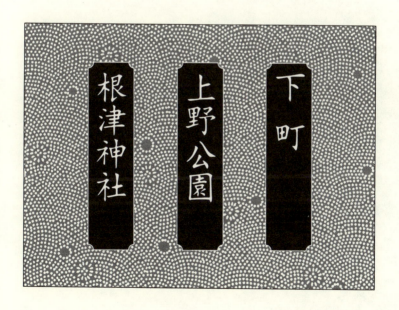

❖ *9* ❖

Shitamachi, Ueno Park,
and Nezu Shrine

根津神社　上野公園　下町

CHINESE geomancy always held an essential place in Japanese life, and it was particularly important when choosing sites for buildings and planning cities. When the Tokugawas made Edo their headquarters after 1603, it was necessary to protect the city against evil forces, which, according to Chinese lore, flowed from the northeast. Thus in 1624 Hidetada, the second Tokugawa shogun, asked Priest Tenkai (1536–1643) to build a temple at the northeast corner of Edo as a protection for the new town. The new temple of Kan'ei-ji was to serve a purpose similar to the one offered to Kyoto by its Enryaku-ji temple, a protection at its vulnerable northeast corner, the Ki-mon (Devil's Gate.)

The temple that arose on Ueno Hill was befriended thereafter by the succeeding shoguns, and by 1700 it had thirty-six sub-temples on 294 acres. As a shogunal temple, it was off limits to commoners. The Ueno Park fountain in front of the National Museum now marks the site where the Kan'ei-ji temple's huge main hall once stood. The temple's pagoda overlooked the city, and after Tokugawa Ieyasu's death, the Tosho-gu shrine to his spirit was raised on temple grounds in the extravagant Momoyama style, which also enriched his burial shrine at Nikko. Kan'ei-ji was truly the shoguns' temple, for it was here that a number of them were buried.

Originally an arm of Tokyo Bay came up to the hillside of Ueno, but in time the low-lying marshland beneath the hill was filled in, and the new land became the *monzen machi* (the town in front of the temple). So huge a temple complex required services, and thus shops came into being in the town below the hill, a portion of *shitamachi* where merchants and craftsmen lived. One modified arm of the inlet did remain, and it became the freshwater Shinobazu Pond.

Yushima Station on the Chiyoda Subway Line provides easy access to the sites of Ueno Park. One leaves the subway and gains Shinobazu-dori, the street under which the subway runs, and heads to the north toward Ueno Park. Shinobazu-dori bends to the left when it reaches Shinobazu Pond at the beginning of Ueno Park, and the street should be followed until one is opposite the second portion of the pond (opposite Benten Shrine across the water). About ten minutes away on the left is a traditional house, the home of Yokoyama Taikan. (**Yokoyama Taikan Hall,** Yokoyama Taikan Kinenkan, open from 10:00 A.M. to 4:00 P.M. Thursday through Sundays but closed for a month in mid-summer and mid-December through mid-January, entry fee.)

Yokoyama Taikan (1868–1958) was an artist who painted in the traditional *nihonga* style but who modified his techniques to include aspects of Western painting, techniques which differed from traditional Japanese approaches. Much of Yokoyama's life was spent in this house at the side of Shinobazu Pond (rebuilt after the 1945 firebombing destroyed it). After his wife's death in 1976 (eighteen years after his demise) the house was opened as a memorial. Some of the rooms are open to the public and these include his tearoom, with fifteen windows looking out upon his garden which has a rivulet running through it. The tearoom has a brazier in its middle with a teapot hanging over it, a *tokonoma* (alcove in a Japanese-style room), and the artist's rare image of Fudo from the 1100s. His studio workroom still retains his working tools. The upstairs bedroom was so planned that the garden could be enjoyed from above as well. Selections of the artist's work are on view, but the house and garden themselves are fine examples of an artist's traditional home and studio. The small garden is a delight with its rocks, carp swimming in the pond, and stone lanterns. A pamphlet in English supplements the labels in Japanese.

Returning to the foot of Ueno Park and the subway exit from which the tour began, one is at Kasuga-dori. A left turn here along that street will, after passing three more side streets, bring one to Chuo-dori, a continuation of the main shopping street in the Ginza. This was an area of shops in Edo times, and so it remains, the Matsuzakaya Department Store being the largest in the area. Continuing along Kasuga-dori at the side of Matsuzakaya, the first street on the left leads into the area known as **Ameya Yokocho.** Ameyoko, which is how most people refer to it, is situated under the elevated railway line which goes into Ueno Station up ahead. (Ueno Station is not only a stop on the Yamanote elevated line, but it is the huge terminal for trains to the north and east of Japan, a station first created in July of 1883.) There are more than five hundred shops in this one-fourth of a mile stretch under the rail line and spilling out into adjacent streets.

The name of the district, Ameyoko, comes from *ame* meaning "sweets," and *yokocho*, meaning "alley," thus Confectioners Alley. After the Korean War, Ameyoko took on new meaning as a play on a contraction of "Ame-rican Market," since this area sold a lot of black-market goods from American military post exchanges during those years. A new central market has been opened, although small shops continue to operate under and around the elevated railway tracks. There is a tremendous variety of goods available, continuing the tradition of *shitamachi* with its small shops and stalls.

The *shitamachi* of early years is recalled in a delightful, small museum at the foot of Shinobazu Pond close to Chuo-dori. Ueno Park begins at Shinobazu-dori, and just beyond the shore of the pond is the **Shitamachi Museum.** Open from 9:30 A.M. to 4:30 P.M. Closed Mondays and national holidays, and from December 29 through January 3, entry fee.

The devastation of the 1923 earthquake, the 1945 bombings, and the inexorable change to the face of the city in the post-1950s economic boom have gradually obliterated the traditional Tokyo that was alive in the late nineteenth and early twentieth centuries. The Shitamachi Museum was conceived in 1980 as an attempt to preserve aspects of the average person's life between 1867 and 1925. Change was to come much more rapidly to Tokyo after that latter year with the rebuilding that occurred after the Great Kanto Earthquake and fire.

The museum helps to recall a past era, and the significance of the displays is made clear in a free English brochure or in a more extensive English booklet, which may be purchased. A single-story tenement from the nineteenth century has been recreated here to illustrate how people lived and worked in close quarters with but scanty belongings in those days. A merchant's shop, a copper boiler craftsman's workplace, and a shop selling inexpensive sweets provide aspects of the mercantile life of Edo days. An exhibition hall on the second floor offers clothing displays, children's games, and household items from the past, some illustrated by photographs and video presentations.

Behind the Shitamachi Museum, a roadway runs along Shinobazu Pond to **Benten Island.** In creating the Kan'ei-ji temple, based on the example of Enryaku-ji in Kyoto, Abbot Tenkai wished to copy other aspects of Kyoto, Japan's capital for nearly a thousand years. An island was built in the middle of Shinobazu Pond with a shrine to the Shinto goddess Benten. The Benten Shrine on the island was an imitation of the shrine to Benten on Chikubu Island in Lake Biwa outside of Kyoto. A shrine on an island should be able to be reached, and thus in 1670 a causeway was built from the shore to the island. Destroyed in the 1945 bombing raids, this seventeenth-century shrine was rebuilt in 1958 in its original style, even down to a painted dragon on the ceiling and painted autumn flowers on the panels alongside the image case. Benten, with her four-stringed lute, still stands before her hall, and the shrine's annual summer festival helps to enliven the warmer months.

In Edo days the pond was surrounded by places where one could eat and drink and admire the deep pink lotus flowers blooming in the water. Here the *bon odori* was danced to welcome the spirits of the dead back for their brief visit to this world each summer. The one and one-half mile circumference of the pond offered a new attraction after 1884: a race track circling the pond, and a royal grandstand alongside the track.

The justification for a racetrack was that horsemanship was

considered a necessary military skill for national defense. This race track "improvement" was removed in 1893. Shinobazu Pond (The Pond Without Patience) is divided into three parts: the northernmost sector is a portion of the Aquatic Zoo and is a haven for birds; the western portion is available for boating; and the southern portion has pink flowering lotus plants. On the hill above the pond is the Seiyoken restaurant, and nearby is the 1666 Toki-no-kane bell, which once sounded the hours for the temple monks. Also above the pond are two shrines and a tunnel of vermilion torii leading to the Hanazono Inari shrine.

Returning to Chuo-dori and passing the entrance to the Keisei Ueno Station, one comes to the main entrance to **Ueno Park.** Here stands the bronze statue of General Takamori Saigo, a reminder of not only the change from the government of the Tokugawa shoguns but of the battle fought at this site in 1868. On April 11, 1868, Takamori had worked out an agreement with the Tokugawa representative on Atago Hill in Edo. The agreement led to the peaceful surrender of the city and the realm to the

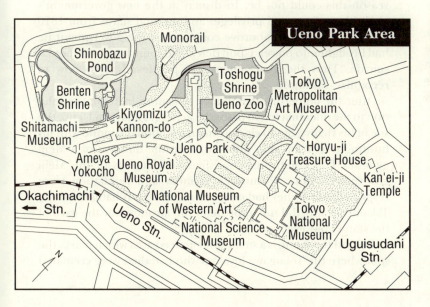

forces operating in the name of the Meiji Emperor. On May 15, 1868, just one month later, two thousand Tokugawa loyalists decided to fight the Meiji army despite the agreement, gathering their forces on Ueno Hill on the grounds of the Kan'ei-ji temple. Here before the Kuro-mon (Black Gate) they took up arms against the more modern army of the Meiji supporters. Besieged by Meiji guns and artillery, the Tokugawa loyalists (Shogitai) were forced to surrender, but not before they set fire to many of the Kan'ei-ji buildings, the protector of the city. Along with the temple buildings, up to one thousand houses were destroyed in the resulting fire. The battle left three hundred of the loyalists dead.

In 1898 a statue to Takamori Saigo (1827–73) was unveiled at the entrance to what had become Ueno Park. He was honored in part for his efforts as chief of staff for the Satsuma and Choshu clans, those Outside Lords who led the revolt against Tokugawa rule, and for his victory at Ueno. The statue should have been erected before the Imperial Palace, but there was one overriding reason this could not be. In dismay at the new government's abolishing of samurai privileges and samurai status from 1870 on, Takamori led an abortive coup against the government he had brought into power. Upon defeat, he committed ceremonial suicide. Thus the government was perplexed as to how to recognize Takamori.

After the emperor rehabilitated Takamori in 1890, the solution to the dilemma was to place the general's image in Ueno, the site of his victory, but to clothe him in traditional kimono with his hunting dog at his side rather than in the uniform of a Meiji general. This compromise satisfied all elements of the Meiji government since Takamori's memory and reputation were respected even if they had not been completely rehabilitated yet. Takamori's wife did not approve of the location nor the garb of the statue, however.

Behind the statue is a small stone-fenced area which marks the spot where the Tokugawa loyalists who had died were cremated and where their ashes were interred. A small museum (open from 10:00 A.M. to 4:00 P.M., closed Thursday) commemorates the vanquished of 1868. An *ukiyo-e* print on the grounds describes the battle of that day in May.

Ahead on the left, beyond the grave of the Tokugawa loyalists, is the **Kiyomizu Kannon-do** above Shinobazu Pond. Abbot Tenkai had this sub-temple built in imitation of Kyoto's Kiyomizu-dera temple. As an imitation it falls a good bit short of the intended goal, for it lacks the huge, intricate, underpinning sub-structure which supports the Kyoto temple. The original copy of the Kyoto edifice was erected in 1631, but in 1698 it was relocated to its present and more auspicious position above the pond. As its main image, the temple holds a Thousand-arm Kannon, which was sent as a gift from the abbot of the Kiyomizu-dera temple in Kyoto. The image that attracts the most attention in the temple, however, is the Kosodate Kannon, a Kannon to whom one prays in the hope of conceiving a child. Those who have been success-ful in conceiving often bring dolls as offerings to the temple, and these dolls may be seen in the left-hand corner of the temple. Here they remain until they are burned in a ceremony of thanksgiving to the Kannon each September 25 at 2:00 P.M., when priests chant sutras. This building was one of the few to survive the battle of 1868 (it was restored in 1994–95). Above the entrance to the hall is a painting which details that 1868 battle. The building is open from 9:00 A.M. to sunset without charge.

The devastated Kan'ei-ji grounds posed a problem as to their future use after 1868. The government favored the creation of a modern hospital on the site, but a consultant from Holland, Dr. Antonius Bauduin, argued persuasively that the grounds be used as a Western-style park and that the hospital be located on the former Maeda daimyo estate to the east (the future University of Tokyo site). As a result, Ueno became the first of five parks in the city, the most important ones being at former temple grounds in Ueno (the Kan'ei-ji), in Shiba (the Zojo-ji), and in a portion of the Asakusa temple grounds. (This latter was returned to the temple by the U.S. military after 1945, and it has now been built over.) In 1877 the first National Exhibition was held on the grounds of the park, as was the 1882 exhibition. At the conclusion of the latter, the Tokyo National Museum and the zoo were established here.

Ueno Park became a cultural center through the years. The Shinobazu Pond was annexed to the park in 1885 while the Tokugawa tombs in a portion of the old Kan'ei-ji temple were separated from it. Behind the Kannon Hall is the **Ueno Royal Museum** (Ueno-no-Mori Bijutsukan), which offers a venue for changing exhibitions by artistic organizations that may rent gallery space on the museum's two floors (optional entry fees). Its current exhibitions are listed in the English-language newspapers. Begun by Prince Takamatsu in 1971, it is an auxiliary of the Japan Art Association. Behind the Royal Museum is the Japan Art Academy, an honorary organization with one hundred and fifty members who are elected for life. The 1974 building was designed by architect Yoshio Taniguchi.

The **Tokyo Metropolitan Festival Hall** (Tokyo Bunka Kaikan) is the next building, designed by Kunio Maekawa in 1961. It has two auditoriums with 2,327 and 611 seats, and is also used as a hall for conventions. Primarily, it serves as a classical music concert hall.

To the left of the festival hall is a stone torii at the entryway to the **Tosho-gu** shrine to Tokugawa Ieyasu. When Ieyasu died in 1616, his ashes were placed in an elaborate shrine which was built in Nikko. Additional shrines were ordered to be built to the deified Ieyasu throughout the nation, and the one on the Kan'ei-ji temple grounds was established in 1627 and was improved in 1651 by the third Tokugawa shogun. The pathway into the shrine is lined with two hundred stone lanterns, one of which, the Obake Toro (Supernatural Lantern), stands eighteen feet tall. Behind these are a double row of fifty bronze lanterns, all gifts from daimyo of the country, their name and the date of the gift recorded on each lantern. They were meant not for illumination but were involved in the purification of the sacred fire for important religious ceremonies. All of the lanterns survived the 1923 and 1945 disasters.

Before the bronze lanterns as one approaches the main hall of the shrine, there is a *kagura* stage on the right for religious dances and then a roofed bell. On the other side of the path is a roofed basin for ablutions. *Koma-inu* (lion-dogs) on either side of the path protect the main building beyond. A fee to enter the main hall is paid on the left, and then one walks to the left and around the vermilion-fenced inner courtyard of the shrine, entering on the right-hand side of the complex. The main building of the shrine (open from 9:00 A.M. to 5:30 P.M. daily but to 4:40 P.M. in the winter, entry fee) is in the *gongen-zukuri* style, that ornate style much favored by the early Tokugawa shoguns. A Karamon (Chinese Gate) in front of the building is in the elaborate "Chinese" carved style with birds, fish, other animals, and shells. It is most noted for its carved dragons ascending on the right and descending on the left, said to be created by Hidari Jingoro, the master carver of the early 1600s. Legend has it that the dragons were so real that they would descend and drink from the Shinobazu Pond at night. It is claimed that wire cages had to be put around the carvings to keep the dragons from wandering.

The main shrine building, the **Konjiki-do** (Golden Hall), is in the ornate Momoyama style which was favored by the Tokugawa. The *haiden* was decorated within by four paintings of lions on a gold background by Kano Tan'yu. Two images of seated shoguns are in the middle of the room with a large dragon head at their side while some thirty-six pictures of officials line the walls near the ceiling. Displayed at one side are the shogun's suit of armor and his sword. The *haiden* is connected by a corridor to the *honden*. The *honden* is where the spirit of Ieyasu is enshrined. The framed tablet on its front with the shrine name on it is in the writing of the Emperor Go-Mizuno-o of Ieyasu's day. The ebony steps leading up to the altar to Ieyasu's spirit are the one element which is not gilded in this small hall. A lion sits at the side of the steps to guard the approach to the shrine itself. Unfortunately, the exterior gold finish of the shrine has weathered and needs refurbishing.

To the left of the shrine is the peony garden (open 9:00 A.M. to 5:00 P.M., entry fee when the plants are in bloom) where the winter peonies bloom from early January to mid-February and the spring peonies are in flower from April to mid-May. About 3,000 peonies of two hundred different varieties bloom at a time, and an annual flower festival is held on April 17. (It should also be noted that the park has one thousand cherry trees, and it is overcrowded in cherry blossom season with people enjoying the transient blooms.)

The 120-foot-tall vermilion pagoda to the Tosho-gu shrine is separated from the memorial buildings since it is now within the confines of the Ueno Zoo. Erected in 1631, it had to be rebuilt eight years later after a fire. Now its top story is covered with bronze roof tiles. The pagoda is not open to the public.

The adjacent **Ueno Zoo** is open from 9:30 A.M. to 4:30 P.M., entry fee. It is in two parts: The Aquatic Zoo on the shores of Shinobazu Pond is connected with the upper zoo area by a monorail train. The zoo is noted for its pandas, its monkey habitat (a "mountain" on which the monkeys roam freely), and its collection of 1,200 animals, which includes more than 950 species of wildlife. Opened in 1882, Ueno Zoo was the first Western-style zoo in Japan.

In the area of the park with the museum buildings, beyond the festival hall is the **National Museum of Western Art** (Kokuritsu Seiyo Bijutsukan), open from 9:30 A.M. to 5:00 P.M., closed on Mondays and from December 28 through January 4, entry fee. The initial building by Le Corbusier was erected in 1959, and a new building by Kunio Maekawa was added in 1979. The core of the collection belonged to Kojiro Matsukata, president of the Kawasaki Ship Building Company, and it was originally housed in Paris. The collection was seized by the French government during the Second World War, but it was released by 1959 and came to the museum. The Matsukata collection, primarily the art of the French impressionists, is housed in the Le Corbusier building while the remainder of Western art is in the newer building where temporary exhibitions are also mounted from time to time. Fifty-seven Rodin sculptures adorn the courtyard, and the museum collection includes works by Cranach, El Greco, Rubens, Tintoretto, Manet, Cézanne, Monet, Degas, Renoir, Picasso, and late twentieth century artists such as Miró and Jackson Pollock.

Behind the National Museum of Western Art is the **National Science Museum** (Kokuritsu Kagaku Hakubutsukan) which is open from 9:00 A.M. to 4:30 P.M. daily except for Mondays and December 28 through January 4, entry fee. Divided into various departments by typology, the museum tries to explore all the areas of modern science. It has five halls: the main hall, a natural history hall, an aerospace hall, a science and technology hall, and a science and engineering hall. A good guidebook to the collections, in English, may be purchased at its shop.

Across the way is the **Tokyo Metropolitan Art Museum** (Tokyo-to Bijutsukan), open from 9:00 A.M. to 5:00 P.M., closed the third Monday of the month and December 29 through January 3, entry fee. This red-brick building by Kunio Maekawa was opened in 1975, supplementing the earlier 1926 building. Housing an art school and studios, the museum displays the work of Japanese artists of recent decades (more than 2,600 items are in its collection) as well as offering rented space for temporary exhibitions, some occasionally showing Western art. The museum library has more than thirty thousand titles which may be used without charge. More than fifty percent of the building is underground so as not to intrude upon the park. In front of the building is the statue of Dr. Antonius Bauduin who, after the 1868 destruction of the Kan'ei-ji temple buildings, suggested that the grounds become a park.

To the left of the bust of Dr. Bauduin is the **Sogakudo,** the oldest concert hall in Japan, and the center for Western music when it was built in 1890 for the Tokyo School of Music. The Sogakudo introduced Western classical music to Japan. Scheduled for demolition, it was saved by public outcry because it was seen as a historic and satisfactory concert hall. The hall is open to tourists on Tuesdays, Thursdays, and Sundays from 9:30 A.M. to 4:30 P.M.

Continuing farther into the park, across the roadway is the huge **Ikeda Mansion Gate,** which once stood before the residence of the Ikeda Lords of Inaba (Tottori) in the Marunouchi district of the city until it was relocated here in 1954. An elaborate gateway, it has two guard houses with Chinese-style roofs. Beyond the gate are four museum buildings around a large central courtyard. These are the four units of the **Tokyo National Museum** (Kokuritsu Hakubutsukan), each one open from 9:00 A.M. to 4:30 P.M., closed on Mondays and December 29 through January 4, entry fee.

To the far left is the **Horyu-ji Treasure House,** a fireproof concrete building created in traditional *azekura* (log cabin) architectural style. In 1878, under pressure from the Meiji government during the period when Buddhism was being attacked by the government, the Horyu-ji temple made a "gift" of 319 items to the Imperial Household from its trove of ancient artistic treasures of masks, paintings, sculpture, ritual implements, and furniture. Labels are in both Japanese and English. This gift protected objects of inestimable historic worth when the art in many temples was being wantonly destroyed with government approval, and it also provided the temple with needed funds to guarantee its continued existence and necessary maintenance. This 1964 building is open only on Thursday, and then only if the weather is dry, so as to protect the ancient art within the building. The quality of these early rare and exquisite pieces is similar to that of items on view at the annual Shosoin exhibition in Nara.

On the left of the large courtyard with its fountain is the **Hyokeikan,** which was built to celebrate the marriage of the

Taisho Emperor in 1909. It is in the Beaux Arts style then fashionable in Europe and America. It contains archeological finds from Japan in its nine rooms, and it is noted for its *haniwa* tomb figures and artifacts from prehistoric Japan through to the 600s. One curiosity in the collection is the wooden figurehead of Erasmus from the wrecked Dutch ship *Liefde,* which stranded William Adams and Jan Joosten in Japan in 1600.

To the right of the large open courtyard, once the site of the residence of the abbot of the Kan'ei-ji, is the **Toyokan,** a 1968 ferroconcrete building by Yoshiro Taniguchi in traditional Japanese *azekura* architectural style, housing the art of other Asian nations. The collection numbers more than 87,000 objects from China, Korea, Thailand, India, and Central Asia. The building has a cafeteria open to the public.

The main building of the National Museum complex, the Honkan of 1937, is at the far end of the courtyard. It houses the main Japanese art collection, the finest and most extensive selection of Japanese art in the world. Among the various Japanese arts and crafts, this collection includes paintings, ceramics, textiles, metalwork, lacquerware, and calligraphy. The objects are so numerous that they are rotated periodically in the building's twenty-five exhibition rooms. In addition, two special exhibitions are offered each year, in April and May and then in October and November.

Behind the Toyokan is the **Jigendo,** or Rinno-ji, the Memorial Hall to Abbot Tenkai, who began the Kan'ei-ji temple in the early 1600s. His posthumous name is Jigen Daishi, thus the Jigen-do (*do* means hall), which was rebuilt in 1720 after a fire. It was one of the few buildings not destroyed in the 1868 battle. (The hall is also referred to as the Ryo Daishi (The Two Great Masters), the first being Abbot Tenkai and the second the tenth-century Priest Ryogen, whom Tenkai revered.) Recently, toward the end of the twentieth-century the main hall was rebuilt and a temple office and hall for religious use has been added to the right side of the main hall. Four bronze lanterns with spiral and dragon-faced decorations stand before the hall. The Kuro-mon (Black Gate) is one of two gateways into the complex. The one on the left, through which one enters, is the newer one. To the right of the bell tower is the original gateway which once stood before the abbot's residence. It was moved here in 1937 when the Honkan was built. Close examination shows the marks of the bullet holes it suffered in the 1868 battle of Ueno.

Turning to the right when leaving the Jigen-do eventually brings one to a cross street beyond the museum complex and to an entrance to the Keisei underground station. Ahead on the left is the **Tokyo University Art Museum** with an extensive collection of the arts of China and Japan. As a branch of a teaching university, its changing exhibitions often reflect the course of study in progress. Open from 10:00 A.M. to 4:00 P.M. Monday through Friday and from 10:00 A.M. to 12:30 P.M. on Saturdays, from April to mid-July and from September to mid-December, closed on university holidays, no entry fee.

A right turn at the Keisei rail entrance takes one past the university's Kuroda Hall and the Ueno library, where a monument to Lafcadio Hearn (also known as Yakumo Koizumi) pays tribute to the writer and early American admirer of Japan. A turn to the left at the road a little beyond the library brings one to the entrance to the **Kan'ei-ji** temple building. It is but a pale remembrance of the grandeur which once existed on Ueno Hill when the full temple was in existence. The temple cemeteries are on the right, beyond the hall. As indicated earlier, the temple was built by Priest Tenkai at the request of Shogun Hidetada in 1625 to "close" the Devil's Gate to the northeast of Edo. Tenkai had been active in the deification of Hidetada's father, Ieyasu, as a Shinto god after Ieyasu's death, and thus the abbot was able to rely on Hidetada to obtain funds for the temple from the daimyo of the nation.

The thirty-six temple halls and the thirty-six auxiliary buildings that resulted from Tenkai's efforts covered the hillside of Ueno. In 1647 the Emperor Go-Mizuno-o's third son was made abbot of the temple, and such royal leadership of great temples continued until the abolition of this practice by the Meiji government after 1868. The temple served the shogunate in an additional way, for the growing interest of the shogunate in the 1600s in Confucian doctrines led to the founding of the Confucian Academy on the temple grounds under the leadership of Hayashi Razan. This important academy was later moved to Yushima, where it remained until its dissolution.

The Kan'ei-ji temple buildings, with few exceptions, disappeared in the 1868 battle in the park. In 1879 the main hall of a temple (built in 1638) in Kawagoe, twenty-five miles away, was moved to what was left of the temple complex, but much of the land had been confiscated for the new Ueno Park. This newly relocated hall came from a large temple which had once been administered by Abbot Tenkai. The hall retains the original main image of the Kan'ei-ji, a Yakushi image of the Buddha of Health. It is a *hibutsu* (hidden image) that is never shown. Newer temple buildings lie behind the main hall. The last Tokugawa shogun retreated to a room in this temple after turning over power to the Emperor Meiji in Kyoto in October 1867. Tokugawa Yoshinobu retired here on February 12, 1868, not knowing what his fate would be under the new government. On April 4 he was pardoned. One week later Edo Castle passed to the Meiji government and Yoshinobu left for his family lands. Since he had surrendered power peacefully and had opposed the Ueno uprising, he was granted the title of prince. Called back from exile in 1911, he presided at the opening of the Nihombashi bridge. He died in 1913, outliving Emperor Meiji by one year. He is buried in an adjacent cemetery close to Nippori Station, less than a mile from the Kan'ei-ji temple grounds.

The land before the temple has been used as a graveyard. Here is a historical marker at the grave of Ogata Kenzan, brother of Ogata Korin. Kenzan died in 1743 and was known for his ceramic art. Nearby is a huge memorial stone, the Mushizuka, erected in 1820 as a memorial to all the insects killed to serve as models for the artistic work of Masuyama Kawachinokami Masakata, head of the Ise Nagashima clan. He is best known for his four-volume work on insect pictures. The artist died in 1820.

Behind the main building of the Kan'ei-ji temple and extending behind the National Museum complex is the Kan'ei-ji Reien, the three cemeteries in which six of the Tokugawa shoguns' remains were buried. The elaborate mausoleums to these rulers were destroyed in the 1945 bombing raids, thus only a portion of the gateway to the tomb of Tsunayoshi, the fifth shogun (1680–1709), with its carved lions, remains (most easily seen from the road behind the National Museum main building). In the second cemetery, behind the National Museum, is the gate to the mausoleum of Shogun Ietsuna (1651–80), the predecessor to Tsunayoshi. Just the stone wall with bronze plaques and the remains of the gates are left to remind one of the former grandeur of the tombs which once housed the remains of the six shoguns interred here. The grounds are open to the public from 9:00 A.M. to sunset.

On leaving Kan'ei-ji, a turn to the right brings one to Kototoi-dori. Opposite is the **Jomyo-in** temple. Built in 1666, this was once one of thirty-six such residences for priests of Kan'ei-ji. The *hondo* of the temple is an unattractive, square, reinforced concrete unit, but the Jizo images to the left of the entry gate, including a large seated Jizo made of bronze, are of interest. In the mid-nineteenth century the abbot of the temple vowed to erect in his temple grounds one thousand images of Jizo, the Buddhist deity protecting children, the dead, pregnant women, and travelers. Having succeeded, he then vowed to increase the number to 84,000 Jizo images. Time ran out on the devout abbot, and the attempt by his successors to reach that elusive goal continues. Each image is numbered, and it is said that the count now reaches beyond twenty thousand.

Each August 15 by the lunar calendar the temple holds the very popular Sponge Gourd Service. It is for those suffering with coughs and asthma, and the grounds of the temple are exceedingly crowded at this time with people seeking relief from their ailment.

A turn to the right when leaving the Jomyo-in leads along Kototoi-dori and brings one after the third traffic light to an addition to the Shitamachi Museum. At the corner of the street is the **Yoshida-ya,** a former saké shop from 1910, a traditional-style building of the late Meiji era which appears to be much older. Within are the bottles, straw-wrapped wooden kegs, and porcelain jugs which contained the alcoholic beverages that delighted Tokugawa and Meiji patrons. The museum-shop is open from 9:30 A.M. to 4:30 P.M., closed on Mondays, no entry fee.

Continuing along Kototoi-dori, at Shinobazu-dori, which has an entrance to Nezu Subway Station, turn right on the far side of the street and walk approximately ten minutes to the fourth street and then turn to the left to arrive at **Nezu Shrine.** A sign at the traffic light indicates that this is the crossing for the shrine. Noted for its attractiveness, Nezu Shrine has a long row of vermilion torii on the hillside leading to a shrine to the goddess Inari. The Nezu Shrine itself honors the sixth Tokugawa shogun, Ienobu (1709–12), who succeeded his uncle Tsunayoshi, the Dog Shogun. Tsunayoshi was not only deeply religious but deeply superstitious. Born in the Year of the Dog, he forbade the killing of dogs under penalty of death. The first thing his successor did was to abrogate such senseless laws, and under Shogun Ienobu's more enlightened rule for the first time the offspring of the Imperial Household were permitted to choose a profession other than that of the temple priests or nuns.

At the tutelary shrine of Shogun Ienobu the grounds are entered through a torii, a pond on the right. The two-story vermilion main gate of Nezu Shrine is similar to that at the Asakusa Kaminari-mon gateway, and this reveals a Buddhist influence. The shrine was created at the time when Buddhism and Shintoism were often allied, a situation destroyed by the Meiji rulers after 1868. The swastika symbol on many of the lamps within the shrine grounds also indicates a heavy Buddhist influence. The

Shinto protectors of the shrine, Udaijin and Sadaijin with their swords and bows and arrows, are on guard in the gateway.

Beyond the main gate, a *kagura* stage for religious dances is on the right while a roofed purification fountain is on the left. Then comes the inner gate, a one-story vermilion gate in the Chinese style, before the shrine main hall, which contains paintings of the thirty-six classical poets. Purification by a priest is necessary before entering this restricted area. This hall is connected to the *haiden,* which stands before the *honden,* where the spirit of the sixth shogun is enshrined. The faces of the beams of this structure are carved in the form of mythical animals while carved pine and plum tree branches enhance the building. Damaged in the air raids of the Second World War, the shrine has been lovingly restored. Its ponds, trees, and three thousand azaleas that bloom in April and May all contribute to a shrine which understandably has been listed as one of the three Important Cultural Properties in Tokyo.

Returning to Shinobazu-dori, one can take the subway at Nezu Station at the Kototoi-dori intersection (Chiyoda Line) to one's next destination.

One other artist's house in the area to the north of Ueno Park is that of Fumio Asakura. It is worth a visit. The house lies to the west of Nippori Station on the Yamanote Line, two stations after Ueno Station. Nippori translates into "Village Living from One Day to the Next." The station should be exited from the front of the train and then the street to the left of the station should be taken. Walking westward from the station to the first through street on the left, a turn to the left will bring one to the **Asakura Chosokan,** an unprepossessing black structure at first glance. The house and sculpture gallery are open from 9:30 A.M. to 4:30 P.M. except on Mondays and Fridays, entry fee. Obviously a disciple of Rodin, Asakura created some four hundred statues during his career. The building is entered through a modern wing which holds some of the artist's sculpture.

The interior of the house and its attractive garden continually bring visitors to this building. A traditional Japanese home surrounding a garden, its tatami-matted tea room overlooks the garden with its pond, islands, ferns, small bushes, and stepping stones. The garden is ideal for a stroll. An iron kettle steams over a small charcoal fire in a traditional burner. It is the house in which the artist lived from 1908 until his death in 1964 at age eighty-one.

The less than attractive black exterior of the house is actually of a practical design and reflects the fact that the studio wing of the complex has been created in reinforced concrete as a protection against fire and earthquakes while the living quarters, easily the main attraction, are made of wood and bamboo and are in the traditional *sukiya* style. The first room to visit is the studio with its lofty ceiling. Here are examples of Asakura's work, some life-size, some greater than life-size, some of nudes. One huge statue of a man in academic cap and gown is of Shigenobu Okuma, a statesman who was also the founder of Waseda University. Another statue of a tall man is that of Shinpei Goto, another statesman and former mayor of Tokyo. The second room is the library with its many books reaching to the ceiling, a number of them in English, including bound copies of *Studio* magazine. The third room is the guestroom with chairs, a couch, and additional books as well as a display of the tools the artist used. A human skeleton and the skeleton of a cat that he used for the study of anatomy are also in this room.

The enclosed garden in the center of the residence is the Goten-no-Suitei, a Japanese landscape garden which incorporates water to symbolize the five Confucianist precepts of benevolence, justice, propriety, wisdom, and fidelity. The water comes from a natural spring. All the rooms surrounding the garden on both floors are tatami-matted, so shoes must be removed before entering these quarters. At the rear on the first floor are the original office and studio of the artist before the 1936 addition of the larger studio. There is a kitchen with its *kamidana* shrine up high to the kitchen gods. A living room and a tea ceremony room with a *tokonoma* (alcove) follow, and then the bedroom with a display of Asakura's kimono.

The staircase to the upper floor has a rustic handrail and an internal "moon" window. Of the two rooms on this floor, the first has a large, low, bright red Chinese lacquered table while the second room is the Poised Mind Room with a *tokonoma,* and a low table with an inlaid mother-of-pearl traditional scene. Old bronzes and ceramics are displayed on a shelf. The third floor also has two rooms, the larger of which is the Morning Sun Room, which contains a huge round table created from two exceedingly large pieces of wood. The ceiling's wood planking is unusually attractive. A corridor runs along two sides of the Morning Sun Room with *shoji* (paper sliding doors) to cut the corridor off from the room if so desired. The outer walls have windows of glass which can be covered with draperies for privacy. An excellent English-language pamphlet concerning the house and its collections is available at the ticket counter.

Much of the city between Nippori Station and Nezu Station has remained untouched by the destruction of 1923 and 1945, and the area is worth a stroll to see a portion of a traditional residential area which is rare in modern Tokyo. The street from the railway station leads down to the subway line in time, and along the way is a local street of fascinating shops. Nezu Station (Chiyoda Line) can be taken into town—or one could always return directly from the artist's house to Nippori Station (Yamanote Line) for a return to the center of Tokyo.

TOUR
❖ 10 ❖

Yushima, Kanda, Akihabara, Jimbocho, Korakuen, and Tokyo University

WHEN one looks at a topographic map of Tokyo, the hills of the High City stick out like fingers into the riverine land of the *shitamachi*. The Yushima and Kanda areas encompass both the high and low sectors, and this tour will alternate between the slightly raised plateau as well as the former meadowland of the city.

Here are ancient shrines to men of valor in centuries past as well as to failed usurpers of the throne. The wisdom of Confucius is enshrined not far from the major universities which continue to search for wisdom of a type unknown to Confucius. Modern shrines to the inventive spirit of the industrial age of the nineteenth and the twentieth centuries can be found in a museum of transportation as well as in the commercial marts in Akihabara where discounts are proclaimed on every corner. Then there is the realm of scholarly bookstores beloved by students and academics, which is followed by another loved retreat of a former Tokugawa lord known as the "Garden of Pleasure Last."

Yushima Station on the Chiyoda Subway Line is where this tour begins. Using exit No. 1 in the subway, turning right at the street and crossing Kasuga-dori, turn right and continue walking uphill on Kasuga-dori with the shrine on the left side of the street. A turn to the left beyond the shrine, since the entrance is down a side street, brings one to the **Yushima Tenjin** shrine, the Yushima Shrine to the God of Heaven. Although the shrine goes back to the fourteenth century, it has burned down many times, and as a result the present buildings date from 1885. It was one of the victims of the 1657 Long Sleeves Fire when monks at the nearby Honmyo-ji temple, just to the northwest of the Yushima Tenjin shrine, burned two long-sleeved kimonos that had been worn by three young women who had died suddenly. After the "cursed" kimonos were set on fire, a strong wind took the embers far and wide, leading to the destruction of much of the city. More than 1,200 houses and 350 temples were destroyed with 108,000 lives lost. The houses of most of the working populace were consumed by flames. Ironically, the next day it snowed.

On a ridge or bluff above the Kiridoshi Slope, the Yushima Tenjin shrine can be reached either by way of the steeper "male" slope to the right of the main hall or the easier "female" slopes. Kasuga-dori provides one of the female and gentler slopes; another such slope will be used when the shrine visit ends. The shrine is said to have been created in 1355 and then restored in the 1400s by Ota Dokan, the founder of the city of Edo. It is dedicated to the ninth-century statesman Sugawara-no-Michizane who was posthumously enshrined as the deity of scholarship. Being as near as it is to Tokyo University and not too far from the other universities south of the Kanda River, it is a favorite among the students who come to petition for divine help in their academic studies.

There was a time when this area was a favorite of the priests of Kan'ei-ji temple and its many sub-temples not far away on Ueno Hill. These men favored the "teahouses" of the area that were served by adolescent boys. The Tokugawa shogunate tried unsuccessfully on various occasions to rid the area of male prostitution, and the Meiji authorities were intent on cleansing the area at the foot of the Yushima Tenjin shrine of these "teahouses in the shadows" as well as the geisha quarter that existed here. The Meiji zeal was occasioned by a concern for the nearby growing Tokyo University, for they wanted the students to concentrate on their studies if Japan was to be an equal with the nations of the West, and not to dally with the *divertissements* of these traditional quarters. One can imagine what success the Meiji leaders encountered, for even today the latest version of an old story can be recognized in the "love hotels" of the area.

The students did flock to Yushima's Shrine of Literature, as it was known, and the area's other attractions, for here they could write their wishes for success on *ema,* small wooden plaques, and then hang them on the overloaded shrine racks in the hopes that Sugawara-no-Michizane, the deity of students and scholars, would smile upon them. While the shrine is quite ancient, its structures are more recent, its bronze torii being about two hundred years old and its main hall dating only to 1885. The shrine had many devotees, not only of its deity but of the lottery which the temple once sponsored, one of three such approved lotteries under the Tokugawas. There is as well another attraction in the springtime, and that is the flowering of the shrine's plum trees from mid-February to mid-March. The plum tree was a favorite of Michizane, and one of them is said to have been so moved by one of his poems, written in exile, that it flew from Kyoto to Kyushu to be near him. The plum trees of Edo, perhaps of a more austere nature, remained in place, and their red and white blossoms are the finest of any plum tree group in Tokyo today. The trees were planted as gifts from area residents. The Ume Matsuri (Plum Tree Festival) is held in February and March.

In late October and November the shrine boasts exquisite displays of chrysanthemums, some of them arranged as human figures in tableaux of the Heian period (794–1185). Court ladies, romantic courtiers, and scenes of the past are recreated in chrysanthemum blossoms.

There are two entrances to the shrine leading off Kasuga-dori. The first, with a stone torii, is the minor entry. The main entrance is further along the street, and a bronze-plated torii marks it. Entering through the minor gate, a modern hall with offices and reception halls is to the left. On the right is a garden with a pond. Past the garden is a large rack to hold *ema* plaques, a rack so loaded with the prayers of students and others that it would seem it might topple to the ground. Behind it is the main hall of the Yushima Tenjin shrine, complemented on the right by a *kagura* stage for religious dances and ceremonies. After exploring the shrine, the grounds can be left by walking straight away from the main hall, noticing on the left, however, the "lost child" stone similar to one which stood on the Nihombashi bridge. The stone still stands in place, even though it is a much later replacement. On the left is a steep staircase, the "male slope" leading from the plateau down to the lower city. Continuing straight ahead from the main hall, one exits the grounds through the bronze torii. A final item to note is the marker just beyond the gate detailing the history of the shrine.

On departing Yushima Tenjin shrine, the street leading south eventually crosses Kuramae-dori, a broad, heavily trafficked street, which has a traffic light. Beyond Kuramae-dori, a street on the left uphill brings one to the front of the **Kanda Myojin** shrine. Located on the same hill as the Tenjin shrine, it looks out over the *shitamachi* to the east. It too has its very sharp "male" slope of steep steps as well as a less harshly inclined "female" slope. While the shrine is said to have been founded as early as 730, it has only been on its present location since 1616. In 730 it would have been solely dedicated to the deity Okuninushi-no-Mikoto, the great deity descended from Susano-o-no-Mikoto and who is the resident deity of Izumo, one of the two most important shrines in Japan. The Kanda Myojin shrine originally was located in the Otemachi area near Edo Castle. It was a most popular shrine since it also had a local hero of the 900s, Taira-no-Masakado, who had later been enshrined here as well. The original shrine was at the spot in *shitamachi* where Masakado's decapitated head is said to have flown in 940 from Kyoto (as described in Tour 2) so as to join his body after his death, a death which was brought about because of his abortive attempt to declare himself the emperor of Japan.

In 1616 Tokugawa Ieyasu had the shrine moved from the lowlands to this eminence, ostensibly to use the shrine site for better securing his castle with its moats and walls. No doubt he was also moving the spirit of a man who had rebelled against established authority, an attitude Ieyasu certainly would not permit. Masakado remained the popular deity with the townspeople despite this move, for they respected his revolt against authority, an attitude they could appreciate but dared not emulate. They could show their affection for this onetime rebel in the great festival which grew up with the shrine. Its *matsuri* (festival) is the oldest of the three great festivals of Tokyo, and in Edo times it was even permitted to pass through the grounds of Edo Castle both as an honor to the townspeople and to permit the denizens of the castle to enjoy the spectacle.

There was a political aspect to the festival as well, for it was held on the fifteenth day of the ninth month, the anniversary of the Battle of Sekigahara in which Tokugawa Ieyasu was victorious over all of his enemies and could thereafter assume complete civil control of Japan. There were thirty-six large floats drawn through the town by oxen, musicians playing from their vantage point atop the floats. Portable *mikoshi* (sacred palanquins) followed. Most of these major floats were destroyed in the 1923 earthquake and fire.

Since that time the Kanda Festival has been moved to May 14 and 15 and is held on alternate years from those in which the Hie Festival takes place, the Kanda festivities occurring in odd-numbered years. Today, three replicas of the emperor's palanquin and seventy-six *mikoshi* on wheeled carts parade through the streets of Otemachi, Marunouchi, and Kanda, the participants clothed in the garb of Heian times (794–1185). Once there were very large festival carts, but these are no longer practical components of a parade in as congested and traffic-ridden a city as Tokyo. Out of season, the shrine *mikoshi* are kept in the *mikoshi* hall to the left of the shrine main hall.

If Ieyasu had his misgivings about a shrine to a rebel so close to his castle, the Meiji authorities were equally queasy about Kanda Myojin. The emperor had been seen in 1868 as the actual ruler of Japan, and the authorities were disturbed when the emperor went to the shrine to do his obeisance to a somewhat questionable deity beloved by the common citizen. Thus they decreed that the spirit of the rebel Masakado had to be removed from the main hall of the shrine and placed in a separate building. The main hall was destroyed in the 1923 earthquake and in 1934, when the older generation of Meiji advisers were gone from the scene, the shrine was rebuilt in ferroconcrete, and at this time Masakado's spirit was returned to his rightful place in the main hall. The shrine was recreated in the ostentatious *gongen* style, an action which, no doubt, would not have pleased the Meiji elders since this was the style favored by their Tokugawa predecessors.

The shrine is entered through a copper-plated torii and then through the two-story, vermilion Zuishin-mon main gateway (refurbished in 1976) with the Shinto guardians on either side of the passageway, the rear niche of the gateway holding the figure of a horse. At the foot of the hill below this main gateway is a large stone torii, and between the two gates there were once traditional shops selling bean paste, pickles, and sweet saké; it is still possible to buy sweet saké with ground ginger in some adjacent shops. Beyond the two-story gateway a *kagura* dance stage is to the left, a gift of the founder of the Matsushita Electric Company, Konosuke Matsushita.

On the right stands a very large statue of Daikoku astride rice bales and with the traditional hammer in his right hand. Daikoku is a popular *kami,* or deity, since he is concerned with the exploitation of land, the development of industry and commercial success, as well as of medicine. He is enshrined here together with Ebisu, who offers protection to commercial enterprises as well. These two figures helped to popularize the shrine in Tokugawa and later times. Beyond the statue of Daikoku is the purification fountain with a crouching dragon from whose mouth a stream of water flows into a basin. On the far right is a long building containing offices and reception halls. A Lion Mountain was created in 1990 between this hall and the main shrine hall to celebrate the enthronement of the emperor. This rock "mountain" has water cascading down it and is graced by two stone lions from 1716.

Two stone lions stand before the prayer hall of the shrine, the figure of a white horse standing to the right side of it since such white horses are favored by Shinto deities. To the left and behind the main hall are small shrines to various Shinto deities, and two *kura* (storage buildings) holding the *mikoshi* of Kanda Myojin. One of these *kura* has glass doors so that the *mikoshi,* large golden dragon heads resting on either side, may be seen.

Once one could look from the plateau on which Kanda Myojin sits to the *shitamachi* area below the shrine. Today the high-rise buildings of modern Tokyo tend to disguise the difference between the two levels of this portion of the Kanda district. As with Yushima Tenjin shrine, Kanda Myojin is noted for its plum blossoms in March and also for its wisteria in May.

Leaving Kanda Myojin through its front gateway, descending to the major Hongo-dori and crossing the street, one is at the rear of **Yushima Seido** shrine (Yushima Sacred Hall). Walking down the side street on the left side of the shrine, the entrance to the shrine can be found at the southeast corner. Yushima Seido had been created in 1632 on the grounds of the Kan'ei-ji temple in Ueno (approximately where the statue to Takamori Saigo now stands) as a hall in which the Confucian classics could be studied. The influence of neo-Confucianism, as Tokugawa Confucianism was known, was to become important since by the 1600s Buddhism had become an establishment which had lost much of its spiritual influence, and Shintoism was so simple a faith, virtually a nature worship, that it did not offer intellectual challenge to the Tokugawa samurai. It was Hayashi Razan (1587–1657), a scholar of the Confucian classics, who was able to reinterpret Confucianism to satisfy the intellectual needs of the period. His version of Confucianism offered a basis for ethics, and it provided a theory of governance which seemed to bolster the political presuppositions of the Tokugawas. Thus Razan's neo-Confucianism became the new ideology of the state, for it omitted the metaphysics of Chinese tradition while reinforcing the elements of government that gave a basis to the feudal system of obedience to one's superior.

The hall for the study of Confucianism was created in 1632 at the Kan'ei-ji temple in Ueno, and in 1691 the devout Shogun Tsunayoshi moved it to its present location where in the second half of the eighteenth century it became an academy for the ruling elite of the Tokugawa regime, much as the University of Tokyo has been in the twentieth century. In fact, in 1872, the first teacher training institute set up by the Meiji government had its origins here, and that new institute was to burgeon in time into the University of Tokyo, not too far to the north in the Hongo district, just beyond Yushima Tenjin shrine.

At the entrance to the grounds of the shrine is the large stone Nyutoku Gate with bronze doors. The pistachio tree at the entrance had significance for those coming to the shrine, for it grew from a cutting from a tree at Confucius' grave. A ferroconcrete office building is on the right, winged dogs decorating its roof. Behind the building is a larger-than-life statue of Confucius. It was in this area that the Shoheizaka College of Confucian Studies existed in Tokugawa times.

Steps to the left of the image of Confucius lead uphill to the main shrine building on a higher level. Here is a large wooden gate, and behind it to the right is the water purification basin, the only two items which survived the 1923 earthquake. Many broad steps lead up to a very large three-part gateway in the front corridor. The corridor surrounds three sides of an inner courtyard, the shrine building itself forming the fourth portion of the court. The dark bronze building with its five massive doors is most impressive. Large roosters surmount the roof of the shrine and two "devil dogs" appear on either side of the roof as well.

This main hall enshrines the spirit of Confucius. Called the Taisei-den, (The Hall of Accomplishment), it was later rebuilt in the Chinese Ming style in 1935 (the earthquake destroyed the former hall). The image of Confucius flanked by his main disciples within the hall was an Imperial gift. The plain building has the heads of devil dogs instead of the traditional dolphins found atop other official buildings of the period. The grounds, which offer access to the statue of Confucius, may be entered on Saturdays, Sundays, and national holidays from 9:30 A.M. to 5:00 P.M., entry fee. The courtyard and Taisei-den, the main hall, may be entered only on Sundays from 10:00 A.M. to 3:00 P.M. Ties between the Chinese Nationalist Government and the shrine have been close, and a building beside the main gateway has reproductions of items in the Taipei National Palace Museum, a gift of the Lions' Club of Taipei. The shrine is no longer connected with the Japanese government, and it is operated by a private organization on the government's behalf. Today it is only a shrine. The Confucian academy no longer exists.

Mounting the steps that lead from the shrine to the street, one crosses Hijiribashi (The Bridge of the Sages) and the Kanda River, a onetime outer moat of Edo Castle. A plaque on the far side of the bridge shows what the earlier bridge looked like. On the far shore of the bridge is the district of Ochanomizu (Honorable Tea Water), so named from a spring of fine water which once existed here. The water was brought to Edo Castle daily because its sweet taste enhanced the shogun's tea. In the distance to the right is the twenty-one story Century Tower. This twin-towered structure was built in 1991 by Sir Norman Foster, whose skyscraper work in Hong Kong has brought him fame. The Century Tower is supported by a huge steel frame on the exterior of the building, thereby freeing the interior of any columns. In the basement of the building is the **Century Museum** featuring Asian art. There is also a museum store here. The museum is open from 9:30 A.M. to 4:30 P.M. except on Sundays, entry fee.

The hill on the other side of the Kanda River has been known as Surugadai, for after Ieyasu's death, land in this area was given to a number of his followers originally from the Suruga area near Shizuoka. Since the 1880s it has been home to more than two dozen educational institutions, some of which, such as Chuo University, have now moved out of the center of the city in order to expand. At the foot of the hill is the Jimbocho district of bookstores and publishers, a natural outgrowth of the educational purposes of this hillside.

Just one street beyond the bridge is **Nikolai Cathedral,** the Russian Orthodox Cathedral built by Ioan Kasatkin (1836–1912). Kasatkin came to Japan in 1861 as a missionary of the Russian Orthodox Church, and he lived here for the next fifty-one years. The 1884 cathedral, which was under construction from 1876, is the largest of the churches Kasatkin built. Josiah Conder was the architect for the building, using plans which came from St. Petersburg. The building originally had a much larger dome, but it collapsed in the 1923 earthquake, and a smaller, flatter dome, 128 feet high, replaced the more traditional and larger Russian onion-dome. The cathedral is open without charge from 1:00 P.M. to 4:00 P.M. Tuesdays through Saturdays. The cathedral bells are rung at 10:00 A.M. and 12:30 P.M. on Sundays only, from the ninety-five-foot-high bell tower, providing what was an unusual sound in the later nineteenth and early twentieth century in this part of Tokyo.

Leaving the cathedral, turn to the left. At the end of the street another left and then a right turn takes one down a narrow street to Ochanomizu-dori. This area has the many buildings of Meiji University, and across the street to the right is the building which holds two of the university's public exhibits. In the Daigaku Kaikan Building (University Hall or Ogawamachi School Building) is the **Meiji University Archeological Museum** (Meiji Daigaku Kokogaku Hakubutsukan), open from 10:00 A.M. to 5:00 P.M., closed Saturday afternoons, Sundays, and university holidays; open August–September from 10:00 A.M. to 3:30 P.M., no entry fee. The museum exhibits artifacts from the Japanese Jomon period (before 200 B.C.) and *haniwa* figures from the Kofun tomb period (A.D. 250–538). Archeological items from Korea and China are also in the collection of more than ten thousand artifacts. The exhibits are labeled in English and Japanese, and the maps and photographs offer further information. (The museum is probably too specialized to be of interest to the average visitor.) In the same building is the **Criminal Museum,** which is open from 10:00 A.M. to 4:30 P.M., closed Saturday afternoons, Sundays, and every afternoon from July 10 through August 31, no entry fee. The collection includes instruments used in capturing criminals in the Edo period, as well as instruments of torture and execution.

On leaving the museum building, turning to the right and

walking down Ochanomizu-dori takes one past the major buildings of Meiji University and eventually down to Yasukuni-dori. At
that intersection the area to the left is filled with sporting goods
discount shops while the area to the right from Surugadai-shita
all along Yasukuni-dori, primarily on the south side of the
avenue, is the bookstore area of **Jimbocho** with approximately
one hundred bookshops. Along the far side of the street to the
right is the Sanseido bookstore with a huge stock of books in
various European languages. The Charles E. Tuttle bookshop is
farther along the street with its many books in English on Japan
and East Asia. The Issei-do shop with its Egyptian-style façade
follows with books on East Asia, *ukiyo-e* prints, and books on art.
Many of these shops have special sales in October and November,
and they are generally open throughout the year from 9:00 A.M.
to 7:00 P.M. Many of the bookshops, however, close on the first
and third Monday of the month.

After an exploration of the Jimbocho district, the Toei Shinjuku
subway train can be taken from Jimbocho Station one stop to
Ogawamachi Station. Five short streets along Yasukuni-dori, in
the direction the train had been taking, brings one to the
Transportation Museum. It is a building which is hard to miss, for
not many structures have a Bullet Train and an old-fashioned
steam engine sticking out of their fabric. Open from Tuesday
through Sunday from 9:30 A.M. to 4:30 P.M., it is closed Mondays
and from December 29 through January 3, entry fee. The
museum includes trains, planes, and automobiles. The first floor
offers trains ranging from model train layouts to actual engines.
One can even simulate driving a train here. The second floor is
devoted to automobiles, while the third floor covers aviation. The
fourth floor contains a library, rest rooms, and a small restaurant
with a limited menu. Late nineteenth-century locomotives from
England and America are on display outside the building, and
the collection is a delight since it includes the first engine to pull
a train between Yokohama and Shinagawa in 1872 as well as the
1877 carriage of Emperor Meiji and the 1916 carriage of the

Emperor Taisho. This is a museum with items of interest for visitors of all ages.

Leaving the museum and walking under the overhead railway tracks on to Chuo-dori and crossing the bridge over the Kanda River leads to the **Akihabara** district with its hundreds of discount shops. Its name, "Akihabara" (The Field of Autumn Leaves), belies its modern commercial nature. What began as a black-market district after the Second World War has grown into a gigantic discount center for modern communications equipment and supplies. Chuo-dori for the next number of streets is lined with a variety of these discount shops, large and small, as are the side alleys and the area under the railroad line. The larger ones offer tourist discounts in their tax-free shops on the showing of a passport. Adjacent to Akihabara Station is the Akihabara Department Store, a normal department store in every respect, except that it also has a wide array of electronic goods that compete with its neighboring discount rivals. Bargaining is a possibility in most of the shops in the district, particularly the smaller ones. Given the pricing situation in Japan, many of the goods sold in the district can usually be bought for less in some of the discount stores of Hong Kong and New York.

For a change of pace, the Chuo Rail Line overhead at Akihabara can be taken to Iidabashi Station for a visit to the **Koishikawa Korakuen Garden.** Leaving Iidabashi Station from the rear, crossing over to the sidewalk under the overhead expressway, and following the expressway to the right brings one after two streets to signs indicating that the Korakuen Garden is to the left. The entrance to the garden is two streets past the Korakuen Hotel. The garden is open from 9:00 A.M. to 5:00 P.M., closed Mondays, entry fee.

The Korakuen Garden today is but a pale reflection of what once was here during the Tokugawa period when this was the estate of the Mito branch of the Tokugawa clan. Then it was three times the size of the present eighteen-acre landscaped park. In 1629 the garden was constructed by Yorifusa, the eleventh son of

Tokugawa Ieyasu and founder of the Mito branch of the Tokugawa clan. It took thirty years to complete this stroll garden in the *tsukiyama* style. The elements of design were meant to reflect classical scenes in Chinese and Japanese culture. It was named Korakuen (The Garden of Pleasure Last), based on the Confucian belief that a gentleman scholar should be concerned with the commonweal first and with his own pleasure only thereafter.

The Korakuen garden was in earlier times a large, shallow lake, an arm of Tokyo Bay, but once the arm of the bay was filled in, the garden preserved a portion of water for an ornamental lake and ponds. Yorifusa's son Mitsukuni continued the work on the garden, and the lake was created by the third shogun, Iemitsu. The miniature lakes and hills were intended to recall a number of classical scenic sites: Mount Lu Shan in China, the famed scenic West Lake in China, and the Togetsukyo bridge of Arashiyama in western Kyoto. An isle in the lake with its shrine to Benten, the Shinto goddess, recalls a shrine on Chikubu Island in Lake Biwa. With its winding paths, stone lanterns, arched bridges, small teahouse, and a small Confucian temple, it was the most noted garden in all of Edo. All those elements which compose the garden and give it greater significance are made more understandable if one purchases the color guide in English. The estate of the Mitos was taken over by the government after 1868, and in 1936 it was given to the city as a public park. The park is rarely crowded, thus it is often possible to enjoy it in comparative solitude.

One cannot escape the amusement and sports center which has been developed on what was once the full extent of the Korakuen Garden, just across the Kanda River from Suidobashi Station. On leaving the garden, the street which parallels the river should be followed toward the "Yellow Building" which is difficult to miss, with its yellow and orange striped façade. Ten stories tall with a glass elevator, the building is dedicated to the sporting life with its bowling, boxing, and wrestling facilities. Behind it is Korakuen Hall with additional sports facilities, including a pool which doubles in winter as a golf driving range. The original and only major facility on the site in 1936 was a baseball stadium. These additional sporting opportunities are post-1950 additions. The original baseball field was torn down to make way for the Tokyo Dome, built in 1988. The dome is affectionately referred to by Tokyoites as the "Big Egg." Home of the Yomiuri Giants, it can seat fifty thousand spectators under its inflatable dome. Soccer, football, and events other than baseball take place here too.

Baseball has become a Japanese addiction. Golf is another addiction, but only the well-to-do can afford the greens fees, and thus baseball games in large stadiums are available to a mass population. Baseball began in Japan in the early Meiji Period, not too long after its beginnings in the United States. Schools and universities in Japan first played the game, and by 1903 Waseda and Keio universities were competing against each other. The game was taken so seriously, and the attitude of the fans became so dangerous that in 1906 the games between the two universities had to be suspended. While the game resembles the American sport, it has become thoroughly Japanese, and it is a team sport in which the individual star is submerged.

The adjacent 1955 **Korakuen Amusement Park** offers more than two dozen rides, parachute drops, and a 328-foot revolving observation tower. Thus Korakuen offers not only an amusement park for children but activities like bowling, swimming, ice skating, bicycling, and swimming. There's also a hall for judo (practice can be watched between 3:00 and 5:00 P.M. by applying to the reception desk at the Kodokan Judo Hall), and for the non-sportsman, there are several cinemas.

Korakuen Station (Marunouchi Subway Line) lies behind the "Big Egg," and it can be entered from the street beyond the Tokyo Dome. From here one can return to the center of the city. Those interested in visiting **Tokyo University** can get off after one stop at Hongo-sanchome Station to walk north on Hongo-dori, crossing Kasuga-dori, to the university entrance at the Aka-mon

(Red Gate), once the entry to the grounds of the mansion of the Maeda lords of Kaga. (Until 1923 a branch of the Maeda family still dwelt in a corner of the old estate.) In 1827, one of Shogun Ienari's fifty-five offspring married into the Maeda family, and this gate was built in celebration of the event. It remains intact today.

The university, as with many urban universities, is not that notable an architectural site. Perhaps its most famous building in the last half of the twentieth century was Yasuda Hall, where in 1968 students barricaded themselves in the battle against the police and other forces. A virtual army besieged the campus at that time and all learning came to a temporary end. The Yasuda Lecture Hall was burned in the ensuing riot, and it has remained as a shell as a reminder of more tumultuous times. On the campus is the University Museum, a six-story museum divided into numerous sub-sections and providing space for changing exhibitions. The monthly guide pamphlet available at the Tourist Information Center downtown and in most hotels lists the current special exhibition.

The university is more familiarly known by its contracted name of Todai (short for Tokyo Daigaku or Tokyo University). It is the most important university in Japan, and many of its graduates can be found in the halls of the bureaucracy, which truly runs the Japanese government. Its 20,000 students are split into various colleges, a number of which have been moved away from the original 1880 campus as enrollment has demanded more space for classes. Law and engineering remain at the main campus. The area to the north of the campus is the Yayoi district, thus named because artifacts from earlier times have been unearthed here and Yayoi is the name of a prehistoric period in Japanese history. A monument on the far (back) side of the university grounds commemorates this find.

Those who make this extra diversion to the university campus can return to Hongo-sanchome for the subway back to the center of the city.

TOUR

■ 11 ■

Atago Shrine, Zojo-ji, Tokyo Tower, Shiba Detached Palace Garden, Sengaku-ji

泉岳寺　旧芝離宮庭園　東京タワー　増上寺　愛宕神社

TOUR 11 encompasses much of the history of old Edo as well as modern Tokyo. The tour recalls the procession of daimyo along the old Tokaido Road from 1632 as well as the 1860s to the final conclusion to the tale of the Forty-Seven Ronin, which has delighted Bunraku and Kabuki aficionados for two centuries and has been held up as an example of samurai loyalty. There is, as well, a tower taller than the Eiffel Tower, from which one can view much of Tokyo.

We start at Kamiyacho Station on the Hibiya Subway Line. From the station from the rear of the train, the first street on the right which goes under Atago Hill through a tunnel should be taken to the north-south street beyond. A left turn here brings one farther along that street to a torii in front of a very steep set of steps to the **Atago Shrine** on a hill eighty-five feet above sea level. Noted for its cherry trees, it is approached by the "male" slope of 85 steps, the adjacent "female" slope of 113 steps being just slightly easier to mount. Two bronze lions guard the approach to the "male slope."

Once a view of the city and Tokyo Bay could be observed from the height of the hill, but modern buildings now preclude the visitor from enjoying such a vista. The Atago Shrine, its teahouse, gardens, stream, small shrine to Benten (on a little island in a tiny pond), and another shrine to Inari all make the hill a delightful spot. The deity of the shrine is the god who protects against fire, a needed deity, given the continuous succession of the "Flowers of Edo" which burned the city to the ground on too many occasions. Unfortunately, the deity was unable to protect his own shrine, for it went up in flames during a 1945 air raid. The present shrine building is a 1948 reconstruction.

Political and destructive events have marked the history of this site. It was here that the eighteen samurai from Mito prayed before setting out to kill Lord Ii Naosuke, the shogun's chief adviser, one snowy day in March 1860. Not too many years later it was here on March 13, 1868, that the leader of the Tokugawa forces met with Saigo Takamori of the imperial army in an attempt to avert an attack on the city by the imperial forces. Pointing out the city, temples, and shrines below, Saigo was cautioned that an attack could see the whole city destroyed by fire in the resulting battle. Common sense ruled on both sides, and thus the city was surrendered with no loss of life or destruction other than what occurred in Ueno by Tokugawa hold-outs one month later. A less happy event occurred here on August 22, 1945, when ten imperial soldiers committed suicide jointly on the loss of the Second World War at the defeat of Japan.

Taking the female slope with its broader steps and more gentle landings, one finds at the top of the hill a modern one-story shrine office. On the left is a pond with a blue torii in its far end and multicolored carp swimming in the water. A small rivulet runs into the pond, and to the right of the rivulet are shrines on either side of the small waterway. The near shrine is preceded by two red torii while the farther shrine is approached through a bronze-plated torii and then a blue-painted torii. Beyond, at the head of the male slope, is a stone torii leading to a roofed, vermilion torii with solid doors. Large bronze lanterns stand before the main shrine building. The shrine has a small *mikoshi* on the right in its *haiden,* while on either side of the unit are large pictures of men on horseback negotiating the very steep shrine steps—a feat which few could accomplish successfully. The *honden* has a snowflake-like golden pendant that can be seen above the innermost shrine area.

A path to the left of the main hall brings one to the **NHK Broadcast Museum.** The initial NHK broadcasts emanated from this building, but today it serves primarily as a museum of early broadcasting, open daily except Monday from 9:00 A.M. to 4:30 P.M., closed December 26 to January 4, no entry fee. An early broadcasting studio can be observed as can other exhibits of the eras before and after television became popular. Tapes of broadcasts are available in the library. Tapes on the history of broadcasting, the production of programs, and the use of the latest electronic means of broadcasting can be viewed.

Returning down the male slope, follow the north-south street to the right to the parkland before the **Zojo-ji** temple complex. The Tokyo Prince Hotel will be on the right at the side of the park. Turning to the left and passing a vermilion gate to the temple, at the corner of Hibiya-dori a turn to the right brings one to the Onarimon gate which was once the shogunal entrance to the temple grounds. Deva kings guard each side of the gate's passageway, the one on the left with a pen and tablet while the one on the right stands guard with a pike in his left hand. The Tokugawa paulownia leaves decorate the closed doors of the gate. Once a brilliant vermilion, the gate needs to be restored. Continuing along Hibiya-dori, one comes to the great Sanmon gateway, the only remaining structure from the Zojo-ji temple's early days.

When Tokugawa Ieyasu established his headquarters in Edo, he was concerned to assure the protection of his city by the deities. Accordingly, the great Kan'ei-ji temple was built in Ueno to protect the city against the "Devil's Corner," the northeast from which evil could flow. A protection to the city was needed from the southeast as well, thus the Jodo Sect, with Amida as its main Buddha, was established at the great Zojo-ji temple, which came into being in the early 1600s. Second in size in Edo only to the Kan'ei-ji temple, the original Zojo-ji had been established elsewhere in 1393, but Ieyasu had it moved to its present site in 1598 to serve as the Tokugawa family temple. The materials to build the temple came by boat from Osaka and were brought from the nearby harbor to the site, for the temple was then close to the bay and the Tokaido Road.

At one time this magnificent temple, established on 164 acres, had forty-eight sub-temples and more than one hundred buildings. The Meiji dislike of the Tokugawas and the 1945 bombing raids reduced the temple and the mausoleums of the shoguns to little more than a memory. Not only did the Meiji government show its disdain for the Tokugawa family temple by confiscating much of its land to create Shiba Park, but the remains of the six shoguns buried here were in more recent times removed and placed within a small enclave to the rear of the main hall of the temple. Meiji religious fanatics set the temple buildings on fire in 1868 in order to cleanse "pure" Shinto from the influence of "foreign" Buddhist influences, and, when the temple buildings were rebuilt on a smaller scale, they were destroyed once more in 1909 in yet another blaze.

In its greatest days, Zojo-ji was the central Jodo sect temple for all the Kanto region, and it served as the main administrative and educational center for Tendai teachings. Its forty-eight sub-temples were served by three thousand monks, and the compound was fifteen times larger than the present sixty-four-acre site. The location of the temple was important since the Tokaido Road between Kyoto and Edo ran beside it, and Zojo-ji was not far from the last barrier or checkpoint on that road. Visiting daimyo on entering Edo could do their obeisance to the Tokugawa clan temple and one of the cemeteries where shoguns were buried (the other cemetery was at Kan'ei-ji). To either side of the temple were the shogunal tombs, an area entered through a black-lacquered gate, and the ornamentation of the mausoleums reflected the extravagant architectural tastes of the late Momoyama period.

Boarding houses and refectories for the staff of the temples abounded, and the grounds included a pagoda and a pond with a Benten Shrine on an island. A nameless seventeenth-century gateway led to the Kodo-in temple, which provided lodging for Tokugawa Inside Lords on their visits to the temple to offer their required respect to shogunal ancestors; it lay between the Daimon gate and the Sanmon gate. Of all the temple buildings of the past, only the Sanmon gate, the plaster sutra storehouse, and one shogunal tomb, that of Ienobu (1662–1712), remain today.

The reconstructed black Daimon (Great Gate) lies to the west off the great Sanmon gateway. The Daimon sits across the roadway leading to the Sanmon. In 1605, a fifty-foot-square, plaster Kyozo (Sutra Hall) was built near the Sanmon (to the left of the Sanmon along Hibiya-dori, behind an entry gateway in the temple wall) to house the three versions of the *Tripitaka,* the complete canon of Buddhist teachings. These Sung and Yuan scriptures from China were a gift from Ieyasu. For the sake of safety, the sutras are now kept in the modern, fireproof Zojo-ji office and reception hall within the temple grounds. Some 18,000 scrolls containing Buddhist sutras remain in the red-lacquered hexagonal sutra case within the Kyozo. This case can be revolved on its base by pushing upon its projecting handles, and one revolution of the case is equal to a complete reading of the sutras. Thus a simple rotation makes efficacious for the worshiper what otherwise would be a most onerous task. The Kyozo is open on four occasions annually, January 15, April 11–15, May 15, and September 15.

A second gateway lies to the left of the entryway to the Kyozo a little farther along Hibiya-dori, and it is the third and only other remaining structure from the original temple. This gateway, erected in 1632, once gave entry to the mausoleum of Shogun Hidetada, the second Tokugawa shogun. It and other shogunal mausoleums were destroyed in the bombings toward the end of the Second World War, and the graves of the shogun were later removed to a corner of the grounds behind the modern Main Hall of Zojo-ji. The former burial area where daimyo came to pay their respects on their periodic visits to Edo is now covered by the Shiba Park golf driving range.

Returning to the great Sanmon gate with its triple entryway on the west side of Hibiya-dori, the main grounds of Zojo-ji can be entered. Standing sixty-nine feet tall and equally wide, this two-story gate was erected in the early 1600s in the Chinese style of architecture, and the gateway is the oldest wooden structure in Tokyo. It is known as the Three Deliverances Gate since the Buddhist faith should help to deliver one from the three evils of anger, greed, and stupidity. On the second floor of this red-lacquered gateway are three images: the main Shaka image is seated on a lotus blossom while at his side are two bodhisattva images (bodhisattvas are individuals who have achieved enlightenment but remain in this world to help others attain this transcendence); a small Monju image is seated on a lion on the left; and on the right an image of Fugen is seated on an elephant. Sixteen *rakan* (early disciples of the Buddha) are also enshrined here.

Within the temple grounds a large stone image of Kannon stands between the gate and the roofed Suibonsha ablution unit on the left, and behind these is the modern Zojo-ji office building with its lecture and reception halls. Within this structure are preserved a number of the temple's treasures, including the sutras donated by Shogun Ieyasu. Beyond this modern unit to the left, up some steps, and through a gateway is a tea ceremony building. Farther to the rear are the temple's nursery school and its Meisho hall with a large collection of books and maps of the Edo period (1603–1868). Back on the path leading from the Sanmon, on the right is the *shoro* (bell tower) with its eleven-foot-tall bell weighing 33,000 pounds. Created in 1673, it is said that the temple was granted a gift of the metal hairpins of the ladies of the shogunal court to be melted as a contribution toward the creation of the bell, which is six feet in diameter. Also in this approach to the main hall is a tree which was planted by former President Grant of the United States in the 1870s.

The Taiden (Great Main Hall), a 1972 reconstruction of the temple's *hondo,* lies directly ahead of Sanmon gate (open from 9:00 A.M. to 8:00 P.M.). This reconstruction is in ferroconcrete, and it has a frontage of forty-eight meters by fifty-two meters in depth. The frontage and the length of the steps (forty-eight meters) are derived from the Amida sutra: forty-eight vows were made by Amida to save all sentient beings. The distance from the Sanmon to the *hondo* is forty-eight *ken* (eighty-eight meters) while the distance from Daimon gate to the *hondo* is one hundred and eight *ken,* representing the number of illusions or shortcomings mankind is subject to. There are twenty-five stairs, symbolizing the twenty-five bodhisattvas who assist the Buddha. The *hondo* has four large golden columns about the altar area, above which are four large golden hangings. By the altar there is also a golden Amida image from the sixteenth century.

To the right of and before the *hondo* are hundreds of small images of Jizo, many of them wearing caps and holding pinwheels that turn in the breeze. Those Jizo represent stillborn or young children who have died, and the images are decorated by grieving parents. To the right of the *hondo* is the Ankokuten (Hall for the Safety of the Nation). Here is found the black Amida image which Ieyasu revered daily. Once an image covered with gold leaf, the smoke of incense offered to it has long since turned it black. It is kept within a case and is shown publicly only on the fifteenth of January, May, and September. Behind the Amida is a row of many Jizo images. Jizo is a guardian of a number of aspects of life, but here the bibs and the pinwheels indicate that he is revered as the protector of children. In this guise he is believed to rescue the lost souls of the young in the underworld.

To the rear of the Ankokuten and behind a handsome wrought-iron gate decorated with dragons are the remains of six shoguns. Of the six tombs with their magnificent architecture, only that of the sixth shogun, Ienobu, remains intact, and above the underground stone tomb holding Ienobu's ashes is a bronze "Treasure Tower." To the south of the temple grounds, once a part of the temple, is the site of the Tosho-gu shrine to the deified spirit of Ieyasu.

On a rise behind the Zojo-ji temple is the **Tokyo Tower,** and a path at the side of the temple leads to the tower which is open from 9:00 A.M. to 8:00 P.M. in the summer but closes at 6:00 P.M. from November to March, entry fee. At 1,089 feet in height, it surpasses by one hundred feet the Eiffel Tower on which it is obviously modeled. The observation hall is at the 820-foot level, and it is the main reason for visiting the tower. On clear days not only much of Tokyo but Mount Fuji and a portion of the Japanese Alps can be seen. A wax museum, an aquarium, and a science museum are located in the base of the structure but they are not exceptional sights. A restaurant and souvenir shops are on the lower levels as well.

Returning to Zojo-ji and taking the street that leads from the Sanmon and through the Daimon, one eventually reaches the **World Trade Center Building,** which is just before Hamamatsucho Station on the Yamanote Line. The fortieth floor of the Trade Center offers an excellent view of Tokyo Bay and the city of Tokyo. Open 10:00 A.M. to 9:30 P.M., entry fee. Inexpensive restaurants can be found in the basement of the building. It is at this building that the monorail line to Haneda Airport, in operation since 1964, has its initial station.

Continuing under the Yamanote Line right-of-way brings one to the **Shiba Detached Palace Garden,** which is open from 9:00 A.M. to 4:30 P.M. but closed on Mondays, entry fee. Three hundred years ago this was the residence of one of the more important Tokugawa officials, Okubo Tadaasa, Councillor of State. The garden was created in the Edo period "go-round" style, being laid out on land reclaimed from the bay. Miniature hills, ponds, islands with bridges, and walkways surrounded by pine trees and stone lanterns made this spot a pleasant retreat on the waterfront. Today, however, the waterfront has receded due to additional landfill projects, but the garden remains a haven in the midst of rail lines, roads, and modern buildings. As with all Tokugawa estates, it came into the possession of the Imperial Household after 1868, and in 1924 it was given to the city, which turned it into a public park.

There are other interesting sites along the waterfront. Today the Tokyo Trade Center lies to the east of the Shiba Detached Garden as does the Takeshiba passenger terminal for boats. The waterbus leaves from Takeshiba Pier for the trip up the Sumida River to Asakusa. Boats also leave from here to a park that has the remains of an 1850s fort and the Museum of Maritime Science to the south and east. Other boats leave from the Takeshiba Pier for the Izu Islands or just for cruises in the bay with variety shows on board.

The Shibaura area south of Hamamatsucho was filled in to create one of the first industrial zones for Tokyo, but the buildings were leveled in the 1945 air raids. U.S. military demands for supplies during Korean War led to the construction of warehouses and port facilities in the area. The filled land of Takeshiba and to the south (the Hinode and Kaigan pier area) has, at the end of the twentieth century, been taken over by artists who have found appropriate loft space in the old *soko* (warehouses). A subway line from Shimbashi to the area makes the waterfront and the **Maritime Museum** across the bay more accessible. This museum is of interest since it has the shape of a sixty-thousand-ton passenger liner, and it exhibits ship models, ship engines, and the like. There is a former Antartic expedition ship, *Soya,* berthed alongside the museum's park (open from 10:00 A.M. to 5:00 P.M. daily). The Maritime Museum Park is but one of some forty seaside parks of varying sizes which are planned for the shores ot Tokyo Bay as reclamation of portions of the bay continues. Until the subway line opened, the Maritime Museum was reached by ferry from Hinode Pier.

As late as 1934 there were 133 geisha registered at Kyodo Kaikan, south of Hamamatsucho and just to the north of Tamachi Station on the Yamanote Line, but times change and the hall housed migrant workers in later years. The central hall from which the geisha were dispatched later became a seventy-tatami-mat community hall with a stage, called the Cooperative Labor Hall (Kyodo Kaikan).

On leaving the Shiba Detached Palace Garden, return to the main highway, the Dai-Ichi Keihin-dori, and go back toward Zojo-ji to find Daimon Station on the Toei Asakusa Subway Line where a train can be taken two stations to Sengaku-ji Station. Exit the station from the front of the train and follow a road on the right at the traffic light that goes up a slight rise (cross to the south side of the street at the traffic light). If one continues straight ahead and does not follow the road as it turns to the right, one arrives at the entrance to the **Sengaku-ji** temple of 1612. Sengaku-ji is famed for its association with the historic tale of the Forty-seven Ronin (*Chushingura*), the popular story and Bunraku and Kabuki play.

In the temple's graveyard is buried Lord Asano, the unfortunate daimyo who was misguided by Lord Kira in shogunal Court etiquette and scorned by Kira. The lord's scorn led Asano to draw his sword and attack the spiteful teacher, a capital offense since it occurred within the castle walls. The hapless Asano was condemned to perform *seppuku,* and his remains were interred at Sengaku-ji. His loyal retainers, having disguised their intentions and plotted revenge, killed Lord Kira on the night of a snowy December 14, 1702, in the teacher's mansion on the east bank of the Sumida River. Parading Kira's head through Edo, they placed it on the grave of Lord Asano to avenge his death. Remanded to the custody of shogunal lords, the Forty-seven Ronin were treated with respect for their loyalty to their former master. The shogunate was in a quandry: the retainers had done what samurai ethics demanded, but they had assassinated a member of the shogunal court. Ordered to commit *seppuku* on February 4, 1703, the forty-seven, ranging from fifteen years of age (the son of Oishi Kuranosuke, their leader) to seventy-seven, are buried here in these same temple grounds as Lord Asano.

The temple is approached through a small gate with a guard-house, a statue beyond it of Oishi holding in his hands a scroll on which was inscribed the oath which the forty-seven retainers took to avenge their master's death. Then comes the 1836 Sanmon two-story gate. The *hondo* lies straight ahead while a museum dedicated to the the Forty-seven Ronin is on the left. Taking the path to the left of the museum, on the right is the well in which the *ronin* washed Lord Kira's head before presenting it to the grave of Lord Asano. A set of steps leads up to the graves, and then one passes a small building selling incense sticks to be burned at the graves. On the right past the small building is the grave of Lord Asano's wife. Beyond is his grave. A short distance beyond and up a few steps are the graves of the faithful *ronin.*

Incense always burns before the graves, placed there by those who continue to honor these men. Oishi is buried at the rear to the far right, a roof over the grave, while his son's grave is in the far left corner, the burials having taken place in order of their precedence in serving Lord Asano. There are times that the area of the graves is almost obscured by the smoke from the many burning incense sticks placed at each grave by visitors.

Returning to the Gishiken (Hall of the Loyal Retainers), one must purchase an entry ticket before visiting the building that holds the personal effects of these Forty-seven Ronin. (Open from 9:00 A.M. to 4:30 P.M.) On the first floor are clothing, armor, helmets, swords, and personal effects of the retainers. Additional personal effects are displayed on the second floor along with an image of Oishi and his son. Two cases on the side walls contain images of the forty-seven men as well as bows and arrows, pikes, drums, and musical instruments.

In front of the memorial hall is a plum tree, planted in memory of Oishi's fifteen-year-old son. Most of the buildings of the temple were destroyed in the 1945 air raids, and thus the reconstructed *hondo* is not of the greatest interest. The two-story gate of 1836 is one of the few early structures remaining.

Back at the main highway, it is difficult to imagine that this broad, heavily traveled north-south road to Yokohama was once the old Tokaido Road which ran along the shore of Tokyo Bay, now filled in to form the railway right-of-way and the port of Tokyo. On the raised land to the west were the mansions of the daimyo and later of the important figures of the Meiji government. Below, along the shore in Tokugawa days, were the houses of the commoners along the great Tokaido Road to Kyoto. It was in Meiji times and later that filling in the bay pushed the waterfront to the east. Across the bay are four small islands which in 1853–54 saw some hurriedly constructed forts built to protect Edo against possible attack by the Western "barbarians." The appearance of Commodore Perry and the U.S. Navy ships that sailed into Japanese waters to demand the opening of the country to commercial intercourse had caused panic in Edo. One such fort, no longer extant, was built at Shinagawa, roughly in the area east of Sengaku-ji.

Here, just to the north of the subway station, once stood the Takanawa-mon, the most important gate to Edo and the checkpoint on the Tokaido where the rule of "no guns in, no women out" kept the daimyos from plotting against the shogunate. High walls on either side of the gate between the waterfront and the hills made for an effective barrier at this natural bottleneck. (Ota Dokan had taken advantage of the narrow passageway in the 1400s by building a castle here.) Obtaining clearance to pass through the gate could often take days, since the government took no chance of permitting interlopers into the capital. Today a mound on the north side of the Dai-Ichi Keihin highway is all that remains to remind one of this gate to Edo on the seashore and the last of the fifty-three stages of the Tokaido.

Between the outer gate to Edo and the area to the south (Shinagawa) was a sector to serve the traveler on the Tokaido. There were inns of varying quality, and, as at all fifty-three stages, there were brothels to serve the passing travelers. While this licensed quarter did not have the reputation or esteem that was enjoyed by Yoshiwara to the north, nonetheless it was a successful red-light district, patronized by samurai and priests; after all there were three thousand novice priests not too far away in Zojo-ji. The poor shogunate tried to restrict such activites by limiting inns to "two rice-serving girls" in 1718, then permitting five "rice servers" fifty years later. If one goes by the reported number of 1,358 "rice servers" at Shinagawa inns in 1843, either the road was overcrowded with inns or the number of "servers" at each establishment had increased drastically.

Be that as it may, the advent of the railroad in 1872 was to see an economic decline for the inns, and the last stage of the Tokaido was to become no more than a memory.

A return to the center of town can be made by means of the subway station back where the visit to the Sengaku-ji began.

TOUR
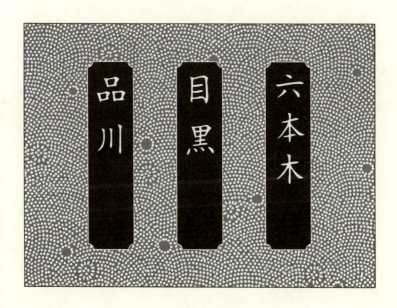

12

Roppongi, Meguro, and
Shinagawa

R OPPONGI is a popular part of the city due to its many restaurants and discos, but it is not the physically most attractive portion of Tokyo since its main intersection, Roppongi Crossing, is darkened by an overhead expressway. The name "Roppongi" means "Six Trees," a reference to the six Tokugawa daimyo who once had their estates in this area, each of whom had the character for "tree" in his name.

Roppongi history has been somewhat darkened by military events, for from 1868 to 1945 the sector to the north of Roppongi Crossing on Gaien Higashi-dori was primarily a military enclave, the imperial army having taken over the land of daimyo estates in that area in 1868. It was here that the drill grounds were relocated when the military gave up the land adjacent to the Imperial Palace so that Hibiya Park could be created. Later the War College for the Japanese army was headquartered in Roppongi, and after 1945 the United States military used the former Japanese army grounds. The American presence brought an international note to the area, and the departure of the U.S. military in 1959 led to the use of the compound by the new Japanese Defense Agency.

The subway came to Roppongi in 1964, and by 1970 the sector took off as a restaurant and entertainment area appealing to the younger working set who might have been attracted to Asakusa in decades past. At the Roppongi Crossing itself there is Almond, a multistory pink building housing a popular café, which serves as a starting point for exploring the restaurants, night clubs, and cafés which can be found along Gaien Higashi-dori on both sides of the crossing. Among these are the Lexington Queen, the Square Building with its many disco spots, and the Roppongi Plaza Building. Many night spots are not on the first floor of their building, and a listing in the monthly tourist guide *Calendar Events,* issued without charge by the Tourist Information Center and at hotels, can indicate the places most popular at any time. Little Beverly Hills, as it has been nicknamed, is down a lane off Gaien Higashi-dori east of the crossing, so called because it's the home of American establishments such as Tony Roma's, the Hard Rock Café, and Spago. A little farther east on the same main street is Forum, a pleasant diversion with its wine bars and specialty shops.

Fashion has not been ignored in Roppongi, and farther along Gaien Higashi-dori is Axis (open from 11:00 A.M. to 7:00 P.M., closed Mondays) with its upscale home interior offerings, galleries, and restaurants. In addition there is the Garden and then the Roi Building (clothing boutiques), of interest for shopping or dining. To the southwest of the crossing, on the street over which the expressway runs and down a courtyard, is Piramide. Wave, farther along the street, is Seibu Department Store's audio-visual enclave in Roppongi, and it has the Ciné Vivant theater showing foreign art films, while an English-language bookshop is on an upper floor. Wave is open from 11:00 A.M. to 9:00 P.M. A number of streets farther along brings one to the Pentax Gallery, which offers an exhibition of photography from its earliest times in the nineteenth century to the present and displays cameras as well (open 10:00 A.M. to 5:00 P.M., closed Mondays).

The **Azabu Museum of Arts and Crafts** is tucked away behind Gaien Higashi-dori. It is most easily reached by walking under the expressway from Roppongi Crossing, past the Mitsubishi Bank to Haiyu-za (the Actors' Theater), where a turn to the left will bring one to the museum after three streets. The museum is open from 11:00 A.M. to 7:00 P.M. but is closed Mondays, entry fee. A bit of a misnomer, the museum is really a gallery for changing exhibitions even though it has its own collection of *ukiyo-e* prints. It has a café and gift shop on the first floor while the exhibition halls are on the two floors above. Another museum worth visiting is the **Striped House Museum of Art,** which is devoted to the avant garde in sculpture. The museum derives its name from the striped effect of its façade, and it occupies the basement and three floors of the building. It can be found down Imoarai-zaka, a street which runs at an angle from behind the Almond Building, and it is open from 11:00 A.M. to 6:30 P.M. except on Sundays and national holidays, free entry. An excellent book shop is in the museum.

In the streets behind Roppongi to the south and southwest is the Azabu district with its many embassies, schools, and expensive residential quarters. Just a few streets south of Axis and other Gaien Higashi-dori shops is the International House of Japan with its coffee shop, restaurant, and lovely traditional Japanese garden of a former daimyo estate.

The Hibiya Subway Line should be taken one stop from Roppongi Station to Hiro-o Station, where a diversion can be made, if one wishes, to a lovely park. A turn to the left at the main intersection above ground brings one to the **Prince Arisugawa Memorial Park.** The prince was a military leader at the time of the overthrow of the Tokugawa shogunate in 1868, and he later made his mark as a statesman. The garden was donated to the city in 1934. On a rise overlooking a pond, with water courses and bridges, it is a period garden of the late Edo period. Of historical note, but not quite worth a visit, is the rebuilt Zenpuku-ji temple a few streets beyond the park. From 1859 to 1870 the temple buildings served as the diplomatic mission of the United States to Japan under Townsend Harris and his successors. A 1936 memorial stone placed by the America-Japan Society was removed during the Second World War, but it has now been re-instated, indicating that, "On this spot Townsend Harris opened the first American legation in Japan, July 7, 1859."

The temple is claimed to have been founded by the great Japanese priest Kobo Daishi in the early 800s, but it has been destroyed by fire on numerous occasions. Once in the 1860s, some of the fanatical imperial adherents, wanting to restore the emperor to power and expel the Western "barbarians," burned down buildings of the temple. Matters were further complicated when Townsend's interpreter, the young Dutchman Henry Heusken, was killed one evening by anti-foreign samurai. Heusken was not permitted burial in the Zenpuku-ji temple cemetery because the temple was within the radius where burial of those not favored by the shogunate was forbidden. He was thus buried in the Korin-ji temple cemetery to the south of Prince Arisugawa Park.

Curiously enough, even Yukichi Fukuzawa, the founder of Keio University, was also denied burial here at his family temple on his death in 1901, and he and his wife were also buried in Korin-ji since Meiji officials considered him too advanced in his ideas. In 1977 the remains of Yukichi and his wife were re-interred at Zenpuku-ji. The present temple structures are post-1945 buildings. The replacement for the main hall is a very ancient temple building which was brought from Osaka after the original main hall was destroyed in wartime. Thus only the memorial stone remains to mark the first American presence in Tokyo.

Back at the subway, the train should be taken one stop to Ebisu Station, where one leaves the subway for the Yamanote Line and takes the train one stop to Meguro. (One curious building in this area is the Physique 2B building which has been designed to give the impression that a portion of the building has collapsed.) In Meguro the station should be departed from its east side. Turn to the left along the main street, which is headed toward the overhead Shuto Expressway. This brings one in a few minutes to the **Tokyo Metropolitan Teien Art Museum** (Tokyo-to Teien Bijutsukan) and the National Park for Nature Study, the entrance of which is one street beyond the expressway. The museum was the onetime home of Prince Yasuhiko Asaka, the uncle of Emperor Hirohito and the husband of the Emperor Meiji's eighth daughter, Princess Nobuko. (The prince served as the general in charge of troops at the time of the Nanking massacre in China.) After being taken over by the government, the villa was subsequently opened to the public as a museum in 1983.

The villa reflects the prince's residency for three years in Paris in the 1920s. It is not surprising that this 1933 building was designed in the art deco style by Henri Rapin, an associate of René Lalique, for this style was just becoming popular in France in the 1920s. Art deco touches can be found in various aspects of the villa, including the opaque glass doors by René Lalique in the entryway. As an art museum, the villa displays temporary exhibitions on loan from other institutions. It is open from 10:00 A.M. to 6:00 P.M. but closed on the second and fourth Wednesday of the month and December 28 to January 4, entry fee. A State Guest House is behind the villa and is not open to the public. The landscaped grounds with its Japanese garden, pond, and large tea ceremony house are, however, open to the public, as are a tea room and restrooms.

The **National Park for Nature Study** adjacent to the villa is a 49.5-acre wilderness which attempts to preserve the condition of the ancient Musashi Plain that once lay to the west of Edo (now Tokyo). The estate of the Matsudaira daimyo of Takamatsu, from the mid-1600s to 1868, was the land taken over by the military in 1868 for a munitions dump before it was ceded to the Imperial Household in 1918. It became a public park in 1949 after the adjacent art deco villa had served as the prime minister's home for a few years after the Second World War. One can wander through overgrown meadowland and by swamps and ponds which are kept as they once would have been before Edo was settled. The park contains 160 different varieties of trees, and the plants of the meadow and the aquatic flora recall those centuries when the Tokyo area was still virgin territory. The hours the grounds are open vary: from May through August they are open from 9:00 A.M. to 5:00 P.M., while the rest of the year the hours are 9:00 A.M. to 4:30 P.M. The park is closed on Mondays, from December 28 through January 4, and the day after national holidays. Admission (with entry fee) is restricted to no more than 300 persons at one time so as to preserve the land from overuse. Since 1962 this reserve has belonged to the National Science Museum and all of the signs are in Japanese.

Returning to the Meguro Station area, one finds a few temples of interest nearby. (In the distance to the west is the Meguro Club Sekitei, a love hotel noted for its appearance as a medieval castle out of a fairy tale.) The JR railway tracks should be crossed by means of the roadway bridge, and at the Sakura Bank Building the narrow street to the left should be taken instead of following the main road to the right. One street down on the left is the small **Daien-ji** temple, which was founded in 1630 but disappeared in the "Nuisance Fire" of 1772.

Rebuilt in the 1840s, the Daien-ji temple is known for its 500 images of the *rakan* (the principal disciples of Buddha). These were created as an offering to the spirits of those who had died in the fire more than three decades earlier. Within the temple grounds the sculptures are to the left against a wall: a series of *rakan* eleven to twelve rows high carved in relief on stone. All are seated, but they differ in their stances and the implements they hold as well as in their individualized faces. Some look amused, some appear to be astonished, while others show disbelief or skepticism. In the foreground is a little pond with a fairly large Buddha on the left seated on a lotus flower with a *rakan* on a lotus to either side. There are numerous free-standing *rakan* with halos and the extended ears that denote their noble status. One image is seated on an elephant on the right while another is astride a monster on the left.

There are another five hundred *rakan* at another nearby temple, the **Gohyaku Rakan-ji.** Turn left and follow the street which runs in front of Daien-ji temple. The fourth intersection ahead is Yamate-dori, where one should turn to the left. The second street to the right leads to the Gohyaku Rakan-ji temple, some three streets away. This second temple of the five hundred *rakan* is a comparatively modern one, for its main hall only dates from 1938. Its present site marks the relocation of a temple which was founded in the seventeenth century. These *rakan* were created by a monk by the name of Shoun who carved them, begging, as a monk traditionally did, for his sustenance. Fortunately the exceedingly religious mother of the fifth shogun, Tsunayoshi, learned in the late 1600s of his efforts to create the *rakan* images, and she prevailed upon her son to provide land for

Shoun to build a temple. Finishing 536 *rakan,* he then carved an image of Sakyamuni, the Indian prince who became the Buddha, and sat the *rakan* about him listening to him preach. The temple building to house the images only came into being after Shoun's death, and the temple led a peripatetic existence before settling in Meguro in 1908.

The temple's ultimate salvation came from an unexpected quarter when it was befriended by a geisha who had married a premier of Japan at the turn of the 1900s. Becoming a nun after a life of various vicissitudes, she determined to see that the images were preserved. Many years after her death, and because of her efforts, a new hall was finally built in 1981 to house the *rakan* and the image of Sakyamuni. Additional images carved by Shoun, including one of himself seated in a chair, are preserved here. About three hundred of the original *rakan* have survived the various moves of the temple, and they still sit, enthralled by Sakyamuni's sermon. The temple is open from 9:00 A.M. to 5:00 P.M. daily, entry fee.

Adjacent to the Gohyaku Rakan-ji temple, and on the hill above it, is **Ryusen-ji** or Meguro Fudo temple. Legend relates that the great priest Ennin (794–864) carved an image of Fudo in 858, which he gave to the village of Meguro. He had envisioned the image in a dream. Ennin is said to have returned fifty years later to create a temple to Fudo, and the wooden figure he had carved became its main image. Today, as in the past, a pond stands before the temple and here two bronze dragons pour a stream of water from their mouths. The waterfall and the pond are a source of religious purification for those who brave these waters, particularly those hardy souls who stand beneath the stream in midwinter. Above the pond is a small hall that originally housed the Fudo image before the post-Second World War *hondo* was constructed. This latter hall not only holds the Fudo image, but it has a dragon painted on the ceiling by Ryushi Kawabata.

Above and behind the temple is the grave of Aoki Kon'yo, the instructor of Maeno Ryotaku who first translated a Dutch volume on anatomy in the late 1700s. Aoki was known by the nickname of Doctor Potato since he had introduced the sweet potato to the Japanese diet. The other grave of interest is located to the left of the gate to the temple, and it has a tombstone to a pair of blighted lovers whose story has become one of the staples of Kabuki theater. Shirai Gonpachi, the man in the tale, turned to robbery and murder in search of funds to be able to visit the courtesan he had fallen in love with in the licensed quarters. Caught and executed for his crimes, he was buried at this temple. When Komurasaki, his beloved, learned of his death, she fled the licensed quarters to kill herself over Gonpachi's grave. They are both buried here under a stone representing two birds who have become one in an embrace.

One street to the south there is another temple associated with Ennin. On his return to the Ryusen-ji, he also carved an image of Yakushi for the Joju-in. Yakushi is the Buddhist deity of healing, and Ennin always carried this image with him. On one occasion, returning from China, a storm endangered the ship on which he was a passenger. Casting his Yakushi image into the sea, the waters calmed, and the ship was brought safely back to Japan. The image he then carved represented Yakushi on the back of an octopus in the sea, and it remains the main image of the "Octopus Yakushi" temple. Ennin also endowed the image with the power of creating magic stones to cure disease, and believers still come to obtain the magical stones to cure diseases and remove warts.

From Meguro Station, one more station to the east is Gotanda Station. The adjacent Toei Asakusa Subway Line can be taken one station to the north to Takanawadai Station. The station exits on to Sakurada-dori, and the street to the west leads to a second street on the left where the **Hatakeyama Kinenkan Museum** is located. The estate on the wooded hill on which the museum sits once belonged to the daimyo of Satsuma (Kyushu), and it still retains its noted garden which can, unfortunately, only be observed from the outside. The museum is situated just five minutes from the station and sits behind the noted Hannyaen restaurant, a traditional Japanese structure surrounded by an exquisite garden. The restaurant is in the wooden house which was once the residence of the industrialist Hatakeyama.

The Hatakeyama Museum is in a ferroconcrete building. It possesses a very fine collection of Japanese paintings by the great artists of Japan's past as well as pottery and lacquerware from the founding of Kyoto (794) to later centuries. Noh robes and Chinese and Korean artistic wares form another portion of the collection. The museum's exhibitions are changed four times a year. Between April and September the museum is open from 10:00 A.M. to 5:00 P.M., but it closes at 4:30 P.M. during the other months of the year. It is closed Mondays and closed from December 16 through January 7.

Return to Takanawadai Station and walk east to the grounds of the Takanawa Prince hotels. The site of three imperial palaces has now become a hotel center. In 1912 Tokuma Katayama, the architect for the Akasaka Palace, and Kozahiro Kigo were retained as architects by members of the imperial court. Here they created two mansions in the French style for Prince Takeda and for Prince Kitashirakawa, and a third mansion in traditional Japanese style for Prince Asaka. Prince Takeda's property was noted for its lovely garden.

After the Second World War the properties were confiscated and placed on the market. The president of the Seibu rail system purchased the land and the buildings in order to create the Takanawa Prince Hotel in 1953 and the New Takanawa Prince Hotel in 1983. The mansion of Prince Takeda has been retained next to the 1953 hotel, and it is used for special events such as private banquets and weddings. The mansion of the other royal cousin of the Emperor Hirohito, the Prince Kaikan (Prince Hall), has also been retained for banquets. Not only has the lovely Japanese garden of Prince Takeda been retained, but a Buddhist temple has also been moved to the grounds with an image of the Kannon in its main hall.

If one walks from the hotel grounds to Shinagawa Station, one has the choice of two sites to visit. These are the Tozen-ji temple and the Hara Contemporary Art Museum. The **Tozen-ji** temple can be reached by heading north (toward Tokyo) on the main north-south highway in front of Shinagawa Station, the Dai-Ichi Keihin road. If one crosses over the highway at the second over-head pedestrian bridge, the first street to the left thereafter leads to the Tozen-ji temple. From 1859 to 1873 the temple was assigned to the British legation because it was sufficiently far from the center of Edo to keep the Western "barbarians" at a proper distance from the shogunal castle, as was also true of the American legation at Zenpuku-ji.

Sir Rutherford Alcock was the head of the legation in 1861 when fourteen swordsmen attacked the legation staff. One lega-tion attaché was wounded by a sword cut, while the visiting British consul from Nagasaki shot one attacker before being slashed on the forehead by another attacker. Edo paid a compensation for the injuries sustained, but the shogunal government was having trouble restraining some of its more rabid anti-Western allies. The building at the rear of the Zen temple held the legation, and the sword marks and the bullet holes are still visible on the pillars of the entrance to the hall. The three-century-old garden and the legation building can be visited by requesting permission at the temple to view them. The temple itself now has modern buildings and a recent three-story pagoda. Tozen-ji is more of a historic curiosity than an important site to be visited.

On leaving the temple, the main highway should be regained and followed to the south to Shinagawa Station. A memorial stone before Shinagawa Station recalls the first train that came from Yokohama in 1872, but no stone or marker recalls the bustling "licensed" district which operated here for 260 years when the area lay just before the last barrier on the Tokaido before entering Edo. The area is a bustling district now with its many hotels, offices, and shops, but it lacks the questionable character of the past.

The **Hara Contemporary Art Museum** (Hara Gendai

Bijutsukan) is the other site which can be visited from Shinagawa Station. Although the walk to the museum is just fifteen minutes, the route can be confusing. It is best to take a taxi and return to the station on foot. The Hara Museum displays changing exhibitions of contemporary art, but perhaps of most interest is the Hara family's 1938 Bauhaus-designed home in which the art is housed. An addition to the house was designed by Arata Isozaki to house the Café d'Art where refreshments can be enjoyed. In warm weather, refreshments can be had in the modern sculpture garden in front of the café. The museum is open from 11:00 A.M. to 5:00 P.M. but remains open to 8:00 P.M. on Wednesdays. Closed Mondays, entry fee.

From the Hara Museum one can walk back to Shinagawa Station, or ask the museum to call a taxi. A Yamanote Line train can then be taken back to central Tokyo.

TOUR

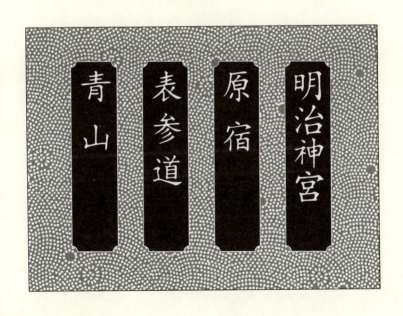

❖ 13 ❖

Meiji Shrine, Harajuku, Omotesando, and Aoyama

青山　表参道　原宿　明治神宮

TOUR 13 is a circular course and so it may be followed in part and then returned to at another time if one finds too many interesting distractions en route. There are many distractions along the way, for the area to be covered offers an amazing number of high-quality shops. Since this volume is meant to be primarily a cultural guide rather than one which dwells upon shops, restaurants, and nightlife, the sites of note historically and culturally will be emphasized. Major commercial establishments alone will be noted, for there are far too many attractive shops to be described in detail.

We begin at the shrine which has been created for the spirit of one of Japan's most noted military figures, a general who was in command of Japan's forces in the fields of war at the end of the nineteenth and the beginning of the twentieth century. General Maresuke Nogi (1849–1912) was the epitome of the role model held up to the youth of Japan by the Meiji government, whose leadership was drawn primarily from the military class of the pre-1868 Outside Lords of Japan. General Nogi not only lived for Japan and for the emperor, but he died for the emperor as well. His home in which he and his wife committed *seppuku* are a part of the shrine to his spirit.

The Chiyoda Subway Line to Nogizaka Station exits onto Nogizaka (Nogi Slope) just before Gaien Nishi-dori. Here is **Nogi Park** in which the General's house, shrine, and Nogi Kaikan (Nogi Hall) are located. The latter is a 1968 building, and its design in red brick with stained-glass windows is meant to reflect the type of architecture which was popular in the early years of the Meiji rule. It was created to honor the general and his wife, and it serves as a wedding reception hall, for, since the severing of Shinto shrines from government support after the Second World War, shrines have to support themselves and raise money through commercial enterprises as well as through the receipt of charitable gifts.

The general's house was situated across the street from the army barracks at the time. The street was named Nogizaka in his honor after his death. A leading military figure in both the Sino-Japanese War of 1894–95 and the Russo-Japanese War of 1904–5, he was responsible on two occasions for the capture of Port Arthur in China. His generalship in the Russo-Japanese War was not particularly glorious since sixty thousand Japanese soldiers died in the capture of Port Arthur, including both of Nogi's sons, his only children. Feeling the disgrace of such a Pyrrhic victory, he requested permission from the emperor to commit *seppuku*. The emperor turned down his request, saying that while he was alive, Nogi should refrain from committing suicide.

Appointed president of the Gakushu-in school (later a university), he was for a few years responsible for training the grandson of the emperor, a child who would eventually reign as Emperor Hirohito. Gakushu-in had been founded in 1842 in Kyoto by the reigning emperor to train the children of court nobility (as distinct from the less important children of the major daimyo). The school was transferred to Tokyo after 1868, and here it attempted to inculcate the ideals of the samurai in the children of the new peerage, composed primarily from the families of the former Outside Lords.

With the death of Emperor Meiji in 1912, Nogi fulfilled the wish he had expressed to the emperor in 1905, and, as the emperor's body left the Imperial Palace for interment in Kyoto on September 13, 1912, the general's wife slit her throat while he performed *seppuku,* thereby fulfilling a very ancient, though seldom followed, custom of following one's lord in death.

The land about the Nogi residence was designated thereafter as a shrine to this exemplar of Meiji virtues. The house has been retained and may be viewed, and a shrine to the general's spirit was created on the grounds. (The general and his wife were interred in nearby Aoyama Cemetery.) Destroyed in a 1945 air raid, the shrine has been rebuilt with a simplicity which reflects the temper of Shinto design, the work of architect Hiroshi Oe who also designed the Nogi Kaikan.

Steps from the street lead to a large torii, a public restroom on the left and steps to the right mounting into the shrine grounds. At the top of the steps, on the left, a row of small vermilion torii lead to a small shrine. The roofed ablution basin is on the left of the path. A modern shrine office unit is also to the left. Two lion-dogs stand before a large stone torii which marks the entry to the shrine proper. A very modern treasury building on the right has a sales counter at its nearest end. On the lower level of the building is a museum with a seated image of General Nogi and materials relating to his life. The Prayer Hall is ahead, and beyond it is the Spirit Hall, containing the general's spirit, the two buildings being connected by roofed corridors. On either side of the Prayer Hall, unusual globular units wait for people to attach fortune slips to them.

Steps lead up from the shrine grounds through what would have been the vegetable garden to the general's house farther up the slope. The simple Nogi house is said to have been designed by the general after a French barracks he had once inspected and admired in Europe when he was there as a student. It is a black, clapboard, wooden structure with as much charm as one would expect from an army barracks, and it was constructed in 1889 when the army moved its drill field from land adjacent to the Imperial Palace to the former daimyo estates across the way. A boardwalk along the exterior of the house permits one to look into the building, and on September 12 and 13, on the anniversary of the death of the Nogis, it is possible for visitors to enter the house.

Large windows with sliding external shutters permit one to peer into the house. There is a large reception room and the family living room on the first floor, sparsely furnished with Western-style furniture of the day, the floors generally being tatami-matted except for the wood-floored corridors. An eight-mat room on the second floor was the general's bedroom while his wife had a six-mat room. Their sons slept in a ten-mat room in the attic. The death clothes, replete with blood stains, are still shown, a rather gory glorification of the death of a belated samurai and his wife. Since the house is built on a slope, the lower, or basement portion, also contains rooms.

Adjacent are the brick 1889 stables in four sections, built before the house was erected. Here Nogi kept the white horse which Russian General Stoessel gave him after the Japanese victory at Port Arthur. The grounds of the residence are open from 9:00 A.M. to 4:00 P.M. daily, free entry. The grounds of the shrine are open at all times, and a flea market is held at the shrine on the second Sunday of each month. (The former military drill grounds across from the Nogi residence became the site of the Japanese War College in time. After 1945 the building was occupied by the U.S. military forces, and it now houses the headquarters of the Japanese Self-Defense Forces.)

The Chiyoda Subway Line can next be taken two stops to Meiji Jingu-mae (In Front of the Meiji Shrine) Station on Omotesando-dori. Just beyond the exit of the subway, the road splits in three directions. The left-hand roadway leads to **Yoyogi National Stadium** and Yoyogi Park. Yoyogi Park has had a mixed history. In the late nineteenth century the Japanese army moved its drill ground from present day Hibiya Park to the site opposite General Nogi's residence. When the War College was built there, the drill grounds were moved to Yoyogi. After the Second World War the grounds became "Washington Heights" with housing for American military personnel and their dependents. Then in 1964, after the departure of the American military, it became the village for the athletes participating in the 1964 Olympics. After the Olympics, the twenty-two-acre tract became a sports center. This park was one of three sites for the Olympics, the other two being the Outer Gardens of the Meiji Memorial Park and in Komazawa in the southern portion of Tokyo.

Two large structures designed by Kenzo Tange for the Olympics continue to serve athletics. The National Indoor Stadium seats 15,000 spectators and is devoted to swimming and diving events. An annex seating 4,000 is built in the shape of a snail with a tail, and it is the basketball court. These buildings may be visited between 10:00 A.M. and 4:00 P.M. when they are not in use. Various analogies have been employed for the unusual architecture of the main structure. It has been described as two huge comma shapes which are out of alignment, or it has also been described as a seashell. The curved roof of tensile steel is hung between concrete masts so as to permit unobstructed sight lines within the structure, there being no posts or beams to hold up the roof. Adjacent is the Olympic Commemoration Hall of five floors housing a sports research laboratory and space for amateur sporting groups. Yoyogi Park beyond the Sports Center provides a green oasis in the midst of one of the largest cities in the world. The park is open from 5:00 A.M. to 5:00 P.M., free entry.

Back at the subway station on Omotesando, Harajuku Station (Yamanote Line) is across the street at the edge of the Meiji Shrine park. This 1924 station is unusual for Tokyo since it is modeled after an English country rail station. On Sundays, in the area between Harajuku Station and the NHK Broadcasting complex behind the stadium, an aspect of Japanese youth culture is much in evidence. Modern dancing of every description is indulged in, boys often dancing with boys and girls with girls, or independent youths "doing their thing." (Whether or not the above is observed largely depends on the current mood of the city authorities, who periodically attempt to discourage the practice of street dancing.)

A bridge from Omotesando leads over the railway right-of-way and into **Meiji Shrine** through the Harajuku-mon (Harajuku Gate). The grounds of the shrine are open from 8:30 A.M. to 4:30 P.M. daily, free entry. The memorial to Emperor Meiji is in two parts: that portion which holds the shrine to the emperor's spirit is known as the Inner Garden; and the portion with the Memorial Art Gallery and the baseball, tennis, and rubgy grounds is known as the Outer Garden (described in Tour 3). The Inner Garden consists of 178 acres with 125,000 trees of 365 species from all over Japan. As the visitor walks down the path toward the shrine buildings, the former Imperial Gardens and the South Water Lily

Pond are on the left. Here is the famed iris garden whose more than 100 varieties of irises bloom in mid-June. The garden is said to have been designed by Emperor Meiji for the empress as part of the original Imperial Gardens in the land which once formed an estate held by the Tokugawa Ii family before 1868. (Entry fee for the iris garden when it is in bloom.)

Emperor Meiji died in 1912, and Empress Shoken died in 1914. This shrine was begun in 1915 and completed in 1920. (The Outer Garden was not finished until 1926.) As with the shrine to the spirit of General Nogi and to that of Admiral Togo (described below), this shrine deified an emperor whom the Meiji government used as a model to inculcate myths of the military spirit and the superiority of Japanese people, ideas that imbued the educational system after 1890 and which would eventually lead the military and Japan to the catastrophe of the Second World War. This and similar shrines were under military sponsorship until the end of the Second World War, when such

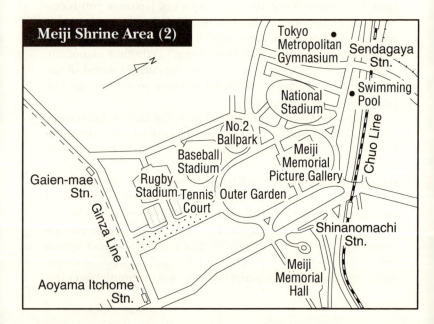

Meiji Shrine Area (2)

shrines were made independent of government financial support and control.

The path from the entry gate turns to the left just before the shrine offices on the right, this new path being distinguished by the O-torii, (The Great Torii). This forty-foot-tall torii, with a top beam fifty-six feet long, is the largest torii in Japan, and it was created from cypress trees said to be fifteen hundred years old. There is an ironic note to the construction of this torii: no cypress (*hinoki*) trees could be found in Japan which were large enough for the design of the torii, thus the planners had to import the tree from Taiwan. After the torii, the path turns to the right and leads to Kita-mon (North Gate), which opens on to the *honden,* the building containing the enshrined spirits of the imperial couple. Created in 1915–20, the shrine burned down during a 1945 air raid and was reconstructed in 1958.

Paths leading off to the right or left can be followed to the far end of the Inner Garden and the Homotsuden (Imperial Treasure House), which holds personal belongings of the emperor and his consort. Built in 1921 of concrete, it is in the style of the *azekura* (log cabin) construction of ancient Japanese treasure houses. These imperial memorabilia include not only personal objects and photographs of the couple but even the carriage drawn by a team of six horses that the emperor used at the proclamation of the Constitution in 1889. The Treasure House is open daily from 8:30 A.M. to 4:00 P.M. from April to November and from 9:30 A.M. to 3:30 P.M. from December to March, entry fee.

Several ceremonies take place at the shrine annually. January 1 is the Hatsumode festival (First Visit of the Year to a Shrine) and it brings some three million worshipers here. January 15 is Adults' Day, and many young women come to the shrine in their best kimono. Ceremonies from April 29 through May 3 celebrate the coming of spring, and *bugaku* (court music) and dances are performed on the stage in front of the *honden*. The same events take place on November 1 and 3. *Yabusame* (horseback archery) also takes place. In October and November there are displays of chrysanthemums, and November 15 is Shichi-Go-San (Seven-Five-Three Day) when children of those ages are brought to the shrine by their parents for a blessing, the children usually dressed in traditional garb. December 31 is Omisoka (Great Last Day of the Year), when people gather at the shrine to pray and the bells of temples throughout Japan are struck 108 times at midnight, signifying the casting out of the 108 failings to which humans are susceptible. The shrine is also a place where wedding pictures and family portraits are taken.

Back to the main entrance to Meiji Shrine at Omotesando, a left turn takes one alongside Harajuku Station to the first street on the right. This is Takeshita-dori, a narrow street of fashions for teenagers and those who still dream of being teenagers. More than a hundred boutiques line this very crowded street, with shop names ranging from those in French to the all-too-cute. It is best to avoid Takeshita-dori on weekends when all of young Japan seems to flock to this 900-foot mecca for fashion. A left turn at the corner of Meiji-dori at the Palais France, with its Café Royal à la Paris and other restaurants in the basement level, leads to the **Togo Shrine.** The army had its enshrined spirit at the Nogi Shrine, and for this reason it was necessary for the the navy to have its leading admiral in the Russo-Japanese War deified too. Admiral Heihachiro Togo had vanquished the Russian fleet in the Tsushima Straits in the 1904–5 war, and thus he was one of the leading heroes of the first third of the twentieth century in Japan. The admiral headed the school in which Emperor Showa (Hirohito) studied at the Togu Palace after 1914. After the admiral's 1934 death at age 87, his spirit was enshrined in this area near the Meiji Shrine. The enshrinement, which took place in 1940, was obviously a nationalistic enterprise by the military of the day.

A path leads from Meiji-dori into the grounds. A stream and a pond enhance the wooded park before the Togo Memorial Hall, a modern building for multiple uses including wedding receptions. Adjacent is Togo Shrine, a ferroconcrete structure that in

1964 replaced the original building that had burned down in a May 1945 air raid. In 1969 the Memorial Hall and the Treasury were added. A stone-roofed gateway leads into the inner shrine grounds, where there is a corridor along which are paintings of the admiral's life. Between the *haiden* and the *honden* is a stage for religious ceremonies. A festival in honor of the admiral is celebrated each May 28, and a flea market is held on the shrine grounds on the first and fourth Sunday of each month.

Back along Meiji-dori, at the third lane on the right after Takeshita-dori is La Foret, another five-story building with 110 boutiques for the younger generation. Following the lane just before La Foret and bearing to the left, one comes to the **Ota Memorial Museum of Art** (Ota Kinen Bijutsukan), open from 10:30 A.M to 5:30 P.M., closed on Mondays and the last week of each month, free entry. The two floors of the museum exhibit changing selections from the twelve thousand *ukiyo-e* woodblock prints that were collected by Ota Seizo, the president of the Toho Mutual Life Insurance Company. The prints include the work of the most noted Japanese woodblock print artists. A pleasant coffee shop that provides a comfortable rest area can be found in the basement of the building.

Leaving the museum, one can continue along the lane to Omotesando, the "Champs-Elysées of Tokyo" as many of its denizens like to refer to it. As the name Omotesando (Avenue in Front of the Shrine) indicates, it originally was an entryway to Meiji Shrine. In the period after 1945, with the American military forces billeted in "Washington Heights" (Yoyogi Park), the street began to blossom with shops aimed at the occupying forces. Then came the 1964 Olympics when Washington Heights became the Olympic Village residence for athletes from around the world, and the street began its more expansive flowering, which still continues. Expensive boutiques, internationally known clothiers, coffee shops, and restaurants make this gingko-tree-lined avenue the equivalent, in Japanese eyes, of the Parisian avenue for which it has been nicknamed.

Along Omotesando in the opposite direction from Meiji Shrine, eventually on the right, is the Oriental Bazaar with its large stone Buddha at the entryway. The shop offers antiques and other items of a Japanese nature which appeal particularly to foreign visitors. Almost opposite, a little farther down the street, are the **Dojunkai Aoyama Apartments.** With the growth of Tokyo in the twentieth century, it was no longer possible for each family to have its own house, and these were some of the first apartment buildings created in 1925 after the 1923 earthquake. The name of the apartment unit was that of the engineering and construction firm which created a series of such buildings in the city. Farther along on the right side is the 1978 reflective glass Hanae Mori Building by Kenzo Tange. It is the headquarters for the display of the designs by this couturière, and upscale antiques are offered for sale in the basement level.

At the Omotesando Crossing with Aoyama-dori, a turn to the right provides additional sites of interest. After the second street on the right is Natural House for natural food items, while across the street is the **Spiral Building** or Wacoal Aoyama Building of the noted lingerie firm who built the "Sewing Machine" building which overlooks the Imperial Palace. Designed by Fumihiko Maki, its nickname comes from the spiral walkway within which leads to the second floor, the first floor having a café (open from 11:00 A.M. to 8:00 P.M.) and gallery and performance areas. Part art gallery, part theater, part boutique, the Spiral Building has a gift shop on the third floor and a theater on the fourth floor. Women's lingerie, Wacoal's staple product, is on the upper floors. Across the street is Kinokuniya (not related to the bookstore chain), a supermarket that sells many foreign products. Since many of its signs are in English as well as Japanese, it is a favorite of foreigners.

Opposite Kinokuniya is Kotto-dori (Antiques Street) which we shall return to shortly, but first **Aoyama Gakuin University** farther down Aoyama-dori should be noted. What began as a missionary school in the Tsukiji area after 1870 moved out here into the countryside in 1883 and blossomed into a full-fledged private university. Across the way from it, along Aoyama-dori, is the new United Nations University of 1993 designed by Kenzo Tange, a complex of glass and concrete units with exposed steel frames and glass walls. Beyond it is the 1985 National Children's Center (or Children's Castle), which includes a swimming pool, a gymnasium, a concert hall for children, a stage, and a library with the latest in audio-visual and computer equipment. This complex was built to celebrate the U.N. Year of the Child.

At the intersection of Aoyama-dori and Kotto-dori, a turn onto Kotto-dori leads to the Shimada Foreign Books shop on the left. This bookstore's proximity to Aoyama Gakuin University accounts for its collection of books in languages other than Japanese. It is open seven days a week. Record shops, discos, galleries, restaurants, and antique shops line this street. A left turn after the fourth lane on the left brings one to the **Nezu Art Museum,** open 9:30 A.M. to 4:30 P.M., closed Mondays and August and the New Year holiday, free entry. The museum holds the collection of Kaichiro Nezu (1860–1940), the founder of the Tobu Railway group. He began to collect the finest of Japanese private art items from daimyo families who were in financial distress at the end of the Tokugawa era, and the collection is thus representative of all the Japanese art forms. The collection contains very fine ceramics, textiles, calligraphy, paintings from China and Japan, and early Chinese bronzes. Holding seven thousand objects, only a portion of which can be shown at one time, the museum holds about eight exhibitions a year, which are generally based on a common theme. A delightful garden with a pond, stupas, a tea ceremony house, and stone lanterns may be enjoyed after visiting the current exhibition.

Turning to the left, back onto Omotesando and after one street there will be the From First Building with a number of noted fashion clothing boutiques and dining places. Farther up the street toward Omotesando Crossing is the Yoku Moku Confectionery shop with a café, and across the street to the left is the Tessenkai Noh Theater. Within the building is a traditional Noh stage created from antique wood. The building is quite revolutionary, in that its exterior walls are of concrete poured on the site, and instead of theater seats there are tatami mats for seating.

At Omotesando Crossing, a right turn onto Aoyama-dori leads to shops specializing in imported wares, an Alsatian cuisine restaurant and others, and a Brooks Brothers clothing store. At the intersection with Gaien-Nishi-dori, on the second floor of the Plaza 246 building on the corner, is the **Japan Traditional Crafts Center,** a collection of the finest in contemporary Japanese crafts. Items can be purchased, or one can just browse here (open 10:00 A.M. to 6:00 P.M., closed Thurdays and December 29 to January 4). Gaien Nishi-dori runs north and south across Aoyama-dori, and its extension to the north of Aoyama-dori has been nicknamed "Killer-dori" due to the number of accidents occur-ring here. Opposite the Plaza 246 Building on the corner across the way is the Aoyama Bell Commons, a popular spot for finding fashionable clothing and for dining at cafés or restaurants. The building even has facilities for tennis and other indoor sports.

If one continues along Aoyama-dori for a brief diversion, there is Tepia, designed by Fumihiko Maki, with exterior waterfalls flowing over marble cladding. The building holds various com-pany-sponsored high-tech displays. Restaurants, a health club, and art galleries complement the advanced technology displays. Beyond, at the Gaien-mae Subway Station, is the 1969 Aoyama Tower Building with its glass curtain walls, one of the early "modern" buildings. The red granite C. Itoh Company Building of 1980 a little farther along the avenue makes a colorful complement to the Tower Building. A 295-foot-high glass-lined, open interior contrasts with the exterior of the building and brings natural light into the structure.

Return to the intersection of "Killer-dori" and turn to the right, to find an amazing number of fashion shops lining the street. After the fourth street on the left is the **Watarium Gallery,** a small gallery of modern art in a building with a façade of alternating black and white stone designed by the Swiss architect Mario Botta; a pleasant café, a gift and art bookshop, and an art materials supply shop are on the premises. (Open from 11:00 A.M. to 7:00 P.M. except Mondays.) Adjacent is On Sundays, an excellent art bookshop. At the intersection with Meiji-dori, a turn to the left will eventually bring one back to Omotesando-dori, where Meiji Jingu-mae or Harajuku Station can be taken to return to the center of the city. (A turn to the right where Gaien Nishi-dori and Meiji-dori meet can lead one to the GA Gallery, the Global Architecture Gallery, which has an excellent bookstore devoted to architecture and excellent galleries for the exhibition of architectural drawings. Open from noon to 6:00 P.M., closed Mondays and mid-August.)

TOUR
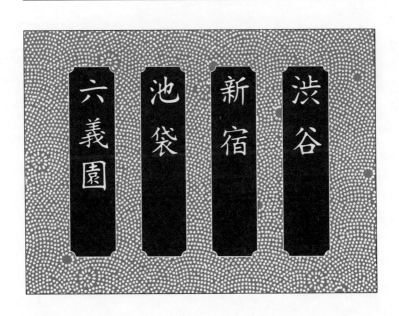
14

Shibuya, Shinjuku, Ikebukuro, and Rikugien

THE Omotesando and Aoyama districts in the last tour presented a panoply of fine shops and boutiques, although no department stores were in evidence. When one turns to the three sectors of Tokyo in this tour, one returns to the world of the department store and the specialty shop. The districts covered on this tour are each served by several rail lines which carry millions of commuters everyday. Since some of the railroads are also diversified corporations, it was natural that they would add department stores to their terminals.

The rail station in Shibuya is in a valley, and thus there is the unusual sight of the Tokyu-Toyoko Rail Station on the fourth floor of the station building, the Ginza Subway Line passing through the third floor, and the Yamanote Line on the second floor. In all, six rail lines converge here to serve this commercial center. Shibuya, as with Ikebukuro and even Shinjuku, is a recent development in Tokyo's long history. Shinjuku had a reason for being during Tokugawa times since it was on the old Koshu Kaido highway into Edo, but all three districts grew as a result of the 1923 earthquake. At that time, inner city dwellers, their homes destroyed, began to move to the outer reaches of the city, a trend that still continues today as part of the ongoing growth of suburban Tokyo. The western suburbs of Tokyo are all served by the various rail lines which meet in the three districts covered in this tour. Shibuya is the first of three sectors which today are commercial centers dedicated to satisfying the needs, but perhaps more the whims and desires, of young consumers.

Where once there were love hotels in Shibuya along Koen-dori (Park Avenue—it leads toward Yoyogi Park), today it is department stores and specialty shops which abound. If one looks at the origin of the name Shibuya (Valley of Shibui), one should recall that *shibui* comes from the fanciers of the tea ceremony and its wares in centuries past. Then *shibui* referred to artistic tastes which reflected austere elegance or restrained beauty, terms which just don't quite capture the atmosphere of today's Shibuya, a modern mecca for the conspicuous consumer.

No account of Shibuya, of course, can be begun without mention of the statue of **Hachiko,** an Akita dog, which stands in the plaza of the station. Hachiko was the pet of a University of Tokyo professor, and he accompanied his master to the train station each day and met him there each evening. One day in 1925 his master died at work, but the dog continued his journey to the station for the next decade, seeking his missing master. The story so captivated the press and the public interest that a statue to the dog was created even before Hachiko's death in 1935. Interest in the tale was so great that Hachiko still exists— since he has been preserved by taxidermy and can be visited in the Natural Science Museum in Tokyo.

The distractions of merchandising cannot be escaped even at Shibuya Station since it forms a part of the Tokyu Department Store (closed Tuesdays), one of a number of Tokyu enterprises in this valley area. To the east of the station, on Aoyama-dori, is the Tokyu Bunka Kaikan, the Tokyu Culture Hall. The complex includes the **Goto Planetarium** (on the eighth floor), which opened in 1957. Here programs of the heavens are projected on the dome. (Open 10:00 A.M. to 6:00 P.M. weekdays, 10:30 A.M. to 6:00 P.M. on weekends, entry fee.) Hour-long presentations are offered a number of times each day, and the program changes monthly. Four cinema halls varying in size from 400 to 1,250 seats form a part of the complex. Behind the unit is the 1980 Shionogi Company Building, whose split thirteen-story façade of reflecting glass provides a mirror of the surrounding area.

The plaza in front of the station has a large Sony television screen on the outside of a building like the one near Shinjuku Station. Jingu-dori rises up the slope from the station and then Koen-dori diverges to the left toward Yoyogi Park, and this is the center of the shopping district, complemented by side streets to the left with their many small shops. Directly ahead on Jingu-dori is the Seibu Department Store and its annex, a store which concentrates on the newest in high fashion (closed on Thursday). Returning to the station plaza, to the right of the station (when facing the station) one sees Dogen-zaka, a slope named for a noted robber, who, as so many of these stories relate, had feelings of remorse late in life and became a monk to repent of his earlier misdeeds. Dogen-zaka today is host to small shops and restaurants, with "love hotels" in the side streets.

At the corner where Dogen-zaka begins is the 109 Fashion Building, an imposing structure with a silver tower. This eight-story complex of one hundred specialty shops appeals to the young. Its restaurants are open from morning through evening every day. A rooftop video studio is the delight of the younger set with its large television screens and live performances. The 109 Building sits in a triangular plot, Dogen-zaka going off to the left while Bunkamura-dori (Culture Village Avenue) is on the right. Uphill on Bunkamura-dori, Sakae-dori takes off to the left, and at this new triangular corner is the main Tokyu Department Store with its **Bunkamura** in the rear. Bunkamura lives up to its name of Culture Village, for it has art galleries, cinemas, concert halls (the Tokyo Philharmonic has its home in the 2,150 seat Orchard Hall), boutiques, restaurants, and even a branch of Les Deux Maggots café of Paris. There are about two dozen restaurants on the top two floors of the Tokyu Department Store.

Returning to the station and going up Jingu-dori to where Koen-dori diverges to the left, one finds **Marui Department Store** on the right. It is popular with the young married set because of its inexpensive wares and its easy credit arrangments (closed on Wednesdays). Further up Koen-dori on the left is **Shibuya Parco,** a three-part complex of boutiques. Two of the centers are opposite each other on Koen-dori (Parco I on the left and Parco II across Inokashira-dori to the right), while Parco III is behind Parco I. Parco I and II offer fashion shops while Parco III provides interior design and cultural exhibits. Parco I has twelve restaurants on the seventh and eighth floors and in the basement. Turning left on Inokashira-dori, between Parco I and II, the **Tokyu Hands** store is ahead on the left. "Hands" began as a shop where hobbyists and those interested in working with their hands and in home improvement jobs could find the needed tools and supplies. Now the store has branched into items ranging from gifts to decorative objects for the interior. It has been suggested that one should start at the top of the store, using the elevator, and then walk down the stairs since the multitude of departments within the building can be quite confusing.

The narrow streets within this general area are filled with bars, inexpensive restaurants, discos, and small shops; one such alley complete with a cobbled path and faux Mediterranean façades is known as Spain-zaka.

At the intersection of Koen-dori and Inokashira-dori, one can continue along that latter street to Jingu-dori, the second street after Koen-dori. Here a turn to the left brings one to the **Tepco Electric Energy Museum** (open from 10:30 A.M. to 6:30 P.M., closed Wednesdays, free entry). A seven-story building of the Tokyo Electric Power Company, the museum offers interactive displays on all aspects of electrical power, from the manner in which it is created to its various uses. If, however, one turns left on to Koen-dori at Parco I and II, at the second street on the right is the **Tobacco and Salt Museum** (open from 10:00 A.M. to 5:30 P.M. except on Mondays, entry fee). Until the 1980s, tobacco and salt were national monopolies. The museum traces tobacco and its uses from the Edo period on. Rock-salt sculptures and the story of the production of salt are also exhibited. Be warned that there are no labels in English, however. The first floor has an information desk, shops, and a lecture hall; the second floor describes "The River of Tobacco" from South America to the world; an intermediate floor offers the history of tobacco in Japan, illustrated by woodblock prints and video displays of the manufacture of cigarettes; the third floor deals with foreign and Japanese salt; and the fourth floor is devoted to traveling exhibitions. The woodblock prints of tobacco and the wooden Indian at the street level holding tobacco leaves in his hand are the more interesting displays in the museum.

Koen-dori leads past the Shibuya Ward Office and the Shibuya

Public Hall at the next major intersection. To the left is the NHK Broadcasting Center. As one of the curiosities of history, just south of the Shibuya Ward Office is a stone memorializing the nineteen soldiers executed here for their part in the February 26, 1936 revolt led by the most militaristic and anti-democratic elements of the army. The revolt attempted to bring down the government in order to institute military rule and to prevent any restrictions on the army's undeclared war in China.

The twenty-three-story **NHK Broadcasting Center** was originally built as the information headquarters for the 1964 Olympics, and it became the center for NHK broadcasts after reconstruction in 1973. Tours of the broadcasting and television complex are offered without charge, but the guided tour is only offered in Japanese. There is viewing of current television programs as they are filmed in the studios of NHK (open 10:00 A.M. to 5:00 P.M., closed the fourth Monday of each month). Next to the NHK headquarters is the 4,000-seat NHK Hall for operas and concerts.

Along the street in front of the NHK Center past Koen-dori, the Olympic stadium lies ahead as does Omotesando in Harajuku. Here one can take the train at Harajuku Station to the next destination, Shinjuku.

Shinjuku is no doubt the most vibrant center in Tokyo today, a fact recognized by the Metropolitan government, for in 1991 it moved its headquarters from the old downtown Yurakucho district to the high-rise district of West Shinjuku. This area has become more the center of the city and its suburbs as people have moved from the old central city and into the outlying districts of western Tokyo.

Shinjuku means "New Lodgings," a name it received in the 1600s when the Tokugawa government required that the daimyo take up residence periodically in Edo. The Koshu Kaido highway came from the mountainous region beyond Tokyo toward the Japan Sea. Having reached the Kanto plain on the Koshu Kaido, the traveler still had a distance to go to reach the Tokaido Road and the last checkpoint at Shinagawa before reaching Edo. Thus it was that the shogun permitted "new lodgings" to be set up to the west of the city in the late 1600s, since Shinjuku was one of the five -*guchi* (mouths) granting entry to Edo. Only twenty years later, in 1718, this new post town was shut down due to a disorderly situation that occurred in a local brothel. A fifty-year hiatus ensued before the post town was permitted to reopen, and in less than a decade this least-traveled of all the highways coming into Edo had fifty-two inns with the appropriate number of "rice serving" girls to please the sexual appetites of travelers. The New Lodgings post town could boast of having one of the six licensed quarters in Edo.

The modern period for Shinjuku began with the coming of the railroad, for a new Shinjuku center developed a mile to the west of the original post town. Today nine rail lines converge on Shinjuku, bringing some two million commuters a day into the station. Aside from the trains, there are thirty bus routes that enter the district. Shinjuku has seen its fortunes change continuously since the first trains arrived here in 1885, for additional lines continued to come into the district. Also, Shinjuku grew larger after the 1923 earthquake, which led to a movement of residents from the inner city to the outer suburbs. This trend continues even today as Tokyo grows more and more populous.

In 1924 Mitsukoshi opened a department store in Shinjuku, and the increase in such shopping facilities has continued ever since. The air raids of 1945 destroyed much of Shinjuku, and a new center for Tokyo's Kabuki Theater was planned for the area, but the plan never materialized. The sector designated for it, Kabukicho, was instead to become a new "pleasure quarter" in both the old and the new sense of that term. As a result, in the 1960s pleasure became one of the great attractions for what became known as Higashi (East) Shinjuku. Here theaters, bars, restaurants, and less reputable places grew in number.

Until 1965 an eight-acre reservoir existed to the west of Shinjuku Station, and its removal was to lead to development of this area for new high-rise buildings. In the 1970s Shinjuku began to attract corporations and financial organizations, thus a business center was added to the district's attractions. In the 1980s and 1990s, Nishi (West) Shinjuku became the locus for a new group of skyscrapers which have totally changed the complexion of the area. The Tokyo city government raised its tall towers here in 1991. From the tower observation floors, one can get an excellent view of Tokyo Bay and Mount Fuji on clear days. West Shinjuku has broad streets in a checkerboard pattern around its skyscrapers, whereas East Shinjuku has retained its narrow streets, alleys and lanes. These two contrasting parts of Shinjuku are separated by the numerous rail lines which run into the central station.

This tour begins at the west exit of Shinjuku Station, a sector bordered by the Odakyu and Keio department stores. The station is so large that it has sixty exits. The Westmouth Plaza to the station was created in 1966 with the development of the forty-seven-story Keio Plaza Hotel, which rose on the site of the former reservoir in 1971, the first skyscraper in West Shinjuku. Its exterior of pre-cast concrete panels were an innovation in Japan at that time. Opposite the station and the Keio Department Store is the bus terminal and the location for taking the limousine to the airport. Just to the south are the Yodobashi and Doi discount camera stores.

Two fountains in the Westmouth Plaza face on to Chuo-dori (Central Avenue), which leads via an underground walkway to the heart of the post-1970s district and the Keio Plaza, an area where thirteen skyscrapers, including three hotels, have arisen over a twenty-one-year period. At the corner of Chuo-dori and Higashi-dori (East Avenue) is the fifty-four-story **Shinjuku Center Building** with a free observation hall on its fifty-third floor. Just to the north is the Yasuda Kasai Kaijo (Yasuda Fire and Marine Insurance) Building with its stone façade reminiscent of ancient Japanese castle walls. It has the **Togo Seiji Museum** on its forty-second floor, a museum named for the Japanese artist whose paintings of young women form the core of the collection. (He did commercial art for the insurance firm and is not among the great artists of Japan.) A very few selections of Western artists have been added to the collection, most notably van Gogh's *Sunflowers,* which set a record at auction when it was purchased by the museum for almost six billion yen (forty million dollars at that time). Other than a Renoir, a Cézanne, and a Gauguin, the collection is not outstanding. However, the gallery does offer an interesting view of East Shinjuku with its love hotels, clubs, theaters, and restaurants. (Open 9:30 A.M. to 5:00 P.M., closed Mondays.) Next to the Yasuda Building is the Shinjuku Nomura Building of fifty floors with a free observation hall on the top floor.

Between Higashi-dori and Shinjuku's Central Park are nine square blocks which contain most of the high-rise buildings in West Shinjuku. Across Higashi-dori from the Nomura Building and occupying the northeast square is the blue, mirror-glassed **Shinjuku Mitsui Building** of 1974. It has an observation restaurant on the fifty-fourth and fifty-fifth floors, and its basement level has a shopping plaza with restaurants. This latter area is pleasant because its outdoor plaza is landscaped with trees and has fountains and a waterfall along with tables where one can dine. South of it in the east-central square are the two towers of the **Keio Plaza Hotel** with an observation hall on the forty-seventh floor. (Open from 10:00 A.M. to 8:00 P.M., entry fee.) The lobby of the hotel is enhanced by the artwork of Takamichi Ito. The southeast square contains the Shinjuku Monolith Building and the thirty-two story KDD (International Telecommunications Center) Building.

The north-central square holds the six-sided **Shinjuku Sumitomo Building** of fifty-two floors with a free observatory on the fifty-first floor. The building appears to be a triangle, despite its six sides, and its central core is an open well from the fourth to the fifty-second floor. Its top three floors have fine restaurants. A glass roof floods the open space beneath it with light. The building is also the location of the Asahi Culture Center, Sumitomo Hall, and the Do Sports Plaza.

The northwest square contains the Shinjuku Dai-Ichi Seimei Building and the Hotel Century Hyatt, while across Kita-dori (North Avenue) to the north is the Shinjuku Kokusai (International) Building and the Tokyo Hilton Hotel. The central square and the west-central square hold the 1991 forty-eight-story, $1.2 billion twin-towered **Metropolitan Government Office Building** (City Hall) and the Metropolitan Assembly Hall. The complex is the work of Kenzo Tange. Each tower has an observation floor which is open from 9:30 A.M. to 5:30 P.M. daily and until 7:30 P.M. on weekends. From these two large galleries one has an excellent view of all of Tokyo, and on clear days Mount Fuji to the west and the Japanese Alps to the north can be observed. Above the large windows are photograph panels showing the view and identifying the buildings one can see in the distance. A coffee and dessert bar in the center of the observation floor provide an added touch to the spacious hall. The buildings' high-speed elevators reach the top of the building in fifty-five seconds. An inexpensive cafeteria is available in the Assembly Hall, and the large sunken plaza before the hall has a wall of falling water. A free shuttle bus runs between the west side of the plaza and the station, making stops at other buildings in the area, too.

The south-central square holds the thirty-story **Shinjuku NS Building** with its multi-colored, see-through glass elevator rising on one corner of the structure. Within the building is a thirty-story-tall atrium with a twenty-four-foot water-powered clock by Seiko. A bridge on the twenty-ninth floor connects the restaurants floors for those who are not queasy about heights. The roof of six thousand pieces of glass illuminates the building's interior by day and night since in the evening it is illuminated artificially. The fifth floor is a popular place because it has displays by twenty computer companies. (The building's name of Shinjuku NS is an abbreviation of the name of the Nihon Seimei Insurance Company.) Across Minami-dori (South Avenue) is the Shinjuku

Washington Hotel with its port-hole windows and curving white exterior.

Opposite the Metropolitan Government Offices, across Koen-dori (Park Avenue) is **Shinjuku Chuo Koen** (Central Park) which occupies the equivalent of three squares. This park is patterned after parks in the West with lawns, flowers, jogging paths, and a manmade waterfall.

Return to Shinjuku Station and leave by way of the east exit. The eastern portion of Shinjuku is much more complicated an area since it is the older portion of the district and does not have the west side's checkerboard layout. Shinjuku-dori and Yasukuni-dori, running parallel to each other on an east-west orientation, divide the shopping and restaurant district from the pleasure sector of Kabukicho, the former enterprises being centered on Shinjuku-dori and the latter being to the north of Yasukuni-dori. Alongside the station to the east is My City Department Store, and across Shinjuku-dori is Studio Alta with its huge external video screen, which marks the building as a television studio and serves as a meeting spot for the younger set.

A large underground promenade with many shops runs beneath this area. Turning down Shinjuku-dori away from the station, one finds the **Marui Young People's Department Store** on the left in the third block. It provides space for more than fifty producers of clothing who can display their latest fashions here. Just beyond it is the **Kinokuniya Building.** The original Kinokuniya bookstore began here in a two-story frame building, and this 1964 structure now offers a diversity of shops. The ground floor and second floor provide a variety of boutiques and restaurants while the second through sixth floors house the stock of Kinokuniya's books, the sixth floor specializing in books in English. The complex also houses an art gallery and a theater seating 426. Camera-no-Sakuraya, another of the major camera discount shops in Shinjuku, is near Kinokuniya.

Opposite Kinokuniya is a branch of the Mitsukoshi Department Store (closed on Mondays), while the Mitsukoshi South

Building lies to the south on Koshu Kaido avenue. The next block has the Marui Fashion Building, and across the way is the large **Isetan Department Store.** Isetan consists of its new and old buildings, and the store's noted art gallery is on the eighth floor of the new building to the rear. It offers a variety of changing exhibitions from 10:00 A.M. to 7:00 P.M., entry fee. On the second floor of the main building is Babington's Tea Room, an offshoot of that English tea room which has been in business at the foot of the Spanish Steps in Rome for decades. Isetan is closed on Wednesdays. To the east of Isetan between Shinjuku-dori and Yasukuni-dori, is Shinjuku 2-chome, an area specializing in gay bars.

Turning to the left at the far side of Isetan on to Meiji-dori and crossing Yasukuni-dori brings one to **Hanazono Shrine,** which dates back to before the founding of the Tokugawa city of Edo. The shrine sits on the site of a garden of the Hanazono branch of the Tokugawa clan, thus the name of this Inari shrine comes from that daimyo family. Inari has many responsibilities, and one of them is the welfare of merchants. Thus this is a favorite shrine for local shopkeepers who come here to pray for financial success. The shrine is entered off Yasukuni-dori through a large stone torii and then a vermilion one. On either side of the entry to the shrine grounds are two large *kura,* which store the shrine's *mikoshi* (sacred palanquins). The shrine grounds run parallel to Yasukuni-dori. There is a large torii on the right, then the water purification fountain. The large vermilion shrine building of a *haiden* and a *honden* are reached via a set of steps. The gold and vermilion interior of the inner shrine is impressive. Between the shrine and the Shinjuku Ward Office are narrow alleys, now the haunt of prostitutes (albeit prostitution was outlawed by the Diet as far back as 1958). The area on the other side of the ward office, between it and the Seibu Shinjuku Station, is the notorious Kabukicho district.

In 1945 Shinjuku was virtually wiped out by the wartime air raids. The Kabuki Theater in the Ginza had been badly damaged, and the idea was generated in Shinjuku of building a new home for the Kabuki Theater here in Shinjuku. Thus the district was renamed in the hopes for the opportunity to upgrade the area with a traditional art form. The hopes came to naught because the Kabuki-za was rebuilt *in situ* in the Ginza. The name of Kabukicho, "Kabuki Ward," remained here nonetheless. The district has everything in the way of entertainment, from legitimate restaurants, movies, discos, pubs, pachinko parlors, and bars (it is said that there are three thousand bars and eating and drinking establishments in the area) to the less than respectable sex shops, striptease shows, topless bars, no-panties bars, soaplands, and *okama* bars for transvestites and the gay crowd. In all, someone has counted more than 130 sex-oriented establishments.

Kabukicho is, nonetheless, an area where one can wander without concern, so long as one avoids the hostess bars and other places where touts try to intrigue one in for an evening of fun—and financial fleecing. The neon signs and the gaudy nature of the district have made it an area of evening entertainment, a district which is always crowded with all sorts of people. After the Second World War the *yakuza* (underworld gangs) controlled much of the black market around the various exits to the Shinjuku Station, and they are still present today, overseeing the less than reputable establishments which they control. About thirty gangs are reputedly in existence.

Kabukicho may not have obtained the Kabuki-za from Ginza, but it does have the Koma Theater which can seat 2,300 and has its own revolving stage . This theater provides all forms of popular entertainment, and within the building's walls one can find discos, bars, and a smaller theater. Coming back to Yasukuni-dori and returning to the station area, in front of Seibu Shinjuku Station one finds the **Shinjuku Prince Hotel,** a somewhat different concept of a hotel for its more than five hundred rooms are on top of the first ten floors of the building, the lower floors containing shopping arcades. The American Boulevard is the name of the ground-floor shops, specializing in American-made products.

In front of the Shinjuku Prince Hotel and running under Yasukuni-dori for six streets is the Shinjuku Subnade, an underground promenade lined with shops and connecting with Shinjuku-dori at Shinjuku Station. Some distance to the north of Kabukicho are two buildings which stand out because of their unusual architecture. These are Ichibankan and Nibankan, Building One (1969) and Building Two (1970), by Takeyama Minoru. The buildings mock the government rules concerning warnings to low flying aircraft by having a façade of black-and-white stripes which no plane could miss—if it were flying that low. The sides of Nibankan form a graphics display as an oversized billboard. The exterior of the buildings is opaque by day, but at night the interior lights provide a full view of the drinking and entertainment establishments within. To the northeast of Kabukicho is Sky Building No. 3 by Watanabe Yoji. The building is composed of steel units which many think resemble mobile homes. This metal collage is topped by a water tank which looks like a submarine, said to reflect the architect's fascination with the type of vessel he was involved with in the Second World War.

The Marunouchi Subway Line can be taken at Shinjuku Station to Shinjuku Gyoen-mae Station for the **Shinjuku Imperial Garden.** Lord Naito, the daimyo of Tsuruga, once had his mansion here after many of the daimyo mansions were relocated from the Marunouchi district following the Long Sleeves Fire of 1657. After 1868 the land was taken by the Imperial Household, and from 1917 to 1939 imperial receptions and cherry blossom viewing parties were held here. After the Second World War the land was given to the state and the park was opened to the public. This public garden consists of 150 acres in two parts: the northern portion is laid out as a Western garden in the French and English styles while the southern portion is in the traditional Japanese manner with paths, artificial hills, islands in ponds, bridges, and stone lanterns. (Open from 9:00 A.M. to 6:00 P.M., to

4:30 P.M. in the winter, entry fee.) Within the garden is the Taiwan-kaku Pavilion, a pavilion in the Chinese style given to commemorate the wedding of Emperor Hirohito in 1927. Cherry blossoms can be viewed in April (the prime minister holds a cherry blossom viewing party here each year), and there is a lovely display of chrysanthemums, considered a noble flower, from November 1 to 15 annually.

To the north of the garden is the **Shinjuku Historical Museum,** built in 1989 (open from 9:00 A.M. to 5:00 P.M., closed Mondays, entry fee). This excellent local museum is northeast of Yotsuya Sanchome Station and southeast of Akebonobashi Station. It is seven minutes on foot from the former station, but a taxi to the museum is the easiest way to find it. Models, including a huge one of medieval Shinjuku, as well as artifacts, and documents illustrate life in old Japan when Shinjuku was still a post town. To the north of the museum, on Yasukuni-dori is the **Jokaku-ji** temple, an insignificant temple as temples go in Tokyo. However, a large communal grave identified by its tombstone as "a grave for children" is of interest. This stone was erected by the innkeepers of the the New Lodging's district in 1860, and it covers the graves of the many prostitutes who died young and were unceremoniously dumped by the innkeepers, employers of these young "rice-serving women," into a common grave at Jokaku-ji, one of the two "dump" temples in Tokyo. The other is in the Yoshiwara district.

Ikebukuro, the newest of the mercantile hubs of Tokyo, can be reached by the Yamanote Line from Shinjuku Station. Its unlikely name, which means "lake hollow," is derived from the area's former swampy nature. A small hamlet out in the countryside beyond Tokyo, it came into its own only after the arrival of the railroads in the late nineteenth century. The introduction of the Seibu Line and then the purchase of a local department store which was to be expanded in 1950 into a Seibu Department Store helped develop this district. This Seibu store claims to cover more ground space than any other such store in Japan. In 1956 a subway line finally connected Ikebukuro with Tokyo Station, and there are now six lines converging on the center of the shopping district.

A rebuilt Tobu Department Store led to an innovative "glass gallery" roofing a plaza and connecting a group of buildings around the station of the Yamanote Rail Line. An underground walkway connects the east and west entrances and exits to the complex and the station, and modern escalators rise to the stores and the street.

Just to the west of the commercial area is Rikkyo University (St. Paul's) which moved here from the Tsukiji district in 1918 in order to handle a growing student body that was attracted by its excellent programs. Begun by an American missionary, C.M. Williams, the new campus had architecture that followed two different styles. A copy of Elizabethan England's architectural heritage can be seen in the classroom buildings while the white, wooden faculty houses reflect a New England heritage.

One other institution was transferred here from the Tsukiji area. It was welcomed by the local inhabitants for the possibility of local jobs,even though it was a prison. At Sugamo Prison the American fliers shot down in General Doolittle's first air raid on Tokyo in 1942 were held and executed; so was Richard Sorge, the dedicated Soviet spy who had wormed his way into the confidence of the German ambassador to Japan and to members of the Japanese premier's cabinet to gain valuable information for Moscow. Here, too, were detained the Class A war criminals tried for starting the Second World War and held responsible for atrocities connected with the war. General Tojo Hideki was the last one hanged in the prison yard on December 23, 1948. (A memorial stone to the Japanese military officers who brought about the war in China and then the larger war in the Pacific has been placed here by unrepentant militarists.) The prison was returned to Japanese jurisdiction in 1958 and was then torn down in 1971 to be replaced by Sunshine City, a rather odd twist of history.

The JR, Tobu, and Seibu rail stations and the Marunouchi and

Yurakucho subway stations are interconnected, and they form the heart of Ikebukuro. Here are the various department stores: Seibu, Tobu, Ikebukuro Parco, and Mitsukoshi. These are all fine stores that are a far cry from the black market which operated along the western side of the station as late as 1961. Seibu has been an innovator in a number of ways, and their art gallery on the twelfth floor of the store has provided visitors with excellent art exhibitions; it was the first store to offer such a gallery. As with most department stores, Seibu has food counters in its two basement levels with some three hundred vendors offering an amazing variety of foodstuffs. (Both Seibu and Seibu Sports are closed on Tuesdays.)

A separate building houses Seibu Sports Ikebukuro, the first sports specialty store of its kind in Japan. Here are all the items needed for the sporting life from fishing gear, to skiing equipment, to martial arts materials. There is even an indoor running track on the eighth floor and a tennis court on the roof. The adjacent **Seibu Saison Bijutsukan** (Saison Museum of Art, open 10:00 A.M. to 7:00 P.M., closed Tuesdays, entry fee) is a venue for contemporary art with changing exhibits. A café and a gift shop are in the museum. Parco is noted for its high-fashion clothing. Mitsukoshi, of course, has the fine offerings that are found in its other branches in Tokyo.

West of the station is Rikkyo University and Marui Department Store. Pride of place goes to the Tobu Department Store on the east side of the station since its Metropolitan Plaza contains not only the Tobu Museum of Art but the Tokyo Metropolitan Art Space and the Hotel Metropolitan. To the east of the station are numerous cinemas, a Seibu Wave store for audio-visual fans, and even a Tokyu Hands store, a branch of the Shibuya shop.

From the east exit of the station, the wide Green Odori street, with its central mall and the statue of two athletes balancing each other in the air, diverges to the left into Rokujukkai-dori. Taking this latter street, just beyond the expressway one finds the **Toyota Auto Salon Amlux** (open 11:00 A.M. to 8:00 P.M. daily but from

10:00 A.M. to 7:00 P.M. on Sundays and national holidays), a five-story temple of praise to the automotive age. Behind it is the **Sunshine City** complex, including the 1978 sixty-story Sunshine Building. (A taxi from the east exit of the station is the quickest way to this area.) The complex of four buildings includes a hotel, a theater, a shopping arcade, a park, a planetarium, a culture center, an aquarium, the Ancient Orient Museum, a concert hall, a trade promotion center, and even a branch of Mitsukoshi Department Store. The management calls the complex "Tokyo's new, complete city within a city." An elevator can take one to the top of the Sunshine Building in thirty-five seconds for a distant view of Tokyo and the Kanto Plain.

The tenth and eleventh floors of the separate **Bunka Senta** (Culture Center) house the Sunshine International Aquarium with seventy-three tanks and about twenty thousand fish (open from 10:00 A.M. to 7:00 P.M. daily, closed December 31 through January 3, entry fee). The Sunshine Planetarium on the tenth floor (open 11:00 A.M. to 6:30 P.M. daily, from 10:00 a.m. to 7:00 p.m. Sundays and holidays, entry fee) has computerized equipment controlling its sixteen projectors that present shows of the stars and planets. The Sunshine Theater is on the fourth through the sixth floor.

The Ancient Orient Museum is on the sixth and seventh floors (open 10:00 A.M. to 5:00 P.M., closed Mondays, entry fee). The museum exhibits artifacts from pre-Islamic Egypt, Syria, and Pakistan that were excavated by a Tokyo University research group. Many of the artifacts were excavated to save them before a proposed damming of the Euphrates River drowned the ancient sites. The collections display the varied arts of ancient Middle Eastern civilization, including glass and mosaics from ancient Iran, gold jewelry from the third century B.C. to the third century A.D., coins, and painted pottery.

The Alpa Shopping Center portion of the complex has more than two hundred shops of all kinds as well as restaurants arranged around a plaza which is enhanced by a waterfall. The

World Trade Center (or World Import Mart) is on the sixth and seventh floor. The adjacent Sunshine City Prince Hotel has 1,200 rooms, and its Le Trianon restaurant is the highest restaurant in Tokyo at 787 feet in the air.

To the south of Ikebukuro is the **Tokyo Antique Hall** (Komingu Kottokan), a center with fifty antique dealers who moved here from Jimbocho in 1987. These dealers operate most of the antique flea markets in the nation.

Returning to the Yamanote Line at the station and taking the train three stations to Komagome, one is but five minutes away from the most delightful stroll garden in Tokyo, the **Rikugien** (The Garden of the Six Principles of Poetry). Open 9:00 A.M. to 5:00 P.M. Tuesdays through Sundays, entry fee. Begun in 1695 by Yanagisawa Yoshiyasu, a confidante of the fifth shogun Tsunayoshi, he designed his own *tsukiyama* stroll garden with a path between hills and lakes. The garden took seven years to make, and was one of the favored resorts of the shogun. After the death of Yanagisawa in 1714, the garden declined. It was purchased by Iwasaki Yataro, the Meiji financier who became wealthy on the wars of Japan between 1895 and 1905, and he had the garden restored. In 1934 the garden was donated to the city and has been open as a public park ever since. As with such feudal "go-round" gardens, the attempt was made to have the scenery evince the eighty-eight sites mentioned in Chinese and Japanese major literary works. The particular desire was to exemplify the scenic spots in the ancient poetry collections of early Japan, the *Man'yoshu* and the *Kokin-wakashu*. There is a pond with its island and pine trees, and a hill with its teahouse, both reflections of classical Japanese gardens. This lovely traditional Japanese garden provides a fitting climax to these cultural tours of Tokyo, and can serve, perhaps, as an antidote to the many commercial enterprises described in this tour.

The JR Yamanote Line and the Nanboku Subway Line bring one from Komagome Station back into central Tokyo.

Appendixes

Appendixes

APPENDIX

1

Getting to Tokyo

Virtually all international airlines arrive at Narita International Airport. Once immigration and customs formalities are cleared, one can change foreign currency into Japanese yen at an exchange desk just before leaving the customs area. An additional money exchange counter can be found in the lobby outside the customs section.

GETTING TO THE CITY

From overseas: Narita Airport is approximately one hour from Tokyo. Tickets for limousine buses or trains can be obtained in the lobby outside the customs sector.

LIMOUSINE BUS service is the most dependable and most frequent. Luggage is placed in the storage compartment of the bus by attendants, and it therefore is no burden to passengers while en route to the city. The bus arrives in one hour (barring traffic problems) along expressways to the Tokyo City Air Terminal (TCAT). A line of taxis is always on hand across the TCAT lobby. Limousines operate from 6:40 A.M. to 11:30 P.M. There is far less handling of luggage when using the limousine to town.

There are limousine buses which go directly to some of the

major hotels, and tickets for those buses can be arranged at the limousine ticket counter. These buses generally are not as frequent as those going to TCAT.

Japan Railways NARITA EXPRESS (NEX) or the KEISEI SKYLINER train are on the second floor below the arrival level. The JR train goes to Tokyo Station (some trains go to Shinjuku and to Yokohama) while the Keisei train ends at Keisei Ueno Station where a transfer can be made to subway or JR trains.

From within Japan by air: Haneda Airport is the domestic terminal for flights to Tokyo. It is at the edge of the city limits and limousine buses can bring one into town by means of the expressway.

Arrival by train: Tokyo Central Station is the terminal for most trains although some from the north or east terminate at Ueno Station. In either case, a taxi can be taken from the station to one's destination.

Transportation within Tokyo: Tokyo has a most efficient system of transportation within the city by means of subways, buses, and taxis.

• *Taxis:* Taxis can be hailed on the street. Taxi doors are opened by the driver automatically on the passenger's side for entry or exit from the vehicle. Taxis are metered, and drivers do not expect a tip.

• *Subways:* There are eight private subway lines and four city subway systems. Each permits transfers within its own system. Travel is charged according to distance, and maps at the automatic ticket machines indicate the fares to various points. If in doubt as to the fare needed, purchase the cheapest ticket and pay the difference at the fare adjustment machine or at the office when leaving the subway.

Tickets are purchased at vending machines in the wall close to the entry barrier. Some machines will take a ¥10,000 bill, and all such machines provide change if you have deposited too great a sum. Tickets are to be inserted in the entry barrier and must be reclaimed as they are returned since the ticket will be necessary to activate the exit gate at your destination.

The private subway lines are Chiyoda, Ginza, Hanzomon, Hibiya, Marunouchi, Nanboku, Tozai, and Yurakucho, and transfers may be made among the lines when they intersect.

The city subway lines are Toei Mita, Toei Asakusa, Toei 12-Go (from 1997), and Toei Shinjuku. Japan Railways runs the Yamanote Line, an elevated line, which circles the major part of the inner city. It crosses a number of the subway lines where one can change trains. The JR Chuo Line and JR Sobu Line provide rapid cross-Tokyo connections.

• *Buses:* Tokyo is crisscrossed by bus lines, but not all buses have their destination in English on their front. Unless one knows the city and is familiar with one's destination, it is better to use the subway or taxis.

APPENDIX

2

General Tourist Information

Money Exchange
Most hotels can cash traveler's checks for staying guests, and a number of the major department stores will also cash traveler's checks as a courtesy to visitors. The exchange rate is posted at 11:00 A.M., and so it is best to go to banks which have money exchange counters after this hour. Banks are open from 9:00 A.M. to 3:00 P.M. on Monday through Friday. Only banks will exchange foreign currencies.

Japanese Currency
Japanese coins come in 1, 5, 10, 50, 100 and 500 yen denominations.
Japanese paper money comes in 1,000; 5,000; and 10,000 denominations.

Tipping
Hotels and restaurants include a service charge in their bills, thus tipping is not expected in Japan.

Rest Rooms
Modern rest rooms can be found in hotels, department stores, and most restaurants. Some public restrooms do not supply toilet paper, so it is best to carry paper tissues. Most rest rooms do not

supply towels, and thus a handkerchief comes in handy as a substitute towel.

Postage
Most hotels will sell stamps and will post one's mail. Larger packages or special handling can be mailed only through a post office, and your hotel can tell you where the nearest branch post office is located. The main post office is across from Tokyo Central Station.

Japan National Tourist Office
Information on travel, events, and even hotels can be supplied by the JNTO office on Harumi-dori just before the overhead rail line. (Harumi-dori is the street running between the Palace grounds and Hibiya Park.)

Electricity
Tokyo electricity is 100–110 watts, 50-cycle AC. American electrical devices can work on this level, but European devices will be inoperable.

Meals
Tokyo restaurants offer all the cuisines of the world to satisfy one's tastes. Hotel restaurants tend to be expensive, but inexpensive dining can be found throughout the city. Restaurants in the basement level of office buildings provide inexpensive dining, and department stores offer moderately priced restaurants on their upper floors. In addition, convenience stores can be found everywhere, and there one can purchase food at a most inexpensive cost. They sell sandwiches and boxed lunches (*bento*) which can be taken on day trips. They also have prepared meals which can be heated for you.

Leaving Tokyo for Overseas
The Tokyo City Air Terminal (TCAT) provides check-in counters for most airlines flying from Narita Airport. Check in three hours early. Also, baggage can be checked through to your destination from TCAT. Immigration clearance can also take place at TCAT.

APPENDIX
3
Holidays and Festivals in Tokyo

The following listing of holidays and events may, in some cases, have dates changed from year to year—particularly those shrine events keyed to the lunar calendar. An up-to-date listing of events with starting times is available from the Tourist Information Center on Harumi-dori between Hibiya-dori and the overhead rail line (Kotani Bldg., 1-6-6 Yurakucho, Chiyoda-ku).

January

1   **Hatsumode.** The first visit of the New Year to a shrine to pray for good luck in the new year. A national holiday.

2   **Ippan-sanga.** Reception of the public by the emperor and family. Palace grounds.

6   **Dezome-shiki.** Firemen's parade and display. At Harumi Pier.

8   **Dondo-yaki.** The ceremonial burning of New Year decorations at the Torigoe Shrine.

15   **Seijin-no-Hi** (Adult's Day). A national holiday. A celebration for coming of age at 20.

Mid-January   **Hatsubasho.** The first sumo tournament of the new year. At the Kokugikan Stadium.

February

3   **Setsubun.** End-of-winter festival features throwing beans to drive out bad luck and attract good fortune. Bean-throwing service at Kanda Myojin, Zojo-ji, Senso-ji, Hie Shrine, and other large shrines and temples.

4   Commemoration of the day on which the Forty-seven Ronin committed *seppuku*. Sengaku-ji temple.

8   **Harikuyo.** Service for worn-out needles. Awashima-do, next to Senso-ji temple, Asakusa.

11   **National Foundation Day.** A national holiday. A celebration of the supposed accession to the throne by the first emperor.

Mid-February   Display and sale of dolls in the Asakusabashi wholesale district in preparation for the Dolls' Day Festival.

Mid-February to mid-March   **Hakubai-sai.** White plum blossom festival. Yushima Tenjin Shrine.

March

3   **Hina Matsuri** (Dolls' Day). Dolls are displayed, particularly those depicting the ancient imperial court.

18   **Kinryu-mai.** Golden Dragon Dance at the Senso-ji temple in Asakusa.

20   **Shunbun-no-Hi** (Spring Equinox Day). A national holiday to show respect for growing things in nature.

April

Early to mid-April   **Cherry Blossom Viewing.** The most popular viewing sites are in Ueno Park, Sumida Park, Chidorigafuchi Park, Korakuen Garden, and the Yasukuni Shrine.

8   **Hana Matsuri.** Celebration of the birthday of Buddha. Children's procession at Tsukiji Hongan-ji, Senso-ji in Asakusa, the Zojo-ji temple, and other Buddhist temples.

13–15   **Spring Festival** at the Zojo-ji temple.

17   **Ueno Toshogu Taisai.** Traditional music and dance are performed in honor of Tokugawa Ieyasu at his memorial shrine.

21–23   **Spring Festival** at the Yasukuni Shrine.

Fourth Sunday   **Confucius Festival** at the Yushima Seido Shrine.

Late April to early May   **Azalea Festival** at Nezu Shrine.

28   **Fudo Ennichi Festival** at the Fudo temple in Fukagawa.

End of April Azuma Odori. Dances by Shimbashi geisha at the Shimbashi Embujo theater.

29 Midori-no-Hi (Greenery Day). A national holiday. The first day of Golden Week. A series of holidays, this week leads to extended vacations. Hotels, trains, and buses are most crowded at this time as all Japan is on holiday.

May

3 Constitution Day. A national holiday celebrating Japan's postwar constitution.

5 Kodomo-no-Hi (Children's Day). A national holiday.

5 Annual festival at the Suitengu shrine. Parade of *mikoshi*, dances on the *kagura* stage, sales at stalls.

12–16 (in odd-numbered years) **Kanda Matsuri.** Seventy *mikoshi* are paraded through the streets of Kanda, Otemachi, and Nihombashi.

Mid-May The fifteen-day spring sumo tournament at Kokugikan Stadium.

Third weekend Sanja Matsuri. Festival and *mikoshi* procession on Sunday at the Asakusa Kannon Temple.

24–25 (or closest weekend) Yushima Tenjin Shrine annual festival.

Late May to early June Iris blooms at Meiji Shrine are at their peak.

31 Potted Plant Fair at Sengen Shrine at the Senso-ji Asakusa.

June

9 (or nearest Sunday) Yomatsuri. A procession of *mikoshi*, including a four-ton unit which takes 200 men to handle. A nighttime festival. Torigo-e Shrine.

10–16 Sanno Matsuri. The great festival held in even-numbered years by Hie Shrine. The procession on June 15 circles the Palace and moves from Ginza to Kyobashi.

July

1 Nagoshi Harai. Torigoe Shrine. Participants believe that walking through a straw ring can protect one against illness during the hot summer season.

9–10 Hozuki-ichi. Chinese lanterns are sold in the Senso-ji temple area of Asakusa. The plants can serve to banish insects.

13–15   **Bon Odori** dances celebrate the festival of the dead at the Tsukuda-jima Sumiyoshi Shrine.

Mid-July to mid-August   Evening festival at Ueno Park.

13–16   **Mitama Matsuri** at Yasukuni Shrine. A service in honor of the war dead who are enshrined here.

Last Saturday   Sumidagawa Hanabi Taikai. Fireworks display over the Sumida River.

August

6–8   **Tsukuda Matsuri.** Held every third year (1998, 2001, etc.), a *mikoshi* is taken aboard a flat barge for a procession on the Sumida River.

15   A memorial service attended by the emperor at the Tomb of the Unknown Soldiers.

13–16   **Obon Celebration.** The annual welcoming home, for a few days, of the spirits of the dead.

15   Bon lanterns are set adrift on the Sumida River in the Kototoibashi bridge area at the end of the Obon festival.

Mid-August   Fukagawa Matsuri. The Fukagawa festival occurs every third year (1996, 1999, etc.) with a procession of 100 *mikoshi.* At the Tomioka Hachiman-gu shrine.

September

1   Memorial services for victims of the 1923 earthquake at the Earthquake Memorial Hall.

15   **Keiro-no-Hi** (Respect for the Aged Day). A national holiday.

Mid-September   The fifteen-day autumn sumo tournament at Kokugikan Stadium.

20–21   **Nezu Gongen-sai.** A parade of *mikoshi* and the setting up of stalls at Nezu Shrine.

23   **Shunbun-no-Hi** (Autumnal Equinox Day). A national holiday. Services for the dead are held at temples.

October

First Saturday   Kakunori. A festival of log-rolling acrobatics in the Sendaibori River at the Kurofunabashi bridge in Fukagawa.

10   **Health and Sports Day.** A national holiday.

17–19   **Autumn Festival** at Yasukuni Shrine.

Mid-October to mid-November Chrysanthemum displays at temples and shrines.

18 **Asakusa Kannon Matsuri.** Golden dragon dance and special offering of chrysanthemums at Senso-ji, Asakusa.

October 31–November 3 **Autumn Festival** at Meiji Shrine. Noh, Bugaku (court dance and music), martial arts, and archery.

November

1 **Azuma Odori.** Dances by Shimbashi geisha at Shimbashi Embujo.

3 **Bunka-no-Hi** (Culture Day). A national holiday.

3 **Shirasagi-no-Mai.** The White Egret Dance at Senso-ji, Asakusa.

On days of the rooster **Tori-no-Ichi** (Lucky Rake Festival). Lucky rakes can be purchased at stalls to "rake in good fortune." Otori Shrine in Asakusa, and other shrines.

15 **Shichi-Go-San.** A celebration at which children aged three, five, and seven are taken to shrines to receive a blessing. (Boys of five and girls of three and seven.)

23 **Kinro Kansha-no-Hi** (Labor Thanksgiving Day). A national holiday.

December

5 **Osame-no-Suiten-gu.** A festival at the Suiten-gu shrine.

14 **Gishi-sai.** A service in memory of the Forty-Seven Ronin on the anniversary of their killing Lord Kira. Sengaku-ji temple.

14 A service to console the spirit of Lord Kira, killed by the Forty-Seven Ronin. At the site of Lord Kira's mansion in Ryogoku.

Mid-December to December 27 **Year-End Fair** at Senso-ji in Asakusa. New Year's decorations for sale.

17–19 **Hagoita-ichi.** Battledore fair at Senso-ji, Asakusa.

23 **Emperor's Birthday.** A national holiday. The emperor greets well-wishers from the Palace reception building.

28 Last official day of work prior to the beginning of the week-long New Year holiday that starts on December 29.

31 **Joya-no-Kane.** The ringing of temple bells 108 times at midnight to absolve mankind of the 108 Earthly desires or passions of humanity.

Bibliography

Enbutsu, Sumiko. *Old Tokyo: Walks in the City of the Shoguns*. Tokyo, Charles E. Tuttle, 1992.

Fodor's Tokyo. New York, Fodor Travel Publications, 1991.

Gluck, Jay and Sumi. *Japan Inside Out*. Ashiya, Personally Oriented, 1992.

Insight City Guides. *Tokyo*. Singapore, APA Publishers, 1991.

Kami, Ryosuke. *Tokyo Sights and Insights*. Tokyo, Charles E. Tuttle, 1992.

Kinoshita, June and Pavlesky, Nicholas. *Gateway to Tokyo*. Tokyo, Kodansha International, 1993.

Look Into Tokyo. Tokyo, Japan Travel Bureau, 1990.

McGill, Peter. *Tokyo: American Express Travel Guide*. New York, Prentice Hall, 1993.

Moriyama, Tae. *Tokyo Adventures*. Tokyo, Shufunotomo, 1993.

The New Tokyo Bilingual Atlas. Tokyo, Kodansha International, 1993.

Richie, Donald. *Introducing Tokyo*. Tokyo, Kodansha International, 1987.

Sansom, George. *A History of Japan 1334–1615*. Stanford, Stanford University Press, 1961.

———. *A History of Japan 1615–1867*. Stanford, Stanford University Press, 1961.

———. *Japan. A Short Cultural History*. London, Barrie and Jenkins, 1976.

Seidensticker, Edward. *Low City, High City: Tokyo from Edo to the Earthquake*. Cambridge, Harvard University Press, 1991.

————. *Tokyo Rising: The City Since the Great Earthquake.* Cambridge, Harvard University Press, 1991.

Waley, Paul. *Tokyo Now and Then: An Explorer's Guide.* Tokyo, Weatherhill, 1984.

Wurman, Richard. *Tokyo Access.* Los Angeles, Access Press, 1984.